Weekday Thoughts

on the

Sunday Gospels

Maurice Taylor

Published by

R. C. Diocese of Galloway
8 Corsehill Road
Ayr   KA7 2ST
Charity No. SC010576

Copyright © 2017 Maurice Taylor

ISBN 978-1-9997602-0-5

Cover photo © Martin Crampin
William Wailes, The Four Evangelists, c. 1860
Church of St Tydecho, Mallwyd, Gwynedd

Printed and bound by

Airdrie Print Services Ltd
24-26 Flowerhill Street
Airdrie
North Lanarkshire   ML6 6BH

With best wishes,
+ Maurice Taylor
11/11/2014.

Weekday Thoughts

on the

Sunday Gospels

Maurice Taylor

Acknowledgement

I wish to acknowledge my appreciation of the help I have received from Nicola and Chris Lawrence. This help includes meticulous proof-reading, ensuring uniform consistency of typefaces, margins, spaces and general layout, and advice (as well as practical assistance) on many aspects concerned with printing, publishing and sale of this book.

Maurice Taylor, June 2017

A note on the use of initial capital letters

When to use a capital for the initial letter of a word can be a problem. The problem can arise more often in writing on religious subjects. In such writing, there are many words that seem to need to start with a capital letter.

One can be so enthusiastic about capitals that every second noun receives the distinction. I have tried, however, to be as restrained as possible and to use an initial capital only when really needed; for example, the names of persons and places as well as some sacred objects, seasons, feasts or actions (eg Mass, Eucharist, Lent, Scriptures, Church when referring to the worldwide community).

The reader may be surprised that I have not given initial capitals to words like baptism, resurrection, messiah and saviour (although the last two receive capitals when they are used directly as names for Jesus). Words like bishop, priest, diocese, parish and even pope are not capitalised, although the last, if used to refer to a particular holder of the office, can have an initial capital.

There are no hard and fast rules about when to use capitals. The decisions are made arbitrarily by writers and publishers. There will always be choices with which the reader will disagree. Moreover, the matter is so complicated that inevitably there will be seeming illogicalities. When you are unhappy with the choice which I have made, please don't be too hard on me. I have done my best!

Contents

Introduction	1
The Seasons and Ordinary Time of Year A	3
Advent and Christmas	3
Lent and Easter	16
Sundays in Ordinary Time	46
The Seasons and Ordinary Time of Year B	85
Advent and Christmas	85
Lent and Easter	93
Sundays in Ordinary Time	112
The Seasons and Ordinary Time of Year C	151
Advent and Christmas	151
Lent and Easter	159
Sundays in Ordinary Time	180
Solemnities and feasts which can occur on Sundays	219
Epilogue	231

Introduction

'Go and announce the Gospel of the Lord.'

With those words, Mass comes to an end. The people disperse, but with that instruction or appeal to proclaim in the world their faith which has been nourished during the celebration of the Eucharist.

I am aware that the instruction or appeal is not made only to the members of the congregation. It is as much for me, the priest who proclaims the words, as for those whom I address. This book, therefore, is an attempt on my part to respond to the call to share the gift of faith which God has given to me.

The book is a kind of companion to an earlier book of mine whose title is '*What Are They Talking About?*' but whose subtitle, though verbose, is more explanatory. '*Help for the puzzled and the patient at Sunday Mass – Short background notes for the Collects and the Readings.*' The idea is to give lay people an idea of the various collects (opening prayers) and Scripture readings that they will hear when they are at Mass on any Sunday in the three year cycle (and on any solemnity or feast which may occasionally displace the Sunday texts).

That book's purpose is merely informative. The present work gives fuller treatment on each of the gospel passages which can occur on Sundays – information, explanation, reflection, suggestion, resolution. It may be useful, therefore, for individual or communal *lectio divina,* for small groups' discussion, for homily preparation or for anyone interested in spending more time with the weekly gospel reading, either before or after hearing it read at Sunday Mass.

Brief background notes are also included about the first and second readings.

I have never had to choose a name for a child (nor even for a pet animal), but I imagine it can be very difficult. Fortunately, Mary and Joseph had no problem since the angel told Mary what her child was to be called. Elizabeth and Zechariah, on the other hand, ran into a serious, though brief, disagreement. My problem has not been with babies' names, but with titles for books I have written. Something informative but dull and stodgy? Or something bright and cheerful but meaningless and unhelpful? I leave a verdict on my choice to you.

The Seasons and Ordinary Time of Year A

Advent and Christmas

FIRST SUNDAY OF ADVENT – Year A

Matthew 24:37-44

Since this is year A of the three years' cycle of Sunday Scripture readings, the gospels are normally passages from the gospel according to St Matthew. This rule does have some exceptions, as do year B (St Mark) and year C (St Luke); such exceptions will be noted as they arise. St John's gospel does not have its own 'year' but many of the gospel passages during the seasons of Lent and Easter, as well as on other occasions, are extracts from the fourth gospel.

For us, the emphasis in the gospels during the first week of Advent each year is on the second coming of Jesus, when he will come in glory to judge all humankind. The gospels teach us that this will happen at the end of the world (at least, of the world as we know it) and when the eternal destiny of each of us is definitively settled. The gospels also indicate that the second coming of Christ will be preceded by various signs. The nature of these signs (as well as the time when they will occur) is unknown to us. It is true that in the gospels and in the book of the Apocalypse the signs are described, but the descriptions are figurative and symbolic rather than literally accurate. Scholars often describe the whole process of the end times and the second coming by employing the Greek word *parousia* (literally, 'presence' or 'coming').

Thus, the gospel today is an excerpt from the discourse which Jesus gave to the disciples on the second coming. He was in Jerusalem and it was in the week which would culminate in the Last Supper and the Paschal Mystery. We are told that the actual scene was as Jesus was leaving the temple area; that explains why the discourse, as well as teaching about the second coming, also foretells the destruction of the city and the Temple (which took place in the year AD 70, some forty years later). The excerpt read today is, however, on the *parousia*.

The burden of Jesus' words is that we must be ready and not be taken unawares at his second coming, especially because that event will occur when we least expect it. This lesson is made emphatically. The evangelist makes sure of this, and probably because, in the very early years of the first generation of Christians, there was a general expectation that the second coming was imminent. When it did not happen, there was a tendency for Christians to cease to be watchful, almost to forget Christ's words. Hence the insistence and stress laid on recalling the very explicit teaching of Jesus.

Two thousand years on, we still await the second coming but, since we are not aware of any signs of its approach, it is only too easy to forget about it, at least in practice. It is salutary to remember that, although the second coming may not be imminent, each of us will face particular judgment by Jesus when we die – a certainty that should keep us vigilant and as prepared as possible. The challenge from today's reading, therefore, is how to maintain, constantly, the required readiness.

Note that, when Jesus is referring to himself, he frequently uses the phrase 'the Son of Man'. Basically, the phrase has little meaning beyond an alternative way of saying 'a male human being' but, in the Old Testament, it is used by Ezekiel and by Daniel. Jesus adopted the phrase, especially on occasions when he wanted to indicate that he should be heard since he had an important point to make.

In today's first reading (Isaiah 2:1-5), the prophet looks forward to the era when the messiah will have used his power to bring salvation and peace to the land of Judah and the city of Jerusalem and in such a way that people from all nations will stream there to place themselves under his authority.

St Paul (Romans 13:11-14) encourages the people to live moral lives since 'the time' of salvation is at hand. Although this advice could be interpreted as meaning that the second coming was imminent, it also means that, since we are in the last age (i.e., the age of Christ and his salvation), we must remain always alert as befits the followers of Christ.

SECOND SUNDAY OF ADVENT – Year A

Matthew 3:1-12

Advent is the season in which we prepare for the coming of Christ. But that phrase has several meanings. In today's gospel, we are called by John the Baptist to prepare for the coming of Christ, no longer a child in Nazareth but grown to manhood and about to begin his public ministry in Palestine.

The Church recognises John the Baptist as a prophet, but very different from the earlier prophets. This is especially true of the location of his preaching, no longer in Jerusalem or directed at the rulers, religious or political, of Israel. Nor is his message about the evils of contemporary Jewish society. His message is timeless, it is for everyone and anyone, and it is preached in the wilderness of the Judean desert. His message is for repentance because the messiah will soon come to establish God's reign on earth.

In the final lines of today's gospel, John begins to describe the mission of the messiah, a mission more important than his own. Whereas he, John, baptises with water in order to convince of the need for repentance, the messiah will baptise 'with the Holy Spirit and with fire', both of which are regarded as even more effective agents of purification than water. Moreover, John the Baptist declares that a complete religious renewal is at hand and that those who reject it will themselves be rejected. For this threat, he uses the metaphor of the threshing and winnowing of wheat in which the grain is separated from the chaff; the former will be kept, the latter burned.

Although Jesus himself does not appear in today's passage, John not only identifies him as the long-awaited messiah but also indicates the mission which he will undertake at the behest of the Father. (Note Matthew's use of the term 'kingdom of heaven' whereas the other evangelists speak of 'the kingdom of God'. Matthew is not denying that Jesus will establish God's kingdom during his life on earth. Rather, since his gospel was written primarily for convert Jews who, out of respect, had never used the divine name, Matthew follows their custom.)

Today's first reading (Isaiah 11:1-10) speaks of a descendant of Jesse (applicable to his son King David but also, and normally, applied to a much more distant descendant, Jesus). This person will have God's spirit in him, as well as the gifts which that brings, and he will usher in to the nations an era of peace.

St Paul (Romans 15:4-9) urges his readers to behave, in their dealings with others, in the same kindly way as Jesus did. He further explains that Christ first preached to the Jews because that was what the Father had long promised them; it gave the gentiles a reason to thank God for his mercy when, unexpectedly, they too received the same gift of faith.

THIRD SUNDAY OF ADVENT – Year A

Matthew 11:2-11

Our first impression of today's gospel may be surprise that it has been chosen for an Advent Sunday. John the Baptist is in prison and will soon be executed; Jesus has already begun his public ministry. Yet, in our quest to discover and know Jesus, this passage is of great use. For us to know Jesus, it is not enough to declare that he is the Messiah, the Son of God born eternally of the Father and born in human nature of Mary. All that is true but, to acquire close knowledge, we must also see how he lives and acts, whom he approaches and befriends, how he chooses to spend his days.

The messengers from John the Baptist with their questions provide the opportunity for Jesus to give witness of himself, witness that is of inestimable value for us who want to know Jesus. He says that he is proclaiming the establishment of God's kingdom (not with a political structure, of course, nor with territorial boundaries nor an army) but one which, in deed as well as in words, will be for everyone, but above all for those who have no authority or power in the temporal kingdoms of the world. As members of God's kingdom, the blind will be given their sight, the deaf their hearing, the diseased their health and the crippled their mobility; even the dead will be raised to life.

Jesus seizes the chance to speak to the people about John the Baptist (since most of them would never have seen or known him). He tells them that his cousin lived a very simple lifestyle, a man of strong character and determination and one, therefore, who was an excellent herald for Jesus himself. What people saw and heard of John the Baptist would prepare them to meet Jesus. (The final words of today's gospel may seem strange. Jesus is not denigrating John the Baptist; only that, since he lived before the establishment of the kingdom, he did not enjoy the graces that are now available in that kingdom.)

Jesus appreciates John's character and behaviour as most suitable for the person who would be his herald. We have a mission not dissimilar to that of the Baptist. Dare we ask ourselves if the way that we live and the example that we set will attract people to Jesus? What do enquirers or the vaguely interested 'hear and see' in us, in the Church? Pope Francis' insistence that we must be a poor Church, that we must show mercy and compassion to those who suffer, is so necessary nowadays. It is essential that we try to be obedient to Christ's pleading – to know who he was and is, how he lived and, through us, still wants to live. If we know Jesus, we know how we should live and thus be his witnesses in the world today.

The first part of the prophecy of Isaiah comes from the eighth century BC; the remainder (often called Second Isaiah or Deutero-Isaiah) is from the mid-sixth century BC. In the days of the first Isaiah, the Jews lived in very troubled times. Internally, there was violence, disruption and even idolatry; externally, there was a constant threat of war and invasion. Yet, in the first reading (Isaiah 35:1-6.10), the prophet looks forward to an era of peace and plenty, when God will be among his people to be their saviour; their suffering will be over, their sorrows at an end, and lasting happiness will be theirs. The passage is recognised as looking forward to messianic times.

The second reading today is, unusually, from the letter of St James (5:7-10), one of the early Christians although not thought to be either of the apostles of the same name. He urges the people to behave in a way that will be given a favourable judgment. Phrases like 'the Lord's coming will be soon' and 'the Judge is...waiting at the gates' contributed to an anticipation of an early *parousia*.

FOURTH SUNDAY OF ADVENT – Year A

Matthew 1:18-24

At last, the Advent Sunday gospel speaks to us of the birth of the infant Jesus or, rather, of the details that occurred shortly before the event itself.

Only the gospels of Matthew and Luke contain information on the birth and childhood of Jesus. These parts of the two gospels are usually called the 'infancy gospels'. They offer many details of the conception and infancy of Jesus and of related events. However, it is difficult to separate which details are meant to be presented as historical happenings and others which, though they have a historical appearance, are included to illustrate teaching about Jesus – who he was, why he came on earth as a human being – as well as to justify various prophetic passages or sayings of the Old Testament. Matthew is particularly keen on this last element since he was writing for Jews who had recently converted and become Christians.

The details differ in the two infancy gospels, although both agree on the virgin birth and on the family's taking up residence in Nazareth. Matthew says nothing of Mary or Joseph living in Nazareth prior to Jesus' birth but, in today's gospel extract, it is Joseph who is the more central and active of the two at that period and to whom the angel's revelation is made. Apart from today's extract, passages from Matthew's infancy gospels are used only twice for the Sundays and feasts of Advent and the Christmas season – the feasts of the Holy Family (year A) and of the Epiphany. All other gospel readings during this time come from Luke's gospel.

Although Mary and Joseph were espoused because a written contract of marriage had been made between them (perhaps by their parents), they would not have been fully married until the bride went to live in the bridegroom's house (the meaning of 'come together' and 'take', verses 18, 20 and 24); if, at that stage, Joseph had repudiated Mary, it would therefore not have been divorce in the full sense.

The word 'virgin' (1:23) comes from the Greek translation (*parthenos*) of the Hebrew *almah*, which means 'young girl' (teenager?). The use by both Matthew (1:23) and Luke (1:27) – and from different sources – of the Greek translation justifies applying the verse from Isaiah (7:14) to Mary and Jesus. 'Jesus' is to be the child's given name; the word means 'saviour' or 'the Lord saves'; a variation of the name is 'Joshua'. The child will be called descriptively or symbolically 'Emmanuel', meaning 'God is with us'. To show the messianic nature of Isaiah's prophecy, Matthew seems to give more weight to its use of the word 'Emmanuel' than the word 'virgin'.

This gospel is an occasion, seldom afforded us, of considering Joseph. Very little is known of him beyond his being a descendant of King David, a resident of Nazareth who worked at a trade, probably in wood. He is often depicted as considerably older than Mary and as dying in the presence of his wife and foster-child. The passage describes him as 'a man of honour', deserved by his careful and caring treatment of Mary when she became pregnant and he did not know how. He is also a person of faith, ready to discern and obey God's will.

The first reading today is the very part of Isaiah (7:10-14) from which the quotation in the gospel is taken. The original context is of King Ahaz of Judah who is fearful of invasion by his enemies (late eighth century BC). The Lord informed Isaiah that he would calm the king's fears with a sign; but Ahaz said he did not wish to put the Lord to the test. Despite this, Isaiah does convey God's message which is in today's reading. Primarily the subject can be Ahaz's son and successor, Hezekiah; but the gospels and the constant tradition of the Church have seen the passage of being of such solemnity that it also includes an assurance of an eventual messianic kingdom.

In the second reading, we have the opening verses (1:1-7) of St Paul's letter to the Christian community in Rome, AD 57/58. Paul greets the Romans, asserts his apostolic mandate to preach the gospel to 'all pagan nations' (i.e., the gentiles) and briefly introduces the subject of his letter: the saving mission of Jesus Christ, the Son of God.

THE NATIVITY OF OUR LORD – Years ABC

Luke 2:1-14	Mass during the night
Luke 2:15-20	Dawn Mass
John 1:1-18	Mass during the day

Luke's account of the birth of Jesus begins with some details from secular history meant to enable us to be aware of the dates to which Luke, writing around the year AD 80, is referring. Augustus was the Roman emperor from 30 BC until 14 AD but the reference to Quirinius is unhelpful for he, it seems, was governor of Syria only around AD 6, yet Jesus must have been born before BC 4, the year King Herod died.

The statement that Mary and Joseph had to travel to Bethlehem, the city of David, is important as it confirms that Joseph was a descendant of King David and so also, as a result, was Jesus his foster-son. The use of the term 'first-born' for Jesus does not mean that Mary had other children but is used only to formally establish the child who will continue the name and enjoy the status and privileges that go with being the first male child in a family, whether or not others follow. The distance from Nazareth in Galilee to Bethlehem in Judea is about 150 kilometres, almost 100 miles.

It is probable that Joseph, and Mary when as his wife she made her home with him, were poor people, certainly not wealthy. Nazareth was a small village and its inhabitants were peasants eking out a living from the land or working at various trades. Joseph is called a carpenter (Matthew 13:55), a term which leaves vague the exact nature of his work with wood. The gospel passages used for the Christmas Midnight and Dawn Masses, in which the second extract follows consecutively after the first, give details which emphasise the impoverished circumstances which Joseph and Mary encountered in Bethlehem and into which Jesus was born. In addition to the details such as no room in the inn, born in a cave, wrapped in swaddling clothes and laid in a manger, we know that the first intimation of the birth was made to some shepherds who were also the first visitors; men who, as shepherds, were regarded as disreputable, irresponsible and untrustworthy. The popular tradition that an ass and ox were present in the cave or stable has, however, no scriptural warrant.

Yet the birth of Jesus is accompanied by unusual and remarkable signs and words – the divine light which frightened the shepherds, the reassuring words of the angel, and 'the great throng' of angels singing the praise of God and proclaiming peace, a peace not restricted any longer to the people of Israel. When, nowadays, so many people do not know what happened at the first Christmas or, if they know, are uninterested, we must take heed like the shepherds and 'go to Bethlehem'. That night the Saviour of all humankind was born, the Christ, the longed-for Messiah. To celebrate Christmas is to know and feel 'the news of great joy'. This good news is the most important we can ever hear, it is the news that should fill us with hope, not only for us but for the whole world, that the injustice of sin which causes so much suffering can be overcome. The birth of Jesus is not just one among many items to make us happy. It is unique – and to appreciate that is the way truly to celebrate Christmas.

In Jesus and through him, God reveals himself; and he does so not in terms of power or authority or domination, nor in ways that only the erudite can understand, but as one who is simply good and truthful and who loves us with unbreakable love. It is Jesus who reveals God to us; he is the human face of God. It is God who, through Jesus, brings us tenderness and affection, assurance and peace. And, since we first meet Jesus as an infant newly born, we are taught how to come close to God – through an approach that is quiet, gentle and free of all pretence or fear.

Let us turn to the fourth gospel, read at the third Mass of Christmas. In the course of the centuries before Christ, God had been slowly revealing himself to his chosen people. In particular, there had been a special development of the appreciation of divine wisdom. The people knew of its influence in the world, not only that it was active in carrying out God's plans but that it also played its part in human decisions and activities; moreover, it never abandoned God but remained always a divine perfection. The appreciation of divine wisdom increased in the years which led up to the birth of Jesus Christ. It was John, the author of the fourth gospel (and writing at or near the end of the first century AD) who recognised that divine wisdom, always active in God's involvement with the human race, was a person, an eternal person, distinct from the Father (yet in some mysterious way within the unity of one God); and that that person had, without surrendering his divinity, also taken on humanity and was Jesus Christ, the Son of God.

Clearly, the gospels of the Midnight and Dawn Masses are of the same nature – their purpose is to give us a description of what happened, and by whom, at the birth of Jesus. The gospel of the Daytime Mass is very different. Reading or hearing it, we are enabled to have, in a way, a glimpse into the interior divine life of the Holy Trinity – not an explanation of the mystery of three Persons in one God, but a mere inkling of their intimate relationship.

The first readings for all three Masses come from the book of Isaiah. In the first Mass, the extract is from First Isaiah (9:1-7); in the other two, the extracts are from Second or Deutero-Isaiah (62:11-12 and 52:7-10). Each looks forward to prosperous times in Israel (the first, written when the nation is threatened with invasion in the eighth century BC; the other two, when exile in Babylon has, or will soon, come to an end in the sixth century BC); but the passages chosen are also, and principally, important as describing messianic times.

At midnight and at dawn, the second readings are both from Paul's letter to Titus (2:11-14 and 3:4-7). In them, he teaches that, through Christ and the salvation he acquired for us, we can be set free from sin and made fit to await with confidence the second coming of Christ. In the third Mass, the author of the letter to the Hebrews (1:1-6) extols Christ who, after his redemptive work for us on earth, is now solemnly glorified by his Father in heaven.

THE HOLY FAMILY OF JESUS, MARY AND JOSEPH – Year A

Matthew 2:13-15.19-23

The gospel chosen for this feast in year A is from Matthew and tells us that Joseph and Mary had to take the infant Jesus and flee urgently to Egypt to avoid their child being killed by King Herod's desperate desire to be rid of the one whom he imagined had been born to usurp his throne. The details of the massacre of the innocent infants (verses 16-18) are omitted from today's excerpt. The Holy Family were refugees in Egypt but we do not know for how long or under what circumstances. Even on their return to Israel, they dared not remain in Judea since the new king, Archelaus, a son of Herod, had a reputation for cruelty. Instead, they went north to Galilee and to the little known and safer village of Nazareth. As a refugee fleeing from danger and as an impoverished exile, the infant Jesus was already sharing the fate of so many millions of his fellow human beings.

In celebrating the feast of the Holy Family and reading this gospel, we can admire the readiness of Joseph, husband of the virgin Mary and foster-father of Jesus, to carry out with extreme caution all that was necessary to safeguard the other two. St Joseph is patron of so many people (workers, the dying, the Church and all its members) but he also provides a clear example for those who, for different reasons, are 'the man in the house' but are not the father of the children who live in the house.

It is salutary to recall that we are celebrating the feast of the Holy Family and that the liturgical prayers present that family as a model for our families. The Holy Family is so unique that the call to imitate can sound unrealistic; but at least we can try to imitate some aspects and qualities of their lives as well as to pray for their help.

Families nowadays can be the scene of so much suffering – marriages that do not last or where one partner is the victim of the other's cruelty; or in which the children are rebellious, out of control, in trouble with the law, or using drugs. In other cases, one partner (usually the father) has gone and a stranger has taken his (or her) place. Unfortunately, complete family breakdowns occur and the children especially are caused to suffer and are exposed to many kinds of danger.

This is not the place to go into details nor to ask what can be done to remedy (or, better, prevent) these tragic situations. But, in addition to anything that public authorities, the extended family or those directly involved may attempt, we should all include the hope of successful and happy family life as a prominent intention in our prayers.

An extract from the book of Ecclesiasticus (3:2-6.12-14) provides the first reading. It was written early in the second century BC by a Jew named Ben Sira. The reading urges children to obey their parents and to treat them always with respect.

The second reading is from Paul's letter to the Colossians (3:12-21). The apostle urges his Christian readers to excel in the virtue of love, especially in their dealings with one another. The final verses have a few words of advice to wives, husbands and children about their relations with each other.

SOLEMNITY OF MARY, MOTHER OF GOD – Years ABC

Luke 2:16-21

New Year's Day, which until the reform of the liturgical calendar in the 1960s was observed as the feast of the circumcision of Jesus, is now the solemn feast of Mary, Mother of God. To an extent it has lost its specific character, in addition to which it has to compete with the celebration of the new year, the World Day of Prayer for Peace and the final day of the octave of Christmas. Further, unless it falls on a Sunday, it is not a day of obligation for Mass. Regrettably, the prominence given to Mary's unique motherhood is less than many would like it to be.

The gospel is the same as that of the Christmas Dawn Mass, with a sentence added to note the circumcision and formal naming of Jesus. However, the passage does contain an intriguing mention of Mary, that 'she treasured all these things and pondered them in her heart' (2:19). These words should be linked with that other reference which Luke notes in his account of Jesus' presentation, when Simeon said to Mary, 'a sword will pierce your own soul too' (2:35).

It is often remarked that Catholics' devotion to Mary is not what it once was. If this is true, it may be as a reaction to the earlier emphasis placed on Mary as our Mother who protects us from all evils and which therefore perhaps lacked stress on our duty of boldly and bravely 'announcing the gospel'. To see Mary as the perfect and idealised mother could foster religious immaturity and even childishness.

Devotion to Mary, properly understood, brings the important and enriching element of the feminine into our prayer and our religious outlook. In particular, it reminds us of those divine qualities which women show forth in a special way – intimacy, affection, tenderness, care and gentleness – as well as woman's likeness to God in her capacity for giving life. A religious faith from which Mary is absent is basically impoverished.

To begin a new year with this feast of Mary seems an excellent choice, and not only because we are within the octave of the birth of her Son. It also allows us to have before us, and to be guided in the months ahead, by her outstanding traits of character: faithful fulfilment of God's will, identification with the poor and lowly, acceptance of her Son's mission, service to the early Church and, undoubtedly, her interest and love for each one of her son's disciples.

The first reading (Numbers 6:22-27) is chosen for its relevance for a Mass on New Year's Day. It comes from Numbers, a book of the Pentateuch or *Torah*, and is a blessing which God gave to be used for the Israelites as they journeyed to the promised land. It is now offered for our use.

For the second reading, a short extract from Paul's letter to the Galatians (4:4-7) is provided. Paul reminds us that, through Jesus, 'born of a woman', we are redeemed and, through the Holy Spirit, are adopted as sons and daughters of the Father and therefore with the right to inherit the fullness of God's kingdom.

SECOND SUNDAY AFTER THE NATIVITY – Years ABC

John 1:1-18

The gospel today is the same passage as is read at the Daytime Mass of Christmas.

In the course of the centuries before Christ, God had been slowly revealing himself to his chosen people. In particular, there had been an evident development in the appreciation of divine wisdom. The people knew of its influence in the world, that it was active not only in carrying out God's plans but that it also played its part in human decisions and activities; moreover, it never abandoned God but remained also a divine perfection. The appreciation of divine wisdom increased in the years which led up to the birth of Jesus Christ. It was John, the author of the fourth gospel (and writing at or near the end of the first century AD) who recognised that divine wisdom, always active in God's involvement with the human race, was a person, an eternal person, distinct from the Father (yet in some mysterious way within the unity of one God); and that that person had, without surrendering his divinity, also taken on humanity and was Jesus Christ, the Son of God.

Reading or hearing this gospel passage, we are enabled to have, in a way, a glimpse into the interior divine life of the Holy Trinity – not an explanation of the mystery of three Persons in one God, but a mere inkling of their intimate relationship.

All the gospels want to tell us that Jesus came to show us how to reach eternal life with God but, more than the other evangelists, John insists that Christ is divine and eternal and that he also became human to live and be visible among us. For this purpose, John relates the miracles of Jesus not just as works of extraordinary power (as the other gospels do) but as signs which illustrate who Jesus was and why he had come.

The opening words of John's gospel (read again today, as well as at the daytime Christmas Mass) plunge straight into these profound truths about the identity of Jesus and the purpose of his incarnation: he is God, the Son of God the Father, eternal; he is the Word of God; although he will be rejected by many, those who believe in him will be adopted as sons and daughters of God the Father, blessed with gifts of grace and truth.

The title 'Word of God' which John uses of Jesus needs comment. The evangelist knows that the events of the Old Testament are meant to be understood as the preparation of God's plan for human salvation through his incarnate son. The very first reported action of God in this plan is to speak – 'and God said' (Genesis 1:3). It is through God's word that the world was created and was given light – God's word is active and creative; John therefore identifies this active and creative word as a person, distinct from, but one with, God the Father; and so the eternal Son of God, the divine agent of all creation, is named by John as God's Word. 'The Word was made flesh and dwelt among us' (John 1:14) to make God's glory present and visible on earth.

The first reading (Ecclesiasticus 24:1-2.8-12) is from the last of the so-called wisdom books of the Old Testament and was written in the early part of the second century BC. Although not yet identifying Wisdom as a distinct person from the Father, the extract is a remarkable piece of writing in which Wisdom, having been called to describe herself, speaks of her creation by God from eternity and of her being sent to live, take root and hold authority in the Lord's city of Jerusalem.

In the first chapter of the letter to the Ephesians (1:3-6.15-18), Paul teaches that God's eternal plan is that, in and through Christ, we are to be his adopted sons and daughters. The passage thanks the Christians for accepting with faith the teaching he has given; he prays that God may give them wisdom and enlighten them so that they may grow in the knowledge of God and be filled with hope as they discover the glories that await those who are faithful.

THE EPIPHANY OF THE LORD – Years ABC

Matthew 2:1-12

'Epiphany' is a word meaning a manifestation, a revealing of someone or something. This solemn feast celebrates the homage paid to Jesus by the 'wise men from the east', the first gentiles to recognise the sacred purpose of his birth. Those visitors to Bethlehem were representing all of us gentiles. The event implies that Jesus is the Messiah not only for God's chosen people of the Old Law but for gentiles as well.

King Herod was greatly upset when the Magi explained the reason for their presence and their enquiries and so also, Matthew adds, 'was the whole of Jerusalem'. The evangelist, as was his custom, justifies Bethlehem as the place of the birth of Jesus by a quotation from the Old Testament, in this case from the prophet Micah (5:1-2) but, whereas Micah describes the town as 'the least of the clans of Judah', the gospel cites him as being much less derogatory: 'by no means least among the leaders of Judah'.

The visitors are 'wise men' who had seen a star which they said was indicative of 'the infant king of the Jews'. Further attempts to be specific regarding the identity of the Magi or of the star are futile. All that we can say is that the region which is now Iraq had a reputation in those days of having scholars who studied the stars for purposes of astrology.

The gifts are sometimes said to have symbolic meanings suitable for Jesus – gold for a king, frankincense for a divinity and myrrh for a burial. There may be a reference here to Old Testament texts that refer to such gifts being made to the God of Israel by important people from the east (for example, Isaiah 60:5-6). However, the presentation of such gifts to the infant in the circumstances in which the visitors found the family seems very incongruous.

The reaction and behaviour of Herod the Great (who died in 4 BC) have all the signs of a man of power ready to do whatever was needed, no matter how brutal and tyrannical, to maintain his position. He serves (if such a verb can be used of Herod) as a terrible example of what the possession of power can do to someone and what suffering will be caused to others in pursuit of his own selfish ends.

It is quite likely that, at this feast, we may ask ourselves what gifts we can ourselves bring to Christ. We may feel that we have nothing to give, nothing, at least, that is of use to him. Yet, what about our prayers, our thanks, our love? And, if we remember that the Church is the (mystical) Body of Christ, each of us has much to offer. The Holy Spirit, at baptism and confirmation, endowed us with gifts, some given to all, others only to some. These gifts are not personal adornments like jewels to make us appear more beautiful or attractive, but gifts to be used in the service of Jesus and for the benefit of the Church.

Most of us have a natural reluctance to step forward and offer our gifts for use. We are not natural volunteers. So perhaps more requests for help are required, not just general and vague appeals but individual requests by those who are aware of the needs and to those who seem suitable. St Paul has a rich theology of gifts from the Spirit and given to be used – if only he were taken seriously, our parish communities would be humming with activity!

Various details of the Epiphany story can also be the source of reflection. The darkness of evil always prevalent in the world, its Herodian character, evident or insidious, its desire to overcome or smother the good; what is its motivation – pride or wealth or fame? On the other hand, the light that, like the star, leads us to Jesus, the object of our homage; can we honestly say that we truly worship Jesus and want to be with him in his kingdom to serve, not to be served?

And a final thought. The Magi were wise, wise enough even to taking the decision to change their route for the journey home. Are we wise enough to change the route of our lives if we know that we should?

As the Jews were leaving exile in Babylon and rejoicing at their homecoming, Deutero-Isaiah (60:1-6) in the first reading apostrophises the city of Jerusalem and its inhabitants. The extract clearly has a messianic application also, and several verses can be referred to the gospel heard today – the star lighting the way for the foreign travellers on their way from the east, bringing valuable presents, specifically gold and incense. The psalm also looks forward to a (messianic) king who will bring justice and peace to Israel and who will attract royal and admiring visitors from the east.

In the second reading, St Paul (Ephesians 3:2-3.5-6) announces the secret plan that God wishes him to reveal, namely that, through Jesus Christ, pagans (i.e., non-Jews) are called to inherit the same divine promise as Jews. This is the truth of which the event celebrated today is the very first epiphany.

THE BAPTISM OF THE LORD – Year A

Matthew 3:13-17

At first sight, the baptism of Jesus by John the Baptist is a very puzzling event. Why did Jesus feel the need to be baptised if he was God and his human nature totally sinless? It is some help towards seeking an explanation if we remember that Jesus, from the very start of his human life on earth, acted with the utmost humility; that his seeking baptism showed his solidarity with all who belong to the human race; and that the baptism provided an 'epiphany', a revealing of himself as he was about to begin his public mission received from the Father.

The immediate consequence of Jesus' baptism is significant and important. Two things happened to manifest divine approval both of the baptism and of Jesus himself. The Father 'spoke from heaven' to identify Jesus as his Son, to affirm his love for him and to declare that he would have his protection and guidance. The other happening was that the Spirit of God came down visibly on Jesus – an occurrence that merits a comment. In the Old Testament, God's spirit is God's breath that creates and sustains life, by which God renews, transforms and empowers its recipients; in the New Testament, the Spirit of God will be revealed as the third and distinct Person of the Trinity. Receiving the Holy Spirit at his baptism can be seen as Jesus, in his human nature, being consecrated, commissioned and empowered for his earthly mission.

All four gospels speak of the baptism of Jesus. Matthew and Luke clearly use Mark's account in their gospels. Matthew does not include the words of John the Baptist who, in comparing his baptism with that which Jesus will confer, declares that, although he, John, baptises with water, Jesus will baptise with the Holy Spirit (and, even if not mentioned by John the Baptist, with the use of water as well). The fourth gospel omits explicit mention of the actual rite of baptism received by Jesus but has the Baptist extolling Jesus as the Lamb of God, God's chosen one on whom he, John, had witnessed the Spirit descending. The term 'Lamb of God' is to teach that, just as the paschal lamb had meant the Israelites' release from slavery in Egypt (Exodus 12:1-14), the sacrifice of Jesus enables us to be freed from the slavery of sin. It is right to note that, at the time of John baptising, various other sects and preachers in Palestine were also carrying out a rite of baptism for forgiveness and purification.

The sacrament of baptism which we receive is, of course, the baptism which Jesus instituted and which gives us the Holy Spirit (and indeed the blessed Trinity) to dwell within us. The Church's development of the theology of our baptism teaches us the abundance and richness of the effects of being baptised: adopted by God as his sons and daughters, forgiveness of all sin, membership of Christ's Church, a participation in his priesthood and the gifts to be actively involved in evangelising and healing, the right to receive the other sacraments, an eternal inheritance, and a close and loving relationship with God even here on earth.

The Church also teaches the necessity of baptism for salvation (but, when actual baptism has not been received, the desire, even implicit, of being baptised is sufficient). The so-called 'baptism of blood' which martyrs receive in accepting death inflicted because of the killer's hatred of the faith is seen as meriting salvation; and, in recent times, the Church has declared that it cannot say that infants dying unbaptised are denied eternal life in heaven.

It is clear that the celebration of the feast of the baptism of Jesus offers us an opportunity to review our knowledge of the sacrament of baptism and to renew our faith and our desire to live as someone adopted as a child of God and a sharer in Christ's priestly mission in the world.

The first reading (Deutero-Isaiah 42:1-4.6-7) is that part of the prophecy called the first (of four) 'Song of the Servant of the Lord'. God speaks of an individual who will faithfully carry out the divine will because he has been given the divine spirit to enable him to bring freedom and justice to the people. The passage is regarded as messianic. Its suitability as related to today's feast and gospel is evident.

Speaking to a gentile household, Peter (Acts 10:34-38) tells them that he now realises that Jesus was sent as messiah and saviour not only to Jews but 'to anybody of any nationality'.

Lent and Easter

ASH WEDNESDAY – Years ABC

Matthew 6:1-6.16-18

The gospel for the start of Lent neatly deals with the three categories in which our good works during Lent can be expressed: almsgiving, prayer and fasting. Jesus tells us that our motivation should be to make ourselves ready and open to receive the graces with which God wants to bless us in this season – conversion from sinfulness and a deeper faith in his promises.

The passage read today is, in fact, included in the Sermon on the Mount, teachings of Jesus which Matthew collects and presents to us as a discourse during which Jesus gives an inaugural instruction on the spirit or ethos of the kingdom of God which he, Jesus, is on earth to establish.

Matthew's gospel was written in the first place for Jewish converts to Christ. For all devout Jews who wished to be considered acceptable to God, the principal activities they had to practise were almsgiving, prayer and fasting. Matthew wishes to ensure that any element of outward show or display is removed from their behaviour and that their only motivation will be to place themselves in the correct relationship with God so that they can receive his graces. The Church has chosen this excerpt of Matthew's gospel as an appropriate one for us to hear and ponder as we begin our Lenten practices.

It is good to remember that the achievement of our chosen penance or good work is not the be-all and end-all of our aim during Lent. What we 'do for Lent' is only the preliminary to being open to that grace of basic conversion of 'turning away from sin and being faithful to the gospel' that is called *metanoia*. During the forty days, we should not forget their culmination in the Easter Vigil at which we are baptised (or, more probably, renew our baptismal promises) to receive the graces of that sacrament and be renewed in faith and holiness.

In the first reading, from the book of the prophet Joel (2:12-18) and dating from around 400 BC, God calls the people to repentance for their sins, a repentance that has to be interior and genuine.

St Paul (2 Corinthians 5:20-6:2) reminds us, in the second reading, that God has granted us salvation through Jesus and that this is a right moment for us to seek that blessing and to be reconciled to God.

FIRST SUNDAY OF LENT – Year A

Matthew 4:1-11

The first Sunday of Lent gives us the account of Jesus' forty days in the Judean desert and the temptations he endured at that time. All the synoptic gospels tell of Jesus' period in the desert and the temptations; John's gospel omits all mention of these matters. The synoptic gospel to be read depends of the year; this being year A, it is Matthew's account that we hear.

After being baptised by John the Baptist and before beginning his public ministry, Jesus is prompted by the Holy Spirit into the Judean wilderness or desert. It is the area between Jericho, the Jordan and the Dead Sea on the east and Jerusalem on the west. The region is barren, rocky and mountainous (not a desert of sand like the Sahara), infertile and inhospitable. Fasting for six weeks had left Jesus physically weakened and vulnerable. It is at this time that he is tempted by the devil.

Matthew describes three temptations, all of which challenge Jesus to determine and declare what kind of saviour or messiah he is to be. If he seeks to have food for himself in his present need, it will indicate that he will be self-centred and set on seeking his own interest. If he seeks to throw himself spectacularly from the temple parapet and thus make a triumphant entry to Jerusalem and the Temple, he will be seen as a messiah who wants to be pretentious and idolised. If he seeks to be a ruler of many nations (provided that he subjects himself to Satan), it will show that he will be a leader who wants to dominate, to have as much power as he can obtain (and by any means whatever).

Refusing all these temptations, Jesus, even before he begins his mission, shows that he is to be a saviour and messiah who thinks of others and not himself, who is humble and wishes to serve, and who is modest and not ambitious for power or domination.

Each of the three temptations and, even more, each of the reactions of Jesus to them provide opportunities for us to ponder our own behaviour. Even although we shall never be offered the rather dramatic scenarios which the devil offered Jesus, what is our reaction to the various selfish traits in our character that the temptations arouse? And yet, if we wish to be faithful disciples of Jesus, this gospel passage tells us what Jesus asks of us. The story gives us some thinking to do in the days ahead and perhaps also some changing.

The same exercise deriving from the three temptations could also be taken up for communal consideration – for the community of the parish; and even in regard to the community of the whole Church (although to embark on the latter, knowing that it would be an exercise in futility since we are neither the pope nor even a synod of bishops, might lead only to dispute or pointless frustration).

A final point. Pope Benedict XVI reminds us of a certain symbolism between the different temptations and three essential aspects of Jesus' subsequent mission: the Eucharist; the Resurrection; the King.

The first reading today (Genesis 2:7-9; 3:1-7) tells the story of an earlier occasion of the devil coming to tempt, in a garden not a desert, and successfully. It is the account of Adam and Eve's original sin which caused God to expel them from Eden and make them subject to all humanity's ills and weaknesses and to death. The story itself is an appropriate 'companion' to today's gospel; moreover, it highlights the need of a saviour who would, in God's plan, mend the broken relationship between God and his creatures.

Paul, in this passage of his letter to the Romans (5:12-19), explains the catastrophic effects of Adam and Eve's sin – that, since all human beings are their descendants, we are all infected and have incurred their sinfulness and its consequences, especially the loss of the privileged relationship that God gave our first parents as well as a sentence of certain death. However, although one man caused so much guilt and suffering, another one man, Jesus Christ, has restored and indeed enhanced the relationship with God, a relationship with all the gifts that we receive through faith and with baptism.

(It is perhaps worth remarking here that, at certain special seasons of the year – and Lent is an example – both the first and the second readings can have a bearing on the gospel of the day. In Ordinary Time, the second reading normally has to stand alone, without any evident relation to the first reading and the gospel.)

SECOND SUNDAY OF LENT – Year A

Matthew 17:1-9

As the gospel for the first Sunday of Lent gives us the account of our Lord's temptations (as narrated in the synoptics), the second Sunday provides us with the story of his transfiguration (again from the appropriate gospel).

The transfiguration reveals once again that Jesus is the Messiah and the divine son of the Father. The event is placed shortly after Peter's profession of faith at Caesarea Philippi and Christ's prophecy of his forthcoming passion, death and resurrection. As is often the case, the accounts of the transfiguration in Matthew and Luke have their source in Mark.

Most scholars understand several of the external features of the transfiguration of Jesus to be a symbolic re-enactment of the meeting of Moses with God on Mount Sinai (Exodus 34:1 and following verses). Hence, although the most common tradition is that the transfiguration occurred on Mount Tabor in Galilee, it possibly had no actual location but may be simply an intimation that Jesus is the new Moses. Jesus is bathed in a luminous brightness that recalls Moses after Sinai when he had to cover his face (Exodus 34:29-35). The appearance of Moses and Elijah are as representatives of 'the Law and the Prophets', a phrase used to indicate the whole of God's revelation in the Old Testament. Hence, when Jesus is in their company, he is seen as the fullness and fulfilment of that revelation. The three tents allude to the feast of Tabernacles (which is a memorial of the Israelites at Sinai when Moses received the law from God) and the cloud reminds us of God's presence on Sinai (Exodus 19:9 and 24:15-16).

The theological meaning of the transfiguration is that Jesus is the Messiah and is so even before that status is revealed in its glory after the resurrection. Further, his status comes from the Father and is the consequence of his humble obedience to the Father's plan which led to his suffering and death. Peter apparently does not understand the greater mission that Jesus has, compared with Moses and Elijah, since he seems to equate the three ('three tents') even though only Jesus is bathed in light. The Father's words are clear – only Jesus is declared to be his Beloved Son; it is only to him that the apostles are told to listen.

The account ends by noting the apostles' great fear, the reassurance that Jesus gives them and his request that nothing should be said of the vision until after he had risen from the dead. This so-called 'messianic secret' (perhaps, rather, secretiveness) is found frequently in Mark's gospel and is usually attributed to the danger that, if such an event had been made public at this time in his ministry, the crowds might well have presumed that Jesus was to be a messiah with worldly power and kingship.

The transfiguration of Jesus can be understood in terms of reassurance – reassurance by the Father to Jesus himself who knew what lay ahead of him and, as fully human, needed to be reassured that the path he would follow was the will of the Father and very much in accordance with the divine plan. The apostles also were reassured, particularly Peter, who had been horrified at the prospect of their imminent departure from Galilee to go to Jerusalem and for the purpose foretold by Jesus.

Personally, I like to consider the transfiguration to be a paradigm or a pattern of God's custom of providing us with little 'transfigurations' of reassurance when we experience fear or dread of forthcoming events. Such reassurance can be given to us in prayer, at Mass and even through the agency of parents or friends. It is very satisfying that St John Paul II, in providing the five luminous mysteries (or the five mysteries of light) to fill the long gap in the rosary between the Finding in the Temple and the Agony in the Garden, should have chosen the transfiguration to occupy one of the places.

In the first reading today (Genesis 12:1-4), we read of Abram setting out on a hazardous mission in obedience to God's will. Abram is obedient and God provides him with a reassuring promise of success beyond all imagining.

St Paul encourages his assistant and delegate (2 Timothy 1:8-10) to accept the difficulties of being a public witness to the gospel of salvation through Christ. He is to rely on the power and grace of God.

THIRD SUNDAY OF LENT – Year A

John 4:5-42

Today and the following two Sundays, the gospels come from St John. They are long accounts of meetings between Jesus and people who are in need. The three gospels can be related to the sacrament of baptism, for which we are preparing during Lent, either to receive it or to accompany those being baptised or to renew our baptismal promises. For the three Sundays, the readings of year A are used in churches and parishes in any year in which there are to be baptisms at the Easter Vigil; and in fact they are considered so relevant that they can be used in any of the three years in any church which chooses to do so.

This Sunday, the connection with baptism lies in Jesus saying to the woman at the well that he can give her living water; there follows a conversation on the subject between the two. In a sense, they are conversing at cross purposes because Jesus is speaking of the 'water' that gives eternal life while the woman thinks he is referring to ordinary drinking water.

The conversation between Jesus and the unnamed woman is fascinating, particularly because it is so unusual. Jesus shows his humanity and his human needs to rest and to quench his thirst while on the long journey from Judea to Galilee. He is in Samaria and there was great dislike and suspicion between Jews and Samaritans. The latter were regarded as heretics by the former since, while in exile centuries earlier, some Samaritans had married pagans so that their religion had become a syncretic form of Judaism unacceptable to strict Jews. Yet, despite this barrier as well as the more basic one of a stranger talking to a woman whom he does not know, Jesus engages in conversation with the woman. Besides, the trend of the conversation seems quite bizarre, almost as if Jesus and the woman were seeking to score points off one another.

But the outcome is serious. The woman is impressed by Jesus, tells him that she recognises him to be a prophet, to which Jesus responds by telling her that he is not only a prophet but indeed the messiah (in contrast with his reluctance, reported in the synoptics, to reveal his identity). The reaction is startling. The woman hurries off enthusiastically to bring some of the townspeople to meet the visitor (what a fine example for all of us of how to share our faith in Jesus!), he is persuaded to stay for two days in the allegedly hostile Samaritan town and many of the citizens became believers. The evangelist even goes as far as to report that their verdict was 'We know that he really is the saviour of the world' (John's gospel having several examples of Jesus being recognised as sent to save the whole world).

The story of Jesus and the Samaritan woman is highly entertaining and we should take time to enjoy the exchanges between the two. Do they not reveal to us something of the nature of Jesus that the gospels, bent on their more serious purposes, tend to hide? But we should also be aware of the reason for the passage being chosen for this Sunday in Lent. The Easter Vigil approaches, the opportunity for us to make a serious and deliberate renewal of our baptismal promises (probably made for us by parents and/or godparents and therefore needing to be ratified by us). The phrases 'living water . . . never thirsty again . . . will turn into a spring . . . welling up to eternal life' provide a basis for prayers of gratitude, of petition and, above all, of faith. This is an opportunity for us to marvel at the truly astonishing privileges which baptism brings us.

The first reading (Exodus 17:3-7) tells us of God satisfying the physical thirst of the Israelites as they trekked through the arid wilderness of Sinai on the way from slavery in Egypt to possession of the promised land.

In today's extract from the letter to the Romans (5:1-2.5-8), Paul explains that we are justified and made righteous, acceptable to God, 'through our Lord Jesus Christ by faith'. Jesus achieved this by 'dying for us sinners' with the result that the Holy Spirit has poured the love of God into our hearts, giving us sure hope of eternal glory.

FOURTH SUNDAY OF LENT – Year A

John 9:1-41

The second of the three special pre-baptismal events in John's gospel is the cure of the man born blind. It is one of the 'signs' which, in John's gospel, witness to the power and mission of Jesus, the messiah. The cure takes place in Jerusalem where Jesus is. He notices the man begging and, having corrected his disciples of the general belief that the blindness must have been God's punishment for sin, either of the man himself or of his parents, Jesus makes a paste of earth and spittle and spreads it on the man's eyes. He then tells the man to wash the mud off at the Pool of Siloam. The man does so and discovers that he can see. Scripture commentators, aware that the receiving of sight has a reference to faith received at baptism, note that Jesus required the man to be himself active in the process, as we must collaborate to receive the effects of our baptism.

There then follow a series of people questioning the man, harassing him and badgering him with hostile severity. He testifies to Jesus as well as he can but knows little or nothing about him apart from his name and has no idea how he was cured. Among his questioners were some Pharisees who condemned both Jesus and the man as sinners and eventually drove the latter out of their presence.

Feeling compassion for the honest and courageous victim of this abuse, Jesus goes in search of him. When they meet, a short dialogue is reported. 'Do you believe in the

Son of Man?' When the man asks who that is and Jesus says that he was speaking about himself, the response comes: 'Lord, I believe'. Jesus has given the gifts both of eyesight and of faith to a person who believes that Jesus can do so. The inference is evident – the waters of the pool, with the power of Jesus, give sight to the eyes of the blind man; the waters of baptism, with the power of Jesus, give the sight of faith to the spiritually blind. The man himself gives great example to us all, catechumens or 'cradle Catholics', by the steadfast honesty and courage with which he fearlessly faces his examiners and, though no scholar, parries their taunts and jibes.

The first reading this Sunday is from the first book of Samuel (16:1.6-7.10-13). It is the story of how Samuel, under God's guidance, chose David to be Saul's successor as king in Israel. In his human nature, Jesus was a descendant of David and therefore belonged to a kingly line.

Paul (Ephesians 5:8-14) reminds the people that they, who once lived in the darkness of sin, now live in the light of Christ. They should therefore discover what God's will is for them and try to live rightly in goodness and truth.

FIFTH SUNDAY OF LENT – Year A

John 11:1-45

'The water that I shall give will turn into a spring inside him, welling up to eternal life'. 'Go and wash in the Pool of Siloam'. 'Unbind him, let him go free'. This Sunday we have the third great story from John's gospel, stories whose purpose is to help us understand the meaning of Easter and, specifically, the meaning of baptism.

Jesus had a close friendship with the family of Martha, Mary and Lazarus, three siblings. They lived in Bethany, a village near Jerusalem and just on the other, eastern, slope of the Mount of Olives. When he visited Jerusalem, Jesus took the opportunity of seeing the trio and enjoyed the hospitality they offered. 'When he visited Jerusalem . . .'. John's gospel indicates several visits to the city during his public ministry of between two and three years. On the other hand, the synoptic gospels speak of only one visit, the visit that led to his arrest, trial and death. Scholars are inclined to think that John is probably correct, the synoptics tending to collect all the Galilean narratives and relate them without Judean 'interruptions'.

The gospel today tells us that Lazarus has died, and that his sisters and Jesus himself are very upset. The two appeal to Jesus and even tend to complain that he could have been there to prevent the bereavement. This allows us to hear Jesus affirm 'I am the resurrection', an incident to which we shall return, below.

Jesus asks to be taken to the tomb. On arrival there with the sisters 'and the Jews', Jesus astonishes them with the command, 'Take the stone away'. Then two further and even stranger commands: 'Lazarus, come out!' and 'Unbind him, let him go free'. No wonder many of those present 'believed in him' though, ominously, some went to report to the

Pharisees. This miracle was performed as a great favour to the family and friends, as well as to Lazarus; and his return to life on earth was not to be permanent, of course. But the Church derives considerable further meaning from the event, since the miracles of Jesus are signs.

The grief that Martha and Mary experienced is a clue of this further meaning. We do suffer greatly when a person whom we love dies, but the miracle teaches that burial (or cremation) of the body is not the end of the person who has died. In the natural order, when the tomb is closed with a stone or the grave is filled in, we have no way of knowing that the person's existence is not finally over. But the command to remove the stone is a powerful symbol that Jesus is breaking that barrier of silence and ignorance and asserting that the dead are alive. Our faith is awakened and restored. We can and do believe that God is already active, infusing life into those who have died.

The raising of Lazarus from the dead is, in fact, the last and greatest of the seven miraculous 'signs' which John's gospel records so that 'through it the Son of Man will be glorified' (11:4). This purpose is made clear not subsequent to the miracle (as with the earlier signs) but prior to it, in the words exchanged between Jesus and Martha (11:21-27).

In thanking his Father for hearing his prayer, Jesus shows that, since he and the Father are one, he can presume the Father's agreement to his performing the miracle; he expresses this aloud for the benefit of the people who are present (11:41-42). At the same time, the description of the event also reveals the complete humanity, emotions and all, of the divine Son of God (11:33-36).

It is time now to recall the words of Jesus, 'I am the resurrection . . .'. Ponder those words and the complete declaration which Jesus made at that moment (John 11:24-27) and let your faith in God's unending and loving care for us be renewed. Let that faith and its fulfilment be recognised as the result of our being baptised children of God.

The words of God in the first reading (Ezekiel 37:12-14) referred primarily to the return of the Jews from exile in Babylon (sixth century BC) but are also understood as a prophecy about messianic times and the inheritance of eternal life promised by God for those who are faithful.

The reading from St Paul (Romans 8:8-11) is also very relevant to today's gospel. He states that, since the Holy Spirit of the Father who raised Christ from the dead is also in us (because we have been justified), then, even if we die, the Father will give life to our mortal bodies. The reasoning is that Christ's resurrection was carried out by the Father because the Holy Spirit dwelt in Christ; therefore, since Christ is in us along with the Spirit, the Father will also raise us from the dead.

PALM SUNDAY OF THE PASSION OF THE LORD – Year A

Matthew 21:1-11
Matthew 26:14-27:66

The first of the two gospel passages is used as part of the liturgy of the blessing of palms and the subsequent procession. The extract contains not only a description of the entry that Jesus made over the Mount of Olives and into Jerusalem but also makes some messianic allusions. The quotation from the prophets Isaiah (62:11) and Zechariah (9:9) is seen as referring to the messiah who will not be powerful or warlike, but gentle and humble. These qualities are illustrated by his riding on a donkey. Matthew has incongruously suggested that Jesus not only borrowed but also rode on two animals, whereas the original prophecy mentions both words but only as 'poetic parallelism' (two names for the same animal).

The journey into the city is a messianic triumphal procession with crowds of people, cloaks and branches of trees spread on the roadway, and shouts of acclamation. 'Hosanna' originally meant 'save, we pray' but here it is just a shout of the crowd. 'He who comes in the name of the Lord' (Psalm 117/118:26) is seen as messianic; so also is 'Son of David' (which Matthew himself adds as heard that day). Curiously, only John (12:13) (and none of the synoptic gospels) mentions palm branches.

The second gospel passage is, of course, Matthew's account of the Last Supper, Gethsemane, Christ's trial, his passion and death. Here are some notes and thoughts.

It is difficult to know on which day of Holy Week the Last Supper took place. The text states that it is a Passover meal (26:17-19). John's gospel (18:28) indicates that Passover that year began on the Friday evening, yet the synoptics set the meal on the Thursday. The more common explanation to solve the problem is that Jesus, knowing that he would be unable to have the meal on the Friday (when he would celebrate Passover very uniquely and individually on the cross), decided to anticipate the meal on the Thursday and, at that Passover meal, he instituted the Eucharist (so closely related to his sacrificial death next day on the cross).

It is during the course of the Last Supper that, according to John's account, Jesus washed the feet of the apostles (13:2-15), addressed them with his farewell discourse (13:31-16:33) and offered his priestly prayer to his Father (17:1-26).

There is a certain confusion about the various authorities before whom Jesus was put on trial. Matthew and Mark say that Jesus was arraigned before the high priest Caiaphas and the Sanhedrin on the night of the Last Supper and Gethsemane. Luke and John, probably more accurately, say that the Sanhedrin session was on the following morning and that the previous evening Jesus was taken to Annas, the previous high priest and father-in-law of Caiaphas, for an informal and preliminary examination. It is while before the

Sanhedrin that Jesus drops the use of the 'messianic secret'. He had already clearly divulged to his close followers that he was the messiah (Matthew 16:16). Now (Matthew 26:63-64) he makes his identity fully and publicly known: he is the messiah and indeed he is divine, seated at the right hand of the Father (see Psalm 109/110:1). The Sanhedrin judged that, in claiming to be divine, Jesus was guilty of blasphemy and deserved to be executed. Moreover, he was seen as a threat to public order. It is during this trial of Jesus by the Sanhedrin that Peter denies his master.

Rome reserved the formal judgment and imposition of capital punishment to its own authority and therefore Caiaphas and the Sanhedrin sent Jesus to the governor of Judea, Pontius Pilate, to impose the sentence which they wished. Pilate was in Jerusalem at the festival in case there was crowd trouble, though normally he lived in Caesarea Maritima. The reply which Jesus gave to Pilate's question, 'Are you the king of the Jews?' (27:11) can be interpreted as 'in a certain sense, yes'. The crowd's cry, 'His blood be upon us and upon our children', was the customary phrase (as shown in other cases) to declare agreement with, and responsibility for, a death sentence.

Pilate was told that Jesus was a Galilean and, knowing that the tetrarch (ruler, but subject to Roman supervision) of Galilee, Herod Antipas, was in Jerusalem at the time, he sent Jesus to be examined by him. Luke is the only evangelist to mention this (Luke 23:6-12). Herod Antipas was a son of Herod the Great and had imprisoned and beheaded John the Baptist. The meeting with Jesus was merely to satisfy Herod's curiosity (since he was without jurisdiction in Jerusalem) but he took the opportunity to further humiliate Jesus before returning him to Pilate.

Crucifixions had, for ritual and religious reasons, to take place outside of the city walls. Although the site of Calvary is now within the city walls, this was not the case in the time of Jesus. Twice on Calvary, Jesus is offered something to drink. First, on arrival on the mount, he is offered wine. This may well be a gesture of pity by the women who had already sympathised with him as he carried the cross. Matthew says that the wine was 'mixed with gall' (27:33-34), but this should probably be 'mixed with myrrh'. Second, just before he died, a sponge soaked in vinegar is held up to him. Although the synoptics suggest that this was an added cruelty, John (19:28-30) suggests otherwise – and perhaps correctly. Jesus cried out the opening words of psalm 21/22 ('My God, my God, why have you deserted me?') which express real suffering and distress but not a sense of despair since the psalm is a prayer which looks forward confidently to God's loving care.

After the death of Jesus, a number of strange occurrences were reported to have taken place in Jerusalem (Matthew 27:51-53). Mention of these happenings can be found foretold in the Old Testament prophets. Since Matthew was writing, in the first place, for convert Jews, he takes advantage whenever he can of citing the sayings of prophets and verses of psalms as being fulfilled by Jesus. It has to be admitted that sometimes the connection is obscure and at other times the quotation has been somewhat altered in order to achieve the evangelist's purpose.

Here are some details of the practice of crucifixion. It was a method of execution introduced into Palestine by the Romans (first century BC). The condemned person, after the mandatory scourging, had to carry a crossbeam to the stake (already in place); the crossbeam could be attached to the top of the stake or lower down. The person was fastened to the cross usually by nails, sometimes by cords. Death came by asphyxiation and especially because, after his legs were broken, the person could not straighten up to breathe.

Pilate, procurator of Judea from 26-36 AD, was highly unpopular with the Jews and had a reputation for ruthlessness and cruelty. He formally condemned Jesus to death because he judged him guilty of sedition. The sentence was carried out by Roman soldiers and according to Roman rules. In all probability, it occurred on a Friday afternoon, a few hours before sunset and the start of 14 Nisan, the feast of Passover. John's gospel regards the raising of Jesus on the cross as the beginning of his exaltation into glory in heaven (John 3:13-14; 8:28; 12:32-34).

A crucified God seems an absurdity. A God who is humiliated and helpless, who suffers pain and death for love of us – such is nonsense or else a completely new and almost incredible truth acceptable only in faith. In this latter case, we begin to know a God who not only loves us but also suffers with us. We learn that, as a result, neither can we be unmoved by the sufferings of our brothers and sisters. To celebrate the suffering of Christ properly we must have genuine compassion, compassion which will be costly, to show Christ-like love and care for those who suffer.

After Peter, in answer to Jesus' question, declared him to be the Christ, the Son of the living God, Jesus told the apostles that he would be put to death and then rise again. Peter was shocked and said that was unthinkable, for which Jesus severely rebuked him. He then went on to declare 'If anyone wants to be a follower of mine, let him renounce himself and take up his cross and follow me . . . anyone who loses his life for my sake will find it' (Matthew 16:24-25; Mark 8:34-35; Luke 9:23-24; John 12:25).

A similar warning occurs at another time: 'Anyone who does not carry his cross and come after me cannot be my disciple' (Luke 14:27; Matthew 10:38). These two texts are prominent in teaching us what is required if we wish to be disciples.

So there is a price to pay if we are to follow Christ. We shall meet suffering, problems, conflict. These will occur in our attempts to make the world more just, the Church more faithful. Although he did not seek to be put to death, Jesus was not deflected from the possibility and its increasing likelihood or from his mission of bringing justice to all the oppressed and identifying himself with the poorest and the despised. His death as a criminal is God's act of infinite love for all of humanity. Our celebration of Christ's passion and death is an act of gratitude for such love as well as a decision to live like Jesus in selfless love for others.

The first reading for this Sunday is from Deutero-Isaiah (50:4-7) and is an extract from the third 'Song of the Servant of the Lord'. The servant declares that he listens to God in order to serve those in need; he then speaks of the suffering that he will endure and affirms that he places his trust fully in God. The passage is messianic and specifically looks forward to the passion of Christ.

The second reading (Philippians 2:6-11) speaks of Jesus, though the equal of the Father, willingly accepting a double humiliation (incarnation and crucifixion) and being rewarded by God with exaltation throughout creation and to the glory of God.

THURSDAY OF THE LORD'S SUPPER – Years ABC

John 13:1-15

John's gospel describes the happenings at the Last Supper in a very different manner from the synoptic gospels. John omits any mention of the institution of the Eucharist (although much is said and implied on the subject in chapter 6). Moreover, the long discourse to the disciples and the prayer that follows are about the divine life that the Eucharist brings us. John starts his account of the Last Supper with tonight's gospel passage, the only one to mention Jesus washing the feet of the disciples (which is also a self-giving, though not Christ's body and blood). There is a discrepancy regarding the days on which the events of the Sacred Triduum took place, but most authorities favour John's information rather than that in the synoptics. Therefore, assuming that the Passover was on the Saturday and that the day began at the previous sunset, the Last Supper was at the start of the previous day (our Thursday night).

The passage begins with the evangelist saying that Jesus had always loved his disciples but he was now going to express that love openly so that they would be aware of it. During the supper, Jesus prepares to wash the feet of those at table, an action usually carried out by slaves and meant not to clean but rather to honour the guests. By washing their feet, Jesus was also expressing the humility that his human nature implied. Peter considers the position incongruous – master washing the feet of servants – and objects. He continues to miss the point by asking Jesus to wash all of him, as if the action were to cleanse the disciples because they were dirty. Jesus explains that his purpose, by using the symbol of washing feet, was to teach his disciples that they also should show the same humility and respect and anxiety to serve others as Jesus himself did.

The liturgy of this Mass envisages that, 'if pastoral reasons suggest it . . . the men who have been chosen' may have their feet washed by the priest. It seems strange that the rubric should seem so hesitant, as if the rite were allowed rather than recommended. And 'men'? Well, perhaps the reason is not chauvinism but delicacy; nevertheless, the highest authority in the Church now considers the restriction no longer necessary.

The rubric does not specify twelve, and rightly because the purpose is not to imitate the precise situation which took place at the Last Supper, but to imitate the spirit of service that Jesus gave.

The rite of washing feet can sometimes appear rather stiff and formal and as if it were being carried out for the benefit of the priest. Sometimes, one also gets the impression that it is those whose feet are being washed who are offering a service and acting humbly. Would there be any advantage and more effective symbolism if, after the priest (who does represent Christ in a special way) has washed some feet, there followed a more general and informal washing of feet throughout the congregation?

Although it is fitting that the rite should be carried out on Holy Thursday, that is often enough. The point is that the rite is a symbol for the service that Christ's disciples should always be ready to offer, service that is by no means available only in this symbolic form or only to those who form the community of participants at Mass.

The first reading (Exodus 12:1-8.11-14) narrates God's instructions to Moses and Aaron on how the Israelites (on that occasion in Egypt and then annually in commemoration of their escape from slavery) are to celebrate the paschal meal and smear the doorposts with the sheep's or goat's blood to avoid the first-born in that house being struck down that night. The death of the first-born was the tenth, final and effective plague visited by God on the Egyptian captors.

In the second reading (1 Corinthians 11:23-26) St Paul provides the earliest extant account in the Scriptures of Christ's institution of the Eucharist at the Last Supper.

FRIDAY OF THE PASSION OF THE LORD – Years ABC

John 18:1-19:42

It is the Johannine account of our Lord's passion and death that is used in the liturgy of Good Friday. Remember that John reports historical details of the events but that he also sees much symbolism in what happens or is said; and that he presents Jesus as in control of the situation (for example, 18:4-9.20-23.34-35; 19:10-11) and, especially in his crucifixion, as one who both suffers and dies but also is exalted (for example, 3:13; 18:36-37; 19:28) and glorified as the conqueror of sin and death.

Pontius Pilate, the Roman governor (procurator) of Judea (26-36 AD) was disliked by the Jews and, from the little that is known of him, deserved his reputation as ruthless and unfair. John gives considerable details of his questioning of Jesus during the trial, details that suggest his interest in the prisoner and his puzzled impressions of him. When he asks Jesus, 'Where do you come from?', Jesus is silent. This is an indication that Jesus is aware that Pilate would be unable to understand his divine origin and mission. Later in the questioning (18:36-37), Jesus declares that he is a king but makes it clear, as the synoptic gospels report he had done when questioned by the Sanhedrin (Mark 14:61-62; Matthew 26:63-64; Luke 22:69-70), that his kingship did not make any claim to worldly power. Despite his frustration, Pilate is reluctant to condemn Jesus to death; but the threat of the people that the Emperor Tiberius would punish him if he did not execute someone who claimed to be king made up his mind.

John asserts (19:14) that Jesus was crucified on the preparation day for the morrow's Passover celebration. On the former, the lambs were killed for the feast and, at the same time as their blood was being shed, so also was the blood of the Lamb of God. A rather similar coincidence is worth noting. Just before he died, the gospels record that Jesus was offered vinegar soaked on a sponge attached to the end of a stick; John alone says (19:29) that the stick was a reed of hyssop – the same plant as was used at the Passover to sprinkle the door posts and lintels of the Jews with the blood of the lambs (Exodus 12:22) to exempt them from God's punishment.

After Jesus has been crucified and when the evangelist is describing the events until and at his death, the gospel makes four references to Old Testament texts being fulfilled in what was happening. We are also told of the words of Jesus: 'Woman, this is your son' and to John, 'this is your mother', words which are usually understood not only in a personal sense but also in a spiritual and symbolic sense with Mary, the new Eve, the mother of all of Christ's disciples, and John, representing them. It is perhaps strange that the synoptics do not even mention the presence of Mary and John beside the cross. John records other words of Jesus on the cross ('I am thirsty' and 'It is accomplished' 19:28 and 19:30) but not the desolate words of psalm 21/22 since he wishes to stress the calm control which Jesus showed during his passion.

That water and blood came from the pierced side of the body of Jesus after death has often been seen as symbolic of baptism and Eucharist; and therefore, just as Eve came from the side of Adam, so the Church (the second Eve) is seen as coming from the side of the second Adam.

Although the principal elements of the passion, crucifixion and death of Jesus are common to both John and the synoptics, there are a considerable number of different details in the four narratives. One final difference may be noted to illustrate this. Before Jesus is entombed, John tells us that Nicodemus, who once had come to Jesus by night (John 3:1), arrived with a large amount of spices, myrrh and aloes; the presumption is that he and Joseph of Arimathea carefully prepared and anointed the body before placing it in the tomb. On the other hand, the synoptic gospels speak of a hurried entombment that provided the motive for the women's arrival at the tomb on Sunday morning to carry out the rites which had been omitted on Friday evening (Mark 15:45-16:2; Luke 23:52-24:1); the fourth gospel, however, says that the women came to mourn (20:1-2.11-14).

Exactly how does the death of Christ save us? Use of the words 'ransom', 'redemption' and 'atonement' in the New Testament and in Catholic theological teaching can suggest a God who demands the dreadful death of his Son as payment for the gift of our forgiveness; or that Jesus had to be punished with death to avenge our guilt. Such ideas are repugnant to the reality of God who is holy and merciful; they cannot be entertained for a moment. The three words (above) do cause a problem, nor is it clear just why God's plan for our salvation involved the death of his Son. One can say that the words are used in a very limited number of cases in the gospels (never in Luke or John, once each in

Mark (10:45) and Matthew (20:28)); and when they occur, they are used in the less strict sense that has become common and merely mean the process of salvation and liberation. I hope that one may correctly express the mystery (because it is a mystery) by saying that it was God's plan, which Jesus obediently fulfilled, that his Son should give limitless love and self-offering, no matter the cost, to the work of saving us from sin and unending death and of enabling us to be adopted as his Father's sons and daughters in the family/kingdom of God; by these actions and his prayers, Jesus intercedes with the Father for our salvation.

The first reading (Deutero-Isaiah 52:13-53:12) is the fourth 'Song of the Servant of the Lord'. It describes the appalling and vicarious sufferings which the servant will suffer for our sins, his death and his restoration in triumph. It is a beautiful and moving reading which is deeply relevant for today's liturgy.

Two short passages from the letter to the Hebrews (4:14-16; 5:7-9) make up the second reading. Jesus is our high priest, now glorified in heaven but who experienced all the sufferings and weaknesses of his human nature in spite of being also the Son of God. He accepted death and thus became the means of our salvation.

THE EASTER VIGIL – Year A

Matthew 28:1-10
[Mark 16:1-7 in Year B]
[Luke 24:1-12 in Year C]

The four gospels state that the first news of the resurrection of Jesus was given by an angel (Matthew), a young man (Mark), two men (Luke) or two angels (John) to Mary Magdalene (and other devoted women disciples, according to the synoptics) on arrival at the tomb early on Sunday to arrange and anoint the body of Jesus, hurriedly buried on Friday afternoon. After this episode, each of the gospels has its own account of appearances of Jesus, which are all different from one another, some being located in Jerusalem or nearby, others in Galilee. Presumably, there were differences in the memories and oral traditions from which the written accounts are derived. However, the one essential truth – that Jesus rose from the dead – is unanimously taught.

It seems probable that the account from the gospel according to St Matthew of the visit to the tomb where Jesus was buried (Matthew 28:1-10) is based on the earlier written account in the gospel according to St Mark (Mark 16:1-8). The two reports are very similar. There are differences, most of which are minor; but there is one important difference. In Matthew, the women, on returning from the tomb, are said to meet Jesus who speaks to them. Mark makes no mention of this but, in fact, reports that the women ran away from the tomb and spoke to no one because 'they were frightened out of their wits'.

Matthew's account of the meeting has Jesus saying the same things to the women as the angel had told them a little earlier at the tomb – that there was no reason to be afraid but they had to tell the disciples to go to Galilee and they would see Jesus there. It has been noticed that this meeting with Jesus also has similarities to the meeting that Mary Magdalene had with Jesus near the tomb and which is reported in John's gospel (20:14-18). So we have to wonder if the women had three encounters (one with an angel and two with Jesus) or two or even only one. We do not know, but it is not impossible that, because of different oral traditions or due to confusion in the reporting, there are inaccuracies in the written accounts.

Mark's silence about a meeting with Jesus near the tomb is significant. On the other hand, the evangelist states (16:7-8) that, although the young man at the tomb asked the women to pass on the message about a meeting in Galilee, they did not do so because of their fear (16:8), a verse which is omitted from the extract used at the Vigil Mass. The ending of Mark's gospel (16:9-20) causes a problem for exegetes. It is a summary of the appearances of Jesus after his resurrection and, since the style of writing is different, there is a theory that (a) the original ending after verse 8 may have been lost, since otherwise the gospel ends very abruptly and on an unsatisfactory note; and (b) as a result, verses 9-20 were added later, either by Mark himself or by an unknown person.

Luke's account, when it is used at the Vigil (24:1-12), is similar to those of Matthew and Mark although there are some differences. He says that the women reported to the disciples that the tomb was empty, but he (Luke) does not say that Jesus had met the women or had given them the instruction about going to Galilee. In fact, Luke does not report any subsequent Galilean appearances of Jesus. Also, the extract used adds a verse about Peter running to the tomb, finding it empty and then going away, puzzled; this, despite John's gospel narrating the visit of Peter and John to the tomb and their belief that Jesus had risen (John 20:1-10).

Today's occurrence is factual. Jesus really rose from the dead. And that fact has great symbolic value; in other words, if we seek Jesus, we shall not find him among the dead. To find him, we must follow in his footsteps and go to where he taught and is still teaching, where he healed and is still healing, where he forgave and is still forgiving, where he brought God's love and gave people hope, as he continues to do today. Faith in the risen Christ does not come merely because we have been told that he is alive. We have to make our own journey of faith and find him among those who are faithful and know that he is with them. He promised that 'where two or three are gathered in my name, I am there with them' (Matthew 18:20).

Earlier in the Vigil there are seven readings from the Old Testament which show us the gradual development of God's plan of salvation. The readings comprise accounts of creation, Abraham's sacrifice and the crossing of the Red Sea, followed by four extracts from the prophets, two from Isaiah and one each from Baruch and Ezekiel. These four contain intimations of the expectation about a saviour/messiah.

The New Testament reading is from Paul's letter to the Romans (6:3-11). He likens our baptism to Christ's entombment and resurrection. We are put into the font (the parallel is clearer if baptism is by immersion) in a spiritually dead condition and emerge alive with the new life in Christ. And since death brings sin to an end, our baptism should mark the end of sin in us.

EASTER SUNDAY – Years ABC

John 20:1-9

The gospel for the Easter Vigil presents us, depending on whether we are in year A, B or C, with one of the synoptics' accounts of the empty tomb. The gospel of the Sunday Mass, read every year, is John's account of the same. The synoptic gospels are in very close agreement about the details. None describes the actual resurrection because, of course, no one was present to witness the moment. John differs from the synoptic accounts in some details, probably due to his gospel being written much later. Presuming that the earlier accounts were known, the evangelist is preparing to describe the meeting between Jesus and Mary Magdalene (20:11-18). For this reason he mentions only her going early to the tomb (though, in verse 2, he reports her use of the plural 'we').

John's gospel does not mention Mary's purpose in going to the tomb nor the appearance of someone (angel or human) to declare that Jesus had risen. This last point is the main difference between John and the synoptics and, although we do not know the reason for the omission, it may be because the detail is subsumed into the incident which is about to be reported (20:11-18) of the meeting between Mary and the 'gardener'.

In today's reading, the fourth gospel tells us that, as a result of Mary's report about the empty tomb, Peter and John ran there and that, on the evidence of the shroud and the cloth which had been on Jesus' head, both of which were still lying in the empty tomb, John (and presumably Peter also) believed. This is the first instance of belief in the risen Lord, without his being seen. The extract ends with a parenthetical admission of their surprise and bewilderment, which would be dispelled by the gift to come of the Holy Spirit.

The Sacred Triduum is our annual and most intense commemoration of the events that are central and crucial in the divine plan for our salvation. The Eucharist is itself a mystery in which some truths are beyond our understanding, above all the real presence of Jesus under the appearances of bread and wine as well as the fact that the rite makes present the saving action or process of the death and resurrection of Jesus. Further consideration of the Eucharist and its mystery will be found elsewhere.

Here, it is right to ponder the challenge that the bodily resurrection of Jesus from the dead presents to us who want to believe and who seek to deepen its relevance to our lives.

Faith, in the sense of believing, is a gift from God which we must want, at least implicitly, before God will grant it. But, as St Paul says, 'They will not believe in him unless they have heard of him, and they will not hear of him unless they get a preacher' (Romans 10:14). In and through the preaching of the radical message of the Good News (such preaching is called the *kerigma* and comprises basic truths such as Jesus is Lord and Saviour who truly died and truly rose to save us), faith is awakened. The *kerygma* has no need to justify itself by reasoning. It is authoritative and is accepted or not, and that's it.

If accepted, faith is born in the sudden and astonishing recognition of the truth of what has been heard.

To accept and grow in faith in the resurrection of Jesus, we have to have a yearning to love and seek him seriously and energetically. We should seek him where the values of Jesus are lived and practised, in communities gathered in his name and who have him at their centre; not among those with a stagnant, tired or purely routine faith but with those actively anxious to bring about the kingdom of God.

It is good to remember that, at the very heart of our faith and of our Church, there is one who, by all earthly evidence, was a failure who died, executed as a criminal; but one to whom the Father has done justice and recognised as triumphantly successful in his mission. So for us who work, suffer pain and apparent failure in reaching out to the needy, the helpless and the rejected, Jesus' life, death and resurrection provide us with reassurance and strength to continue, rather than lamenting the evil in the world or the apathy and criticism we meet. True Christians have to give their time, their efforts, even perhaps their health and their lives because they love both Jesus and those in need in whom he lives. And it is faith and hope and love, God's gifts, that sustain them.

The first reading, as throughout Easter time, is from the Acts of the Apostles (10:34.37-43). Peter is preaching to a gentile family, telling them about Jesus and his saving work, and declaring that the salvation won by Jesus is for all, gentiles included.

The second reading offers us a choice of two passages from St Paul: either Colossians (3:1-4), in which we are told that, because we have been given a new kind of life by Christ, our thoughts and hopes should be on him and on heavenly concerns; or first Corinthians (5:6-8), to learn, appropriately using metaphors from the Jewish rites of Passover, that we should rid ourselves of the yeast of evil and make ourselves into a new and unleavened bread of sincerity and truth.

SECOND SUNDAY OF EASTER – Year A

John 20:19-31

The disciples had been told by Mary Magdalene about the reported resurrection of Jesus but their main concern on that first Easter Sunday seems to have been their own safety. They were behind closed doors 'for fear of the Jews'. The risen Lord, whose body is glorified now and no longer subject to earthly limitations, enters the room. He greets them with the familiar words, 'Peace be with you', and their timid caution is replaced by joy. On that occasion, he gives them the gift of the Holy Spirit as well as a mission and the authority to forgive sin in his name. Note that he breathes on them; breath (which in Hebrew is the same word as for spirit: *ruah*) is a symbol of the Holy Spirit. Also worth noting is the similarity in several points between John's account of this Easter Sunday appearance and the account by Luke of the Lord's appearance to the apostles on that same day (Luke 24:36-49).

It has to be kept in mind that, for the apostles, chronology was of less importance than the meaning and significance of events. So, for John, since Jesus is glorified at the resurrection, he has already been reunited with the Father although also present and seen on earth; consequently, John considers that the resurrection and ascension of Christ have occurred before Jesus meets the disciples. For Luke, especially in the Acts of the Apostles, the ascension is the close of the period of Christ's being visibly with the disciples and Pentecost is the start of the apostolic witness – and he affirms this by separating in time the three events. For those writers, chronology is not the issue here. Scholars also note that the Jewish feast of Pentecost commemorated God's law being given on Mount Sinai during the Jews' trek through the desert from Egypt; the inference here being that the Holy Spirit fulfils and completes that law and in a sense supersedes it.

Jesus reappears to the group a week later and Thomas, previously absent, is there. 'My Lord and my God' is the most explicit profession of faith in the divinity of Jesus that is found in the gospels and paradoxically it is made by 'doubting Thomas'. The response which Jesus makes is very important. Miracles, historical arguments, even the reported visible appearances are useful in leading us to belief in the risen Christ but it is the preaching of the Good News that is the authentic and universal motive for faith. The gospels have been written so that we may come to faith and continue to deepen it (20:29-31). 'Doubt no longer, but believe' (20:27), Jesus said to Thomas; it is an invitation which, though we may have become sceptical, comes to each one of us whether we are seeking it or not.

The gospel tells us that 'the disciples were filled with joy when they saw the Lord' (20:20). This is the joy we experience when we are aware that Jesus is present with us, in our midst. Sometimes however, even in our gatherings, even for Mass, we do not have that experience; the gospel is read and proclaimed as 'the gospel of the Lord' but we did not hear it as such; or we exchange the sign of peace, Christ's gift, but it is only a brief flurry of a few words from the person beside us. It is as if Jesus were absent, blocked by routine or apathy or inattention. The risen Lord is at the centre of our worship and of our Church, but that is too often forgotten or unknown. Is he no longer loved and followed by his disciples? Have we become like the disciples early on the first Easter Day, with the doors closed, afraid to be seen or known as disciples?

The conclusion of today's passage is interesting and important. It speaks of the events in the fourth gospel, both recorded and unrecorded, having been 'signs' and explains their purpose of revealing the identity and mission of Jesus (20:30-31). It is these signs that we commemorate in the third mystery of light of the rosary.

The Acts of the Apostles contain three short word-pictures of the lives of the earliest Christian community. The three passages are the first readings on this day in years A, B and C. Today we are told of the community's exemplary lives of worship and charity (2:42-47).

The second readings today and for the next five Sundays of year A are extracts from the first letter of St Peter. The letter, which seems primarily for the newly baptised, may originally have been an instruction or a homily.

The authorship is very doubtful but the letter is 'canonical', i.e., recognised by the Church as inspired Scripture. Today's passage (1:3-9) encourages us to be faithful and to bear the burdens of this life because, through the resurrection of Jesus, we have been reborn as God's adopted sons and daughters and with a glorious inheritance awaiting us in heaven.

THIRD SUNDAY OF EASTER – Year A

Luke 24:13-35

For most of us, the appearance of Jesus to the disciples on the road to Emmaus is our favourite post-resurrection story. It is a story with a plot and a good ending, and it rings true. Moreover, as we shall see, it has real relevance for us.

The opening phrase of the story has been cut from the gospel reading: 'That very same day', namely Easter Sunday. It is difficult for us to grasp the feelings of all Jesus' disciples that day. Most seem to have been so disheartened that they had no hope and were in hiding from hostile mobs. Others had heard reports and rumours that the tomb was empty and even that perhaps he had risen. A few were really hopeful and excited. And the two disciples in today's story had urgent business to attend to in Emmaus and had only heard vague rumours before leaving Jerusalem; but they had discounted these and felt let down, their previous hopes dashed.

Jesus joins them, unrecognised because now glorified. He pretends to be ignorant of the rumours, even of the crucifixion. Then he changes his tune and scolds them for their lack of faith – 'so slow to believe' – despite all the teaching of the law and the prophets that, after suffering, the messiah, Christ, would be glorified. Consoled, they persuade Jesus to remain in Emmaus with them. They gather to eat, Jesus takes bread, blesses and breaks it and gives each a piece – Eucharistic words and actions. The truth dawns on them, but Jesus has disappeared. However, their minds are made up and their duty is clear. They must return to Jerusalem at once to tell the Good News.

No matter how often we have heard the story, we like to hear it again. It is a story that catches our attention and grips our emotions. It is a story of faith lost and faith regained; perhaps we can relate to that. It is a story of a journey; we can all relate to that – particularly if we are thinking about a journey, not of seven miles but of a lifetime. And, like those two disciples, do we share our story so that others may believe?

A final point. Did you notice the sequence? Hearing the Scriptures and their message, followed by a meal with Eucharistic characteristics. When we are at Mass, we have the chance of enjoying an Emmaus experience with our faith in the risen Lord renewed and strengthened; then, 'Go and announce the gospel of the Lord'. No need to say any more!

In today's first reading (Acts 2:14.22-33), Peter, emboldened by the presence of the Spirit, preaches to the crowd 'in a loud voice' (what a transformation in Peter!). He tells them about Jesus, his miracles, his death and resurrection – and uses a passage from the Old Testament (psalm 15/16) – to show that Jesus was the messiah long awaited. Peter's teaching method is the same as Jesus used on the road to Emmaus.

The second reading (1 Peter 1:17-21) warns that, since our salvation cost something very precious (the blood of Christ), we must take care to live good lives if we want to receive a favourable judgment.

FOURTH SUNDAY OF EASTER – Year A

John 10:1-10

This is Good Shepherd Sunday, the day each year when we pray that those whom God is calling to a share in his Son's ministerial priesthood and/or to consecrated life will hear and respond to that call. For most of us, the need for such prayer is very urgent.

In the Old Testament, God frequently describes himself or is described as the shepherd of his people Israel. Jesus uses the same title for himself and his teaching on the subject is found, above all, in the tenth chapter of St John's gospel (the chapter of which three extracts form the gospels of this Sunday of Easter in years A, B and C). Jesus is in Jerusalem and is talking with some Pharisees who had shown their displeasure with him for giving sight to the man born blind. The tense atmosphere that resulted from that cure explains the evangelist's remark today (verse 6) that 'they' did not understand the parable that he was now using.

Later in the chapter (year B), Jesus will assert that he is the Good Shepherd. But today, he describes himself as 'the gate of the sheepfold'. This image can be puzzling if one subconsciously imagines the gate as closed. I think that a more helpful word would be 'the entrance', which can be closed when necessary but is generally open for the sheep. Those who enter through this gate will, says Jesus, be safe, free to go in and out, and assured of the sustenance they need. They will be safe because protected from those who would harm them; free because the sheepfold is not a place of detention and the shepherd will lead them in and out as required; and nourished because all the pasture that is necessary will be provided.

The image of the entrance to the sheepfold allows us to maintain the Old Testament view of God the Father as the shepherd who always cares for the sheep, whether they are in the sheepfold or not, and who leads them out when that is appropriate and looks after them so that they know and trust him (especially Ezekiel 34:1-16). The same image of the sheepfold also lets Jesus speak of 'thieves and brigands' who try to enter the sheepfold undetected but who are unsuccessful in their attempts to lure the sheep away. The failure of these people in their nefarious purpose is due to the close relationship that the sheep have for their true shepherd whose voice they recognise and obey.

Most people are of the opinion that, nowadays, we have an increasingly worrying shortage of men offering themselves and seeking to be priests. And, even if there are some who dispute that statement, everyone must recognise our duty to pray for, and try to foster, vocations to the priesthood (that is, a response from those whom God is calling). Without priests, we are deprived of the Eucharist, the very source and summit of our relationship with God through Christ.

Here are a few comments on this subject of vocations to the ministerial priesthood. Vocations come from God and sometimes go to unexpected and unexpecting persons. So we should not hear assertions such as 'I'd never want to be a priest'; much better to ask 'how would I respond if I thought God was calling me?' However, it is unlikely that such a call will be heard or heeded unless we promote a culture for vocations (prayer, support, encouragement, readiness to accept). It is very sad, but admittedly understandable, to hear Catholics say something like 'I hope very much that no son of ours becomes a priest'. This particular vocation and, in fact, any vocation from God is a privilege; for the priesthood, courage and unselfishness are needed, but not fear since every vocation from God is accompanied by all of the graces and helps needed.

The first reading (Acts 2:14.36-41) describes the scene after the Holy Spirit came to the disciples. Peter's earlier fear is changed to courage, he speaks to a large crowd about the salvation to be obtained through faith in Jesus Christ and by being baptised. The outcome is spectacular.

The extract from the first letter of Peter (2:20-25) encourages us to follow the example of Christ and accept suffering even if undeserved. He was guiltless of any wrongdoing but he bore torture and even death without resisting; his selfless conduct brought us salvation.

FIFTH SUNDAY OF EASTER – Year A

John 14:1-12

Although we are celebrating the resurrection of Jesus, today's gospel is part of the long discourse which he gave to the apostles at the Last Supper. The extract is meant to calm their fears, because he has been talking about going away as well as of being betrayed by one of them and of Peter disowning him. They naturally ask Jesus where he is going and today's gospel is his response to that question.

He says that they cannot go with him, not yet anyway, but he will be preparing places for them for later. Thomas, the practical one, asks a practical question. If they don't know where he is going, they will not know how to get there. Then Jesus, having told them that his destination, and later theirs also, is his Father's house, adds 'I am the Way, the Truth and the Life'. He leads us to the Father, he is the teacher of truth so that we can know the Father, and eternal life is precisely knowing the Father.

So far, so good. But then comes another request, this time from Philip. 'Can you not let us see the Father now, to calm our fears in the meantime?' The request allows Jesus to take them, and us, some way into the life of the Trinity. He says that, if we see and know him, we see and know the Father since, through faith, we believe that Jesus is in the Father and the Father is in him; the two do not exist apart. At least, if for no other reason, we can believe that fact on the evidence of the work that Jesus is doing, works of goodness and love, of mercy and forgiveness, of healing and compassion for those who are in need. He then adds that, if we have that awareness through faith, we will do the same kind of work as he does. This is because, when Jesus is glorified and with the Father, they will send the Holy Spirit to empower the disciples. The phrase 'even greater works' is best understood not in terms of more impressive miracles but in the sense that the Church will be much greater both geographically and in numbers.

The prospect of death and separation from those we love is upsetting but this discourse of Jesus can be very comforting. Two things that Jesus declares are especially consoling: that he has gone to prepare a place for us in the Father's house and that, if we know Jesus, we also know the Father. The latter assurance in particular encourages us to try to learn as much as we can about Jesus, his life, his works and his character; and, as we know about him, we discover that we know him as our brother who loves us and wants our love in return.

If it is our vocation to be a parent, a teacher or a priest (or even to help others to know Jesus and therefore the Father), this gospel passage should be encouraging and enabling as we fulfil our responsibility of sharing our faith with love.

The first reading (Acts 6:1-7) continues to describe the earliest days of the Church in Jerusalem. The passage explains the awareness of the apostles of their need for help and their decision to choose deacons to carry out the duties of helping others in want.

The letter of Peter (1 Peter 2:4-9) teaches us that the Church is a building made up of the believers, its living stones; and that, as such, they are chosen to share a royal priesthood and be consecrated to worship God in gratitude and love.

SIXTH SUNDAY OF EASTER – Year A

John 14:15-21

John devotes four chapters of his gospel (13-16) to his report of the discourse of Jesus at the Last Supper, then a further chapter to the prayer that Jesus offered for the apostles. So, like last week, the gospel today is part of the discourse. The general context today is that, since Jesus will no longer be with them in the way that he was present during his public ministry, what can be done to provide help for them?

The solution comes from Jesus himself. 'I shall ask the Father and he will give you another Advocate to be with you for ever, that Spirit of truth . . .' (14:16). Scripture scholars find the Greek word *parakletos* difficult to translate since it can have various meanings – advocate, counsellor, protector, intercessor, defender, mediator, helper – but, since the Spirit will do the same work for the apostles as Christ (the latter being the first Advocate, the Spirit 'another Paraclete'), Jesus is speaking of a personal being, the Holy Spirit, the third Person of the Trinity.

The Spirit will preserve the apostles from anything that could separate them from Jesus, thus enabling them to continue being aware of the presence of Jesus in them and with them. Jesus assures the apostles of this because they love him and are obedient to his commandments. Those who love and obey him, Jesus says, will be loved by him and the Father and, since he and the Father live in each other, both will dwell in the apostles and he will make that presence of both known by the vision of faith.

Today's gospel passage is not an easy one to follow or to understand. The extract ends at verse 21; if the following verse had been included, we would have heard one of the apostles ask (and perhaps putting our thoughts into words): 'Lord, what is all this about?' In line with Jesus' words today, it has been suggested that, to help us understand this excerpt, we need to move from a routine and merely verbal attachment to Jesus to one rooted in 'the Spirit of truth'.

The reading from the Acts of the Apostles (8:5-8.14-17) shows Philip preaching to Samaritans (whom the Jews despised since their religion was a mixture of Judaism and some pagan beliefs) and baptising them. The problem here, however, is what is meant by 'baptism in the name of the Lord Jesus' but which did not confer the Holy Spirit.

St Peter's first letter (3:15-18) encourages the converts to be ready to explain their reasons for the faith and hope that they possess, whether the questioners are friendly or hostile. If the latter, they must still reply with courtesy and, if they are made to suffer, they should remember that Jesus himself also suffered.

THE ASCENSION OF THE LORD – Year A

Matthew 28:16-20

For this feast, the principal text must be from the first chapter of the Acts of the Apostles (1:1-11). That report forms the first reading in all three years, A, B and C. The synoptic gospels also refer to the event and the three references form the gospels of the three years.

With regard to the date and place of the ascension, the gospels and the Acts of the Apostles offer differing accounts which suggest that the details given are presented for symbolic reasons or to show fulfilment of Old Testament prophecy, and not with the intention of providing factual information. The place named varies between Galilee and the Mount of Olives, near Jerusalem; and the time or date depends on whether Jesus is reckoned to have returned at once to the Father after he rose glorified (though able, when he wished, to be present to the apostles in the glorified state which made him difficult to recognise) or if it is supposed that there was a gap of some (forty?) days between the resurrection and the ascension.

Matthew's account is set in Galilee, on a high place there (a symbol of Christ's authority). There is still some dubiety among the apostles with regard to the identity of the person they had come to meet. Jesus declares that he speaks with total authority given to him in his glorified state following the resurrection. He then instructs the apostles to go throughout the world and call people to become his disciples, being baptised and obeying all his teaching (which he has already given to the apostles). The exact words of baptism given by Matthew may be that of a formula used in the early Church, but the reality and the effects are those we know. Matthew's account ends with Jesus assuring the apostles of his continuing presence with them for ever – a matter on which they had earlier shown much concern (for example, John 13:36; 14:5; 16:17-19).

This pledge of Jesus to be ever present in the Church with his disciples is not just something which Jesus said to his apostles but it should be firmly believed by us and be a permanent source of reassurance. The Church, whether universal or local, wherever his disciples are, has Jesus alive in its community, teaching us how to live in imitation of his life on earth, healing, forgiving, welcoming. And where the glorified Jesus is, there also are the Father and the Spirit. The life and activities of the Church provide a constant testimony of the presence of Christ. (The close relationship between the gospels for the previous Sunday and for this feast now becomes evident.)

Today's first reading is from the Acts of the Apostles (1:1-11), written by the same author as wrote the third gospel and both works dedicated to Theophilus (identity unknown). The passage provides a description of several of the details of the ascension (including citing the Mount of Olives as its location). Since it is by far the most detailed account, the details given have now been incorporated into the popular idea of the event (including a stone showing the footprints of Jesus as he 'took off').

St Paul (Ephesians 1:17-23) prays that God may give us a vivid awareness of the inheritance that awaits us as a result of what God did to save us through raising Jesus from the dead and investing him with all authority as head of the Church, his body.

SEVENTH SUNDAY OF EASTER – Year A

John 17:1-11

All twenty-six verses of the seventeenth chapter of St John's gospel are taken up by the priestly prayer of Christ at the Last Supper, but only the first eleven verses are used in this Sunday's gospel. The prayer affords us a summary of the purpose of Christ's life on earth. The synoptic gospels often mention that Jesus prayed but, apart from teaching the apostles the Lord's Prayer, they do not, as here, tell us the content.

Jesus asks his Father to glorify him so that he can glorify his Father. He says that he has glorified the Father by revealing him through his own words and life to those chosen to be his disciples; now the Father can glorify him by restoring him to the glorious state he had before he accepted the humble conditions of his life on earth. Jesus then extols the fidelity of the disciples to God's call and, anticipating the action of the Holy Spirit soon to come, he asserts that the disciples now are fully aware of the relationship between Jesus and the Father, as well as the mission he received from the Father and that the teaching he gave them came from the Father.

The last part of today's excerpt has Christ praying, on this solemn occasion, for the disciples themselves (in fact, therefore, for Christ's Church), who belong to both Father and Son. Jesus again speaks of his glorification, this time by his disciples (by their fidelity and probably also in anticipation of their future missionary work) before alluding to the reason for the special need of guidance for the disciples – that he will no longer be visibly present with them.

Although those present with him were the primary object of Jesus' prayer, the limitless intention of that prayer and its efficacy reach down through the centuries to the disciples of today. Guided by the Holy Spirit and with the graces for which Jesus prayed, the knowledge and faith which the apostles and the first disciples received from him have been faithfully transmitted to us through parents, teachers, priests and bishops. It is our sacred responsibility and privilege to be today's links in the chain by our lives, our example and our words. For our faithful completion of this duty, Jesus prays, interceding with the Father in the words he used at the Last Supper.

The first reading takes up the Acts narrative (1:12-14) to inform us of the apostles' return to Jerusalem after the Lord's ascension. Mary was there as well as some others, including some friends and relatives of Jesus. We are told that the group engaged in 'continuous prayer' (to which John's gospel (20:19) adds the further detail: 'the doors were closed . . . for fear of the Jews').

The final excerpt from the first letter of St Peter (4:13-16) speaks of suffering, not as a result of wrongdoing and punishment, but inflicted because we are Christians. We should thank God if we suffer for that reason since thus we can have a share in the sufferings of Christ.

PENTECOST SUNDAY – Year A

John 20:19-23

In the Acts of the Apostles (2:1-11), Luke gives us a description of Pentecost and the coming of the Holy Spirit on the apostles, a description with which we are familiar. It strikes us at first as something of a surprise when we realise that, in the gospel passage chosen for today, John indicates that the Holy Spirit was given to the apostles on Easter – and he was there! There is apparently a conflict here due principally to the fact that the human authors of the Scriptures were intending to teach the actual mysterious events themselves and not the accurate chronology. When Jesus rose from the dead, it is clear that he lived a different and glorified human existence (the apostles had difficulty in recognising him, he was able to appear and disappear without being seen to make his way in the normal manner, nor was he constantly in the apostles' presence). The conclusion is that, when he rose he also returned to the Father, and that the 'forty days' is not the period before he went to the Father but the period during which he made appearances to the apostles (as well as being with the Father). When he was with the Father, they could together send the Holy Spirit on the nascent Church. Perhaps, then, it may be that, in imitation of the two Jewish feasts of Passover and Pentecost, the early Christians did the same in their (separate) liturgical observances of the resurrection and the coming of the

Spirit. Our custom, therefore, of having separate liturgical observance of resurrection, ascension and descent of the Spirit gives us the advantage of being able to reflect more carefully on the meaning of each mystery.

In the gospel today, we hear that Jesus came to the disciples on Easter Sunday evening and, of course, they were overjoyed. His next words are important. He gives them the same mission as the Father had given him – to reach out to those in need, to bring forgiveness and freedom to those who are oppressed by sin or injustice, to give them the new life of the sacraments – and he shows the wounds of his crucified body to show that the task requires total and unconditional commitment. Since he is very aware of their weakness and inexperience and that he will no longer be visibly present with them to lead, he confers on them the Holy Spirit, the Paraclete, the Advocate, literally to be their inspiration in fulfilling their mission even to death.

The gospel links the words of Jesus conferring the Spirit to his giving the Church the power to forgive sin in his name. While this particular privilege is exercised only by those who have a share in Christ's ministerial priesthood, the same Spirit is given to us all in baptism and confirmation in order that we take our share in continuing the mission of Christ and doing so in countless ways.

Prayer addressed to the Holy Spirit is not common in the Church's liturgy, but it does occur, perhaps most notably in the so called sequence (*Veni, Sancte Spiritus*) at Mass on Pentecost Sunday and in various other hymns. Best known of these are *Veni, Creator Spiritus* and, in English, *Come, Holy Ghost, Creator, come.* And the conclusion of the collect prayers at Mass, although addressed to the Father and through the Son, ends with a profession of faith 'in the unity of the Holy Spirit'.

Given our awareness of the essential work of the Holy Spirit in the Church, it would be no bad thing if our prayers were more frequently said directly to the Spirit. For example, prayer that we be more alive to the presence of Jesus among us, more courageous in following his example, more open to accepting change when it is needed. We might also seek the Spirit's help in being constantly reminded of the teaching and message of Jesus so that our witness does not become routine, uninspired and uninspiring, but rather that the gospel we proclaim is genuine good news for a vibrant community of disciples. And what about the mission of Jesus, now committed to us to continue, the mission of building the kingdom of God, a kingdom of justice and peace, of a more caring world in which, sadly, unfairness and greed and violence are still so evident, of a world of generous love for others and especially for those in need? For many of us, the work of the Spirit in the Church and in ourselves remains in the background, even forgotten. So, 'Come, Holy Spirit' into our thoughts and prayers; make us gratefully aware of your loving presence in our midst.

The first reading (Acts 2:1-11) is Luke's familiar account, beginning with 'When Pentecost day came round' and providing a graphic description of the coming of the Holy Spirit and of the galvanic effect it had on the apostles and their preaching.

An extract from the first letter of St Paul to the Corinthians (12:3-7.12-13) provides today's second reading. He explains the work of the Spirit, both in the great variety of gifts conferred to different people and in the unity of the multitude of people who receive the gifts, all of whom are united in the (mystical) Body of Christ, all baptised in the one Spirit and recipients of that Spirit.

THE MOST HOLY TRINITY – Year A

John 3:16-18

Nicodemus is a rabbi, a Pharisee and a member of the Sanhedrin who is intrigued by Jesus and attracted by his teaching. He comes to Jesus to seek clarification and the two engage in a conversation about the fact that baptism can be described as being born again. The dialogue, as it is reported by John, develops into a monologue from Jesus and the subject becomes more general. It is from this section of the narrative that today's gospel passage comes.

Jesus says that the world, now in a sinful state, could be saved only by God. The fact that he intervened by sending his Son to be our saviour proves the great love that God has for us. So, if we wish to be saved, we must believe in God's Son. (The final phrase of the extract speaks of belief 'in the name of God's only Son', the use of the word 'name' being a Hebrew and Aramaic custom, meaning 'person'.)

The love of God for us is so fundamental in our faith that we can perhaps fail to recognise its crucial importance. Yet, the manner in which Jesus fulfilled his mission on earth is an image of that love. In a similar way, our conduct as Christians ought also to reflect that basic truth, so often overlooked but, if recognised, so comforting.

It seems strange that this gospel excerpt, chosen for the feast of the Blessed Trinity, makes no mention of the Holy Spirit. However, it is helpful to recall the opening words of the second reading last Sunday (Pentecost): 'No one can say, "Jesus is Lord"' unless he is under the influence of the Holy Spirit' (1 Corinthians 12:3). The second reading today is equally helpful.

The first reading (Exodus:4-6.8-9) has Moses ascending Mount Sinai in the desert in order to have a meeting with God, who declares himself to be a God of love and fidelity (which is confirmed in today's gospel). It is worth remembering that, although the Jews were prone to fall into polytheism from time to time, God himself insists always on his being the only God, a truth that we firmly maintain as basic to our faith.

The final words of St Paul's second letter to the Corinthians (13:11-13) provide the second reading. Paul is bidding farewell to the Christians in Corinth and, as he often did in his letters, he invokes the three Persons of the Trinity. This instance is particularly explicit (and therefore is also used as the opening greeting of our liturgy).

THE MOST HOLY BODY AND BLOOD OF CHRIST – Year A

John 6:51-58

Although Holy Thursday is a celebration of the Eucharist and the annual commemoration of its institution, the fact that, on that day, we are on the eve of Good Friday and the Easter Vigil prevents our full attention being concentrated on this great feast. So at today's celebration, we can give our undivided attention to the Eucharist, the central and most crucial gift of Jesus to his followers, the source and summit of our worship and indeed of our lives. The synoptic gospels and St Paul give accounts of that first Eucharist which took place during the Last Supper. St John's gospel concentrates on other aspects of that Supper but, in the discourse of Jesus which he reports in his sixth chapter, he provides us with some very full teaching on the Eucharist. It is from that chapter that today's gospel extract comes.

Jesus had, with five loaves and two fish, fed several thousands of those who had been listening to his teaching. The following day, at least some of them were again in his company when he resumed teaching in the synagogue at Capernaum. He told them, 'You must believe in the one whom God has sent'. They ask for a sign to justify that he is the one sent. He says that he will feed them with the bread of God which gives life to the world – and he himself is that bread. He then goes further in his explanation: 'Anyone who eats this bread will live for ever; and the bread that I shall give is my flesh for the life of the world' (verse 51, the first verse of today's extract from the discourse). It could have been assumed that Jesus was speaking only metaphorically and the 'bread' was his teaching, to nourish their faith. However, the rest of the passage removes any doubt. The crowd understood the literal meaning of his words. Christ did not correct them as if they had interpreted erroneously, but reaffirmed the literal meaning, and he did so several times. The remainder of the narrative (not read today) tells us that many found his teaching unacceptable and left him; and that, when he asked the Twelve if they also wanted to leave, Peter replied in their name: 'Lord, whom shall we go to; you have the message of eternal life, and we believe' (verses 59-69).

Later, the apostles were to be alarmed when Jesus spoke of his leaving them. But, in today's great discourse we have the reassurance that, though he may no longer be visible to those who believe, he will still be really present when we celebrate the Eucharist, present in several ways as the Second Vatican Council asserts, and above all in his teaching (Liturgy of the Word) and in his flesh made present and eaten (Liturgy of the Eucharist). The Council, while maintaining the essence of the rite of the Eucharist, recognised that certain additions, made during subsequent centuries, had obscured the necessary clarity and simplicity of the rite and that some parts had been removed; it therefore decreed a reform of the rite to enable it to be better understood by those present so that their participation might be as full, active and effective as possible. Among the reforms was the restoration of Holy Communion from the chalice in addition to the form of bread, a practice that seems to be presumed by Jesus in the gospel read today.

There is a great deal of necessary catechesis implied in today's gospel passage, as well as from reflection on its words – the sacredness and mystery of the Eucharist, its fundamental importance for our growth in faith, hope and love, the need to participate and to do so with as much care, understanding and devotion as possible. We should be aware of the 'community' nature of the Eucharist, its renewal of the covenant between God and ourselves, its commitment to evangelisation and loving care for the needy, and its aspect of being a pledge and foretaste of the joy of heaven.

This is a suitable place to note that, although this feast was inaugurated in order to express our gratitude and devotion to Jesus for having bequeathed the Mass to the Church, the primary reason for celebrating the Eucharist is not to worship Christ made present on the altar, but to remember and re-present his total self-giving, above all on the cross, and to commit ourselves to copy him, as members of the community which he established, ready to give all that we have for the sake of our brothers and sisters. In the celebration of Mass we both recall the last meal on earth which Jesus had with his disciples and anticipate the feast we hope to have with him in heaven.

There are some elements in our Mass, especially for instance, the dual elevation of host and chalice (introduced in the Middle Ages for popular devotional purposes) which tend to distract us from our main reason for celebrating the Eucharist. We may also lose sight of the Mass as a community celebration which commits us to the way in which we are to live and act in this world, rather than an opportunity for me, as an individual, to gain the graces I need in order to get to heaven. Thus, Holy Communion ought to be a public and radical commitment, as a member of the Church, to follow Jesus in his work of building God's kingdom on earth.

Note that, in the prayers that we say during Mass, and above all in the words of the Eucharistic prayer, we are addressing God the Father, not Jesus. Remember also the words which Christ used at the Last Supper. 'This is my body' and 'This is my blood', to which he added not 'for you to worship' but 'which will be given up for you' and 'which will be poured out for you'. If we understand that the Mass is a commitment to action now, in this world, perhaps those who dismiss it as boring and irrelevant will be able, instead, to appreciate it as relevant and pertinent to the real world in which we are living.

In the Old Testament reading (Deuteronomy 8:2-3.14-16) Moses reminds the Israelites of God's care for them on their way to the promised land. He not only freed them from slavery in Egypt but, when they were hungry and thirsty in the desert, he provided them with manna to eat and water to drink. These gifts are seen as signs and figures of Holy Communion.

Paul (1 Corinthians 10:16-17) speaks of our union (better, communion) with Christ which occurs in the Eucharist. That many share in the one loaf is a powerful sign that we are one body. (Admittedly, the sign value of Holy Communion is diminished when the 'loaf' is actually individual little pieces of bread previously prepared in that form).

Sundays in Ordinary Time

SECOND SUNDAY IN ORDINARY TIME – Year A

John 1:29-34

Although the Sunday gospels of year A are usually from St Matthew, this Sunday's choice is from the first chapter of St John. The verses preceding today's passage have John the Baptist at the Jordan encountering a deputation of priests and Levites come from Jerusalem to check on his identity and the orthodoxy (in accordance with the law given by God) of his teaching. The first part of the Baptist's testimony (just before today's passage) is about himself – who he was not and then who he was.

Now we come to today's gospel excerpt. John the Baptist recognises Jesus as the messiah whom Israel awaited and testifies to that effect. It is noticeable that John's gospel does not explicitly say (as the synoptic gospels do) that it was his cousin who baptised Jesus, but the Baptist does make clear the distinction between the baptism he (John) was conferring and the baptism which Jesus would confer: baptism with water compared with baptism with the Holy Spirit.

John the Baptist had not recognised Jesus as the messiah and possessing the Holy Spirit until he saw Jesus coming to him. He is reported as having used two descriptive phrases about Jesus: 'the Lamb of God' (a phrase that recurs several times in every Mass) and 'the chosen one of God'. The source of these phrases is unclear. Was the first phrase a reference to the paschal lamb (which, however, has no direct reference to the remission of sin)? Or, perhaps more probably, a reference to 'the lamb led to the slaughter house' (Isaiah 53:7) which the Old Testament prophet uses as a description of the suffering 'Servant of the Lord'. The second phrase may well be a reference to 'my chosen one in whom my soul delights' (Isaiah 42:1) in which the prophet is also referring to the 'Servant of the Lord'. Some early manuscripts have 'the Son of God' (rather than 'the chosen one of God') but this is thought to be an editor's desire to employ the same word as is used in the synoptic gospels.

Therefore the great difference between the two baptisms is that Jesus, possessing the Spirit, was able to confer it on those who receive his baptism; his therefore is a baptism in which we not only confess our sinfulness but also receive forgiveness, adoption into God's family, membership of a sacred community, a share in Christ's priesthood of the New Law and empowerment to assist in God's plan of salvation. These are breath-taking gifts which too easily can be overlooked or forgotten or unappreciated. So, when we read about the baptism of Jesus, it is good to take time to renew in faith our awareness of the associated gifts and our desire to use them for the purposes that God calls us to fulfil.

It perhaps should be noted that John the Baptist, in proclaiming that he saw the Spirit coming and resting on Jesus, would have understood 'the Spirit' in the Old Testament sense of God's power; while John the Evangelist would have known that 'the Spirit' was a distinct Person in the Trinity.

We should keep in mind that, each Sunday in Ordinary Time, the first reading is a passage from a book of the Old Testament. The passage is chosen because of its relevance to the gospel passage of the day. The second reading, nearly always from St Paul's letters, has no such relation to the gospel but, during the sequence of Sundays when the extracts are from the same letter, they maintain a certain consistency of theme from week to week.

Today's first reading (Isaiah 49:3.5-6) is a happy choice to accompany the gospel passage since (a) it comes from the second 'Song of the Servant of the Lord' while the gospel seems to have allusions to the 'fourth and first songs'; and (b) God declares that the future messiah will bring salvation not only to Israel, but to 'the ends of the earth'.

In each of the three years of Ordinary Time, the earliest five to seven Sundays have passages from St Paul's first letter to the Corinthians as the second readings. The nineteen extracts are more than those taken from any other Pauline letter. Corinth was a large and influential seaport where Paul spent eighteen months (end of AD 50-mid-52). Thereafter, he kept in touch with the Christians in the city and knew of the progress of the faith as well as the problems which the community faced. He wrote a letter to them which is not extant and then, in AD 57, he wrote the letters that we call First and Second Corinthians. In year A, excerpts from the former provide the second readings for seven Sundays, from today to the eighth. In this first introductory extract Paul sends complimentary greetings to the Christians of Corinth (1 Corinthians 1:1-3).

THIRD SUNDAY IN ORDINARY TIME – Year A

Matthew 4:12-23

The early years of Jesus' life are described in the first two chapters of Matthew's gospel. All of chapter three and the first eleven verses of chapter four deal with John the Baptist at the Jordan, Jesus meeting him there and then going into the Judean wilderness for forty days. Today's gospel takes up the story from there.

The excerpt begins by making the point that, in going to Galilee and specifically to the town or village of Capernaum, Jesus was fulfilling a prophecy of the Old Testament. Such assertions occur frequently in Matthew's gospel, indicating that his gospel was written primarily for a group of Jewish converts to Christianity and therefore to reassure them that Jesus was the messiah foretold and expected.

The remainder of the passage is a succinct description of Jesus' ministry: calling disciples, travelling from place to place in Galilee preaching repentance, 'proclaiming the Good News of the kingdom' and healing the sick. In contrast to the other evangelists who speak of 'the kingdom of God', Matthew uses the term 'kingdom of heaven'. The kingdom which Jesus proclaimed was inaugurated on earth by him; it developed slowly, not widely noticed, and is still growing among us on earth. It will reach its perfect fulfilment only after Jesus' second coming.

Matthew's use of the word 'heaven' was out of courtesy to those for whom he was originally writing, Jews who did not use the sacred word 'God'.

Jesus chose Capernaum as the centre of his missionary work because in those days it was a bigger town than Nazareth and better located on the lakeside and on a route that saw many more travellers. Nazareth was an insignificant village and indeed is never mentioned in the Old Testament. Another reason for Jesus' choice may well have been the hostility he met in Nazareth (Luke 4:28-30). Nowadays, of course, Nazareth is a large thriving town and Capernaum is an archaeological site and a place of ruins for pilgrims to visit.

The invitation which Jesus gives to the brothers Peter and Andrew and to the other brothers, James and John, is remarkable for its apparent suddenness and for the immediate response and definitive commitment of the four. One admires their singlemindedness, although we must have sympathy for Zebedee, left without the help of his two sons. Did he manage to continue his work, perhaps finding two other men who were looking for employment?

The gospel begins with Matthew quoting a passage from Isaiah (which, in fact, is also the first reading today: 8:23-9:3). Zebulun and Naphtali were areas near Capernaum and were among the first parts of northern Israel to be conquered by the Assyrians in BC 733 with many of the people taken captive into exile. In Isaiah, God promises a time of liberation and happiness for the district, a prophecy which Matthew and the early Church saw realised in the arrival of Jesus.

'The day of Midian' is probably a reference to the occasion on which the Israelites, under Gideon, defeated the nomadic tribe called Midian, a group which from time to time invaded Israeli territory. Some details are at Judges 7:12-25.

Following today's gospel, we should look forward to learning more about Jesus and his way of proclaiming the Good News. How did he live? How did he preach and to whom? How did people react? Although we have a general idea on these matters, succeeding Sundays' gospels will give much more detailed information to help us to know Jesus Christ.

Brief comments on the first reading (Isaiah 8:23-9:3) are today incorporated in the gospel reflection above.

In the second reading (1 Corinthians 1:10-13.17), Paul wastes little time in getting to the point in his letter. Writing from Ephesus, he deplores the divisions among the Christians of Corinth, each of the various factions claiming to be followers of a different leader. The reading ends with Paul mentioning another theme: the Good News of salvation does not need to be preached in philosophical terms.

FOURTH SUNDAY IN ORDINARY TIME – Year A

Matthew 5:1-12

It is useful to note that, in all probability, Matthew and Luke for their gospels use Mark, adding material obtained from other, now unknown, sources, the principal one being arbitrarily called 'Q'. Because of their similarities, these three gospels are called the synoptics. John's gospel is very different, one of the principal differences being that, while according to John, Jesus makes several journeys to Jerusalem during his public life, the synoptic gospels have Jesus remaining in Galilee until, near the end of his life, he goes to Jerusalem.

Matthew's gospel has seven sections, including an opening (Christ's infancy and childhood) and an ending (his passion, death and resurrection). Between these, his public ministry is divided into five sections which purport to show the stages of the establishment of God's kingdom here on earth. The stages can be described successively as proclamation, preaching, obstacles, embryonic existence, definitive arrival. Each of these five sections is further subdivided into (a) narrative material and (b) a discourse by Christ. The five discourses run from 5:1-7:29; from 10:1-11:1; from 13:1-13:53; from 18:1-19:1; and from 24:1-26:1. We shall see that the divisions and subdivisions are not always obvious and free of extraneous material; nor is chronological order observed.

The first of the five sections that comprise the public life of Jesus, 'Proclamation of the kingdom', has its narrative subsection in chapters 3 and 4. So today, in chapter 5, we reach the second subsection, an inaugural discourse, popularly called the Sermon on the Mount, in which Jesus outlines the character of the kingdom that he has come to establish (chapters 5, 6 and 7). The discourse today is a list of the 'beatitudes', the eighth and last being expanded by a later explanatory addition. (Note that Mark's gospel omits the beatitudes, while Luke's gospel, read on the sixth Sunday of year C, has a rather different 'take' on them than Matthew's.)

The beatitudes in Matthew are descriptions of the qualities needed in us to be good members of God's kingdom which Jesus came to establish. They may also be seen as illustrating the commandment to love our neighbour. The qualities are characteristic of the poor and powerless, the opposite of the conventional values of the world. God's kingdom, therefore, will involve a moral revolution, turning common standards upside down. The beatitudes illustrate that Jesus came not to abolish the precepts of the Old Law (the ten commandments above all) but to 'perfect' them, to raise the standards even higher. As God gave Moses his commandments of the Old Law on Mount Sinai, so Jesus, the new Moses, climbs 'the mount' to deliver the revelation of the precepts of the New Law. Jesus himself is the perfect embodiment of someone living the beatitudes. And remember that the beatitudes are not only for us as individuals but also for us in communities, especially for us as the Church. English translations vary between 'happy' and 'blessed' to list the beatitudes; personally, I prefer the latter.

'The poor in spirit' is the first beatitude, the most described and discussed especially because, in Matthew's version, the words 'in spirit' qualify the poverty which Jesus requests of his followers. It is not only individuals who are called to be poor in spirit but also, as Pope Francis frequently teaches, the Church itself. What exactly does the phrase mean? Much has been written on this; perhaps the meaning is well expressed in a few phrases: knowing how to be content to have little; trusting in God's care; attentive and generous to those in need.

'The gentle/meek' can perhaps be best understood by what they are not – not violent, aggressive, bullying, selfish, fierce, uncontrolled; so to be gentle suggests patience, tolerance, forbearance, understanding. These qualities should be found in each of us as individuals and in all of us, the Church.

'Those who weep/mourn' include those who grieve for the sadness caused by the death of those we love; but we can also weep with regret for our sins, our mistakes, our sufferings and those of others too, especially if we are the cause. To weep or mourn is not a futile activity if it leads us to consolation and, if necessary, repentance; and at least it shows sensitivity.

'Hunger and thirst for what is right' is the desire to do God's will and to ensure that justice prevails in the Church, in the secular world, in our families and in our own activities. Primarily, it is our own behaviour that should be under scrutiny, but, when others are responsible for injustice, our response should be more than annoyance or anger. Injustice, whether caused by us or by others, should impel us to seek to restore what has been damaged or lost.

'The merciful' are those who act with compassion for others, especially the poor, the hurt, the defenceless. It is a God-like activity since God promises mercy for the merciful. In Matthew's gospel, almsgiving and forgiveness are prominent.

'The pure in heart', different from the ritual purity sought by the Jewish religious leaders of the time, are those with an honesty and rightness of thoughts and desires, manifest in their speech and actions. It does not admit of hypocrisy.

'The peacemakers' are those who patiently and honestly work for the good and the happiness of all. They try to bring reconciliation where there is discord, confrontation and violence. The theatre of their activity can be anywhere and at any level. (It is unfortunate that we still use gender-limited words, such as here: 'sons' of God.)

'Those who are persecuted in the cause of right' overcome evil with good because they suffer injustice, persecution and violence, determined to remain obedient to God's will and without attempting retaliation or revenge. (This beatitude has had an expansion or explanation added subsequently, probably to comfort the early Christians who were subjected to persecution or exclusion; but it is a pity, I think, that the expansion is included when the beatitudes are the chosen passage to be proclaimed in liturgies.)

The beatitudes represent a radical change from the moral values of the world, then and now. Wealth and status are rejected, as well as what can be secured by selfishness or violence. They summarise the qualities which Jesus wants to find in those who are, or wish to be, in the kingdom of God which he established on earth. That kingdom will reach its perfect fulfilment in heaven, the eternal home of those who tried to be faithful to Christ's vision. It is, therefore, highly appropriate that this extract from Matthew's gospel should also be read in the liturgy of the solemnity of All Saints.

The Old Testament first reading is from an unusual source – the minor prophet Zephaniah (2:3; 3:12-13). He lived in the later seventh century BC, troubled times in Judah, which were to end in conquest by Nebuchadnezzar and exile in Babylon for many. Zephaniah calls the people to integrity of life, humility and honesty – values which are prominent in Jesus' preaching of the beatitudes.

In the second reading, St Paul (1 Corinthians 1:26-31) explains that those who had become Christians in the city were not from powerful or aristocratic backgrounds but from those who, in ordinary estimation, were powerless, common and even contemptible. The converts' wisdom, holiness and freedom were not inherited but were gifts from God. By coincidence, therefore, the second reading today is in accord with the gospel passage.

FIFTH SUNDAY IN ORDINARY TIME – Year A

Matthew 5:13-16

Matthew continues to present the teaching of Jesus as part of his Sermon on the Mount. Christ calls his followers to be genuine and honest disciples and he does so using the metaphors of salt and light. Provided that the salt has not lost its savour and the light is not concealed, our good works will manifest the goodness of God. Salt without a taste and a lamp whose light is not visible are useless; likewise, our duty to witness will not happen unless our lives, words and actions are such as to produce their effect. Neither inaction nor mere outward pretence will do.

Isaiah (58:7-10) also uses the metaphor of light to explain how our behaviour can be effective. God asks us to feed the hungry, shelter the homeless, clothe the naked and free the oppressed; to avoid injustice, violence, evil and hurtful speech.

In the first letter to the Corinthians (2:1-5), Paul continues in similar vein to last week. He writes that he taught them in simple language and thus their faith depends not on human philosophy but on the power of God. It would be lawful for us to make a link with the gospel by saying that Paul's teaching is therefore an example of salt with savour, lamp with light; whereas the use of human philosophy in this case would have been unauthentic pretence.

SIXTH SUNDAY IN ORDINARY TIME – Year A

Matthew 5:17-37

The gospel passage deals with the relationship between, on the one hand, the law which the Jews followed, which had 613 different precepts, and which they considered to be God's definitive revelation and, on the other hand, the teaching of Jesus. The problem was of the utmost importance especially for those first Christians who were converts from Judaism, the very people for whom Matthew composed his gospel. Jesus says that he does not reject the Law and the Prophets (a phrase which denotes the entire Old Testament) but his mission is to fulfil or complete them, to bring them to perfection.

Jesus gives an assurance that nothing 'will disappear from the law until its purpose is achieved'; this phrase is explained as 'until it has been perfected by the work of Jesus'. Hence, the law which the disciples are to 'keep and teach' is similarly qualified.

There follow, in today's gospel excerpt, examples in which Jesus 'fulfils' the law. The law is stated along with its traditional explanation, followed by Christ's 'but I say this to you', demanding a deeper or wider response.

First, to murder, Jesus adds anger, the verbal expression of anger, and indeed mutual dislike. Note that, although worship was regarded as one's most sacred duty, it had to be postponed, to allow reconciliation first.

Second, to adultery, Jesus adds lustful gazing. The reference to the hand (from Mark 9:43-48) is less relevant than the reference to the eye.

Third, to a loose paraphrase of Deuteronomy 24:1 (which allows a man to divorce his wife if he has found an impropriety or something shameful concerning her), Jesus forbids divorce absolutely. At least he does according to Mark (10:11-12) and Luke (16:18). Matthew, however, includes the phrase 'except in the case of fornication'. This causes a problem because, apart from its going against the other two gospels, it makes little sense in the context. One possible explanation is to suggest that the Greek *porneia* can mean concubinage and Greek has no separate word for 'wife'. So, instead of 'He who dismisses his wife, except for adultery, makes her commit adultery', the sentence would read 'He who dismisses his woman, except for concubinage, makes her commit adultery'. A certain solution of the problem seems impossible.

Fourth, to a paraphrase of various texts in the law, Jesus forbids the use of oaths since, although meant to guarantee veracity, the practice provides various means of evading the truth and even of mendacity; further, it encourages distrust between persons. In the new morality, truthfulness will depend on a person's own integrity.

The excerpt from Ecclesiasticus (15:15-20) calls on us to behave morally and obey the commandments, for God sees our every action.

St Paul (1 Corinthians 2:6-10) continues to emphasise that his teaching comes not from human wisdom but from God. The truths are now revealed to us through the Holy Spirit and were previously unknown; otherwise, people would not have crucified 'the Lord of Glory'.

SEVENTH SUNDAY IN ORDINARY TIME – Year A

Matthew 5:38-48

Jesus gives another two examples of the ways in which his teaching does not destroy the moral precepts or values of the past, but makes them even more demanding in accordance with standards of the kingdom he has come to establish.

First, in relation to revenge (which the Pentateuch allows, but only in proportion to the injury inflicted), Jesus forbids any resistance or retaliation by a victim of injury or damage. He gives a few examples. Some Scripture scholars find it hard to 'rationalise' these commands of Jesus (in the sense of mitigating their severity) or to justify any suggestion that they are impractical or exaggerations; rather, they suggest, Christians simply seem unwilling to accept the teaching of Jesus in these matters.

Second, the law enjoined love of neighbour (Leviticus 19:18) but not hatred of our enemies. The latter seems to have been a popular opinion or dictum, not part of the law. However, Jesus requires us to love both friends and enemies and to treat both with the same kindness and consideration. After all, we are children of God who treats all, whether good or bad, equally.

The commands contained in the two final examples of Jesus' demanding more than the Old Testament Law required are extremely rigorous, even extreme. In the first reading today (Leviticus 19:1-2.17-18), God instructs the Israelites on how to be holy. The objects of our good conduct which are given in the text are brothers, neighbours, 'children of your people'.

However, Paul's injunction in his first letter to the Corinthians (3:16-23) that 'the wisdom of this world is foolishness to God' and that a Christian 'must learn to be a fool before he really can be wise' is a very relevant admonition which helps prepare us for the shock of today's gospel passage. Christ's teaching there is not only in regard to behaviour in our family or in our parish; it is unconditional and applies also to relations between nations. It calls us to pacifism. How do we react to that?

EIGHTH SUNDAY IN ORDINARY TIME – Year A

Matthew 6:24-34

Jesus presents us with alternatives. We must choose between God and material possessions ('mammon'). We can choose love and service of God or give the things of this world priority of importance in our lives. We cannot do both. Having put that choice before us, Jesus goes on to encourage us to choose the first alternative and gives reasons for us to do so. God's loving providence will ensure that we will be looked after materially. If the flowers and the birds are cared for, then surely God can be trusted to provide us with our needs. The explanation that Jesus gives for such confidence in God's kindness is offered as thoughtful entreaty. In today's conditions, savings can be considered prudent; unnecessary and excessive accumulation is not. It should be noted that the final short sentence in the gospel passage, which introduces a rather sour note, is a later addition which unfortunately provides an irrelevant distraction to Christ's teaching.

Reflecting on our Lord's teaching, we can see that his examples of flowers and birds are not meant to suggest that we need neither earn nor buy food or clothes. Rather, the point is that we tend to worry too much (and even make ourselves ill) because we lack trust in divine providence.

There is, of course, something else – if the acquisition of material wealth becomes our god; in that case, we become alienated from God and in a very sorry state, morally speaking. Perhaps such a situation is more typical of what is called western society rather than of us, as individuals. We are members of that society and therefore have a certain amount of responsibility that it exists and that it continues. It is not only that millions – rather, billions – of our fellow human beings are without sufficient food and water, adequate housing, education and health care; but the economic system that the wealthy nations impose on the world – consumerism, capitalism, the arms trade – contribute to the increasing impoverishment of our 'brothers and sisters' living in what is euphemistically called the developing world.

These are serious considerations that, probably, do not give us much concern because they are unpleasant matters that are of little interest to our politicians and the media. But, as with wars that are irresponsibly begun and that cause such enormous misery and suffering – deaths, injuries, refugees – not to mention the cost, we should, as Christians, deplore that they are the reality of our world. Moreover, we should be aware of our duty to do what we can to oppose injustices and enable people to live in a world that, at least, is less violent and unjust.

The first reading today is from the prophecy of Isaiah (49:14-15) and offers us a few words about God's providence, a promise of loving care that is immensely consoling. However, it does not say anything about our human reaction to God's providence or to our duty of being agents of that providence for others less fortunate than ourselves.

Undoubtedly, St Paul (1 Corinthians 4:1-5) chose to serve God rather than opting for a life of selfish ease. He knows that he will be judged by God but, aware of human propensity to judge our neighbours, he reminds us that God alone has the right to judge because only God can know the 'dark and secret intentions' in our hearts. It is salutary to be aware of this when discussing the apparent failings of others in the light of today's gospel.

NINTH SUNDAY IN ORDINARY TIME – Year A

Matthew 7:21-27

Today's gospel is the final excerpt from the section called the Sermon on the Mount, a number of teachings by Jesus which Matthew has gathered and presented as a discourse to the disciples on the general theme of Jesus proclaiming that he has come to establish God's kingdom. In today's passage, the message which Jesus imparts as the essential requirement for his would-be followers is to listen to his words concerning the will of his Father and to act on those words, to carry them out. To stress this message, he compares two houses, one built on rock by a sensible man, the other built on sand by a stupid man – one house withstands the storms, the other collapses.

It will not be sufficient, Jesus warns, to claim on the day of judgment that you have done marvellous or spectacular things, if you have neglected to do what the Father asked of you and which was taught to you. This is crucial teaching, for us as much as for those who actually heard Jesus speaking. It shows the importance of knowing what Jesus asks of us, knowledge obtained from the New Testament and especially from the gospels. It would seem to indicate the need for an examination of conscience on this subject, not only as individuals, but also as parish, diocese, the entire Church. Have we been doing what our own impulses suggested? Have our activities, while perhaps not sinful, been the result of human decisions, even of false complacency or self-deception? Knowledge of Christ's teaching is needed. So also is prayer.

Moses has a similar warning for the Israelites as they make their way from Egypt to the promised land. He enjoins on them (Deuteronomy 11:18.26-28.32) the necessity of knowing what God has commanded them, as communicated to them by Moses. The specific danger of disobedience is idolatry, of worshipping the gods of other tribes or peoples whose beliefs have attracted them. Despite the efforts of Moses, however, the Jews frequently fell into the sin of idolatry, both on the journey and also subsequent to their arrival. Do we, Christians, fare any better?

For sixteen Sundays beginning today, the second readings are from St Paul's great theological treatise, the letter to the Christians of Rome. This excerpt from chapter 3 (verses 21-25.28) speaks of God's justice. By 'justice', Paul means God's promise to save his people. This salvation is called 'justification' which cannot be acquired by our own actions but only by God's free gift through the self-sacrifice of Jesus. This justification we obtain through having faith in the redemptive plan of God. The plan was known from the Old Testament but, since it is offered to everyone, it is revealed now by God through Jesus.

TENTH SUNDAY IN ORDINARY TIME – Year A

Matthew 9:9-13

The gospel of Matthew sees Jesus' public ministry as the inauguration of God's kingdom or reign. This is given in five stages, each stage or section having a subsection of narrative and a subsection of teaching or discourse. The gospel passage today is an extract from the narrative subsection of the second stage which is sometimes described as 'The kingdom is preached'.

The event occurs in Capernaum, situated on the shores of the Sea of Galilee. It was on a route used by many travellers and traders moving between Jerusalem and further south on the one hand and Damascus and further north and east on the other. There were taxes to be imposed on those passing through. The collectors were employed by the Roman rulers and, for that reason and because of their reputation for extortion and enriching themselves, the collectors were very unpopular and generally despised.

Apparently, Jesus noticed one of them and called him to be a follower of his. The person was named Matthew (although, in the corresponding accounts in Mark and Luke, he is called Levi). Matthew obeyed and then occurred the extraordinary sight of his inviting Jesus and some disciples to go to his house and have a meal there. There were more guests – other 'tax collectors and sinners'. The scene was deeply shocking for those Pharisees who saw it happen – Jesus with his disciples sitting and eating with a number of disreputable people, social outcasts and ritually unclean because of their employment or their immoral behaviour.

The Pharisees were scandalised. Here was this preacher, this man who claimed to be teaching God's message – did he not know what kind of people he was dining with? Did he not care? The response which Jesus makes helps us to understand how he views his mission. He is sent not to people because they already consider themselves virtuous and God-fearing; not to people who punctiliously fulfil the externals of religion but do little more. He comes to people who need him and the loving care that he brings from God. He comes to them, treating their sinfulness as illness that requires to be healed. They are in need of mercy and help rather than judgment and condemnation.

Jesus' attitude is reassurance and consolation for us. But it should also be a warning, teaching us that we must treat others as Jesus did and does, especially those whom society and popular opinion reject.

The first reading (Hosea 6:3-6) is from one of the earliest of the prophets who have left written accounts of their teaching. Hosea lived in the north of Israel in the second half of the eighth century BC, at a time of frequent rebellions, widespread corruption and the threat of invasion by Assyria (which did happen in 721 BC). He is the first to depict the love of God for his chosen people as a marriage. Today's excerpt speaks of God's disappointment that the love he expects in return for his constancy is so uncertain and transient. The final verse of the passage is quoted by Jesus in today's gospel: 'What I want is mercy, not sacrifice'.

In the second reading (Romans 4:18-25), Paul continues on the theme of faith. Abraham was favoured by God, he was 'justified', receiving God's 'justice' because he believed. It was faith in God's promise that enabled him to be justified. (Not included in today's reading is the assertion that it was not the law given to Moses by which Abraham was justified – he lived long before the law existed.) So it will be by faith that we are saved, if we believe in God who raised Jesus from the dead.

ELEVENTH SUNDAY IN ORDINARY TIME – Year A

Matthew 9:36-10:8

After last Sunday's brief visit to the narrative subsection of the second stage of Christ's 'programme' of establishing the kingdom (a section which records a number of miracles of healing), this Sunday's extract is from the discourse of the same stage.

Jesus is aware that, by and large, the people that he met as he moved around the villages were spiritually as well as materially neglected. 'Like sheep without a shepherd' is his description. These words above all refer to their ignorance of the good news of God's plan of salvation. They must be evangelised (to use theological language) and he must take measures to ensure that they are. These must have been the thoughts and decisions that caused Jesus to choose twelve men, 'the Twelve', to whom he gives the commission to go to the people and bring them the gift of the Good News. It may be noticed that, whereas both Mark and Luke distinguish between the call of the apostles and their being sent out to preach, Matthew assumes the former which here is subsumed into the latter.

In the meantime, the gospel is to be preached only to 'the lost sheep of the House of Israel', those who, in their history, were God's chosen people. Not even the Samaritans, let alone any gentiles, were to hear the Good News while it was being explained to the Jewish people. (In the Acts of the Apostles, we read of the controversy among the first generation of Jewish Christians on the subject of the rightness of preaching the faith to gentiles.)

So Jesus sends out the apostles (the word means a person sent) and, in the gospel, the words which describe their mission are important. They are to proclaim that God's kingdom is at hand – with words of explanation, undoubtedly, and the witness of their lifestyle; but perhaps more importantly with their activities in the name of Jesus – healing of both body and mind and even raising the dead. And since these powers are not the result of their own studies or training but are given to them as gift, so also they must on no account use them as a means of financial or material enrichment.

Those who, today, bring divine gifts (especially the sacraments) to those who need them must try to conform to the instructions which Jesus gave to the apostles. Like them, they have to be sustained with shelter, food, clothes and other necessities but they must not see their sacred ministry as a means of financial gain or enrichment. In addition, of course, the Church forbids any practice of 'simony', the sin of selling spiritual gifts in exchange for money or any material benefit. And how sadly true even today is the lament of Jesus about the scarcity of labourers for the abundant harvest. Surely the Lord is not complacent about the situation, is he?

Once again in today's passage, we see some of the characteristics of the 'kingdom' which Jesus is inaugurating. It is for everyone, especially for the poor and powerless, it confers forgiveness and healing, not this world's power or wealth or status, it brings an awareness of God's love and seeks that we may respond to that love through love of God and all others, shown through our humble and unconditional service of them.

The first reading this week is from the book of Exodus (19:2-6). As the Israelites travel from slavery in Egypt to the promised land, God orders Moses to tell them that they are his favoured people; this is the basis of the instruction Jesus gave to the apostles to go and instruct only the Jewish people. (The terms of God's declaration that the Jews are 'a kingdom of priests, a consecrated nation' are applied in the New Testament to Christians in 1 Peter 2:9.)

In the letter to the Romans (5:6-11), Paul explains that, not only are we reconciled to God and justified through the death of Jesus, but Jesus gave his life for us while we were sinners. This fills us with trust that God does indeed love us.

TWELFTH SUNDAY IN ORDINARY TIME – Year A

Matthew 10:26-33

The gospel today is another extract from the discourse of Jesus to his disciples, which Matthew presents as the instruction to the Twelve as they were sent to proclaim the kingdom. This extract contains a warning by Jesus that they will encounter hostility on their mission; but they must not give in to fear – the Father is protecting them.

Jesus wants those who speak and act in his name to be brave and bold and never to be deterred by opposition or hostility. In telling them of the Father's certain care for them, he uses language and examples reminiscent of his teaching on divine providence (Matthew 6:25-33). Not only will the Father protect them, but he, Jesus, will be their advocate on the day of judgment, putting their case to his Father.

Today's gospel passage is relevant for us also. If we express our beliefs openly we shall, on some occasions, meet opposition; it will probably come not in the form of martyrdom or physical persecution or torture, but through criticism, ridicule, embarrassment and, perhaps most frequent of all, apathy. To be without fear, to be courageous in our beliefs and our witness, we need the support of family, friends, community and, most essential of all, the promise of God's help which Jesus guarantees in today's gospel.

The first reading (Jeremiah 20:10-13) is well chosen and appropriate for the gospel. The prophet Jeremiah was born in mid-seventh century BC and seems to have been taken to Egypt shortly after Nebuchadnezzar and his Chaldean army, in 587, captured Jerusalem, destroyed the Temple and removed many of the citizens to captivity in Babylon. Jeremiah was a man of peace, gentle and devout. But since he lived in very troubled times with vice, corruption and violence rife, his prophecies foretell catastrophes, threaten punishment and speak of disaster. This brought him public and sometimes violent opposition and great suffering, but he remained steadfast, trusting in God's protection throughout the task he had to fulfil. The first reading is an example of the situation in which Jeremiah found himself.

St Paul (Romans 5:12-15) teaches the famous doctrine of original sin. His argument is that death is due to sin, we all die so we must all have sinned. Moreover, our sin is not due to breaking the law which God gave to Moses since death was happening before that law. In fact, our sinfulness does not come from breaking a law since, in the time between Adam (who broke a law) and Moses, there was no law. It is due to Adam that we are all sinners and that we all die. Similarly, but contrariwise, we have all been offered the free gift of God's grace of justification through one man, Christ.

This doctrine that original sin is inherited by each of us (except Mary) and makes us truly sinful (and not only with a tendency to sin), was defined by the Council of Trent in 1546. The Council added that, by Adam's sin, he and all of us lost the holiness and justice with which it was God's wish to endow us. Paul's teaching, confirmed by Trent, has been constantly discussed and debated and remains a difficult and controversial doctrine.

THIRTEENTH SUNDAY IN ORDINARY TIME – Year A

Matthew 10:37-42

Today's gospel comes at the conclusion of the discourse which brings to an end the second stage of Matthew's unfolding of the Good News of God's plan of salvation. The discourse is presented as an instruction to the Twelve on their duties in proclaiming the gospel and on the reception they are likely to receive.

Jesus tells them that, for the true disciple, the mission to be his witness must take precedence over everything else. He especially emphasises that even family ties or concerns must yield to the importance of work carried out for him. Although Matthew does not deal specifically with the manner in which Jesus recruited the Twelve, we know some details from the other gospels. The apostles seem to have obeyed a sudden, peremptory call and given up their previous occupations there and then. That may well have involved leaving their families behind also. So the instruction in today's excerpt may have been confirmation of the rightness of their response; or is the point being made here as a general rule for all who would follow Christ?

To be a disciple requires not only leaving one's family, says Jesus, but also accepting the inevitable 'cross' that it will bring. The cross that Jesus encountered was 'the real thing'. For his disciples, it may be likewise or it may be metaphorical; but if the latter, it will still bring suffering. Are we ready to accept (or have we already accepted and borne) our cross – in the great inconvenience of giving Jesus and his call absolute priority, in the resulting criticism, scorn and even rejection, in the cruel apathy?

The final sentences of the passage are reassuring and comforting. There will be a welcome sometimes for the disciples of Jesus Christ and especially for those who spread the Good News as well as those of evident holiness. And God will reward those who recognise and welcome Christ's disciples.

This last point is exemplified in the first reading (2 Kings 4:8-11.14-16). In the ninth century BC, Elisha received hospitality from a childless couple. The prophet was able to tell them that God was going to reward them with the birth of a son.

In today's second reading (Romans 6:3-4.8-11), Paul teaches that baptism is the God-given way for removing sin and receiving new life. He uses the image of Christ's lifeless body being placed in the tomb; 'he died, once for all, to sin'. Then being raised, he was given new life by God. So, continues Paul, our 'tomb' is the baptismal font (the parallel is more evident if baptism is by total immersion) from which we emerge 'dead to sin but alive for God in Christ Jesus'. That, of course, is the ideal and is certainly true in regard to original sin. Unfortunately, we retain our capacity for personal sin – for which the Lord in his mercy has provided the sacrament of reconciliation.

FOURTEENTH SUNDAY IN ORDINARY TIME – Year A

Matthew 11:25-30

We now move to the third stage of Matthew's describing how Jesus revealed God's kingdom. Although this is the so-called narrative subsection of the stage, today's gospel has Jesus apostrophising the Father. Mark's gospel makes no mention of this episode, but Luke's is very similar to Matthew's account (thus indicating that, in this instance, the two evangelists were using the same, but now unknown, source which scholars call 'Q'). Luke, however, says that Christ's words were a joyful reaction to the return of the seventy-two disciples from the successful mission on which he had sent them. His introduction to Jesus' words is: 'Filled with joy by the Holy Spirit, he said . . .' (10:21). In the circumstances, Luke's mention of Christ's joy and the Holy Spirit is understandable; but it also should be noted as one of several instances in which Luke affirms the presence and activity of the Holy Spirit in Jesus.

The incident shows Jesus thanking his Father that the message of salvation has been understood by the simple people, the Galilean peasants who listened to him and his disciples. The educated and learned religious leaders failed to appreciate the teaching because they disdained its simplicity, in contrast with the complexity of their knowledge. In adding that 'no one knows the Son except the Father . . .', the account of the incident shows that, in the synoptic gospels as well as in John, the divine sonship of Jesus is known.

Having expressed his delight that the poor and unlettered were receiving his teaching, Jesus then shows his compassion for them (in opposition to the oppression they suffered from their rulers, both civil and religious). He makes a threefold invitation: if you are weighed down by the burden of the law and additional observances, then come to me; change your present burden and take on mine, which is bearable and relevant and motivated by love; let me teach you, by words and example, and you will discover gentleness and humility.

The first reading (Zechariah 9:9-10) dates from the end of the fourth century BC and is a prophecy about the messiah who will come to bring freedom to the Israelites. In character and behaviour, he will be gentle and humble. This makes the reading a very apt preface for today's gospel.

St Paul (Romans 8:9.11-13) explains that we have two sides to our characters, the spiritual and the unspiritual. It is the former that we should adopt so that the Holy Spirit may be living in us. In this case, we shall belong to Christ and the Father will give us immortal life through the Spirit in us.

FIFTEENTH SUNDAY IN ORDINARY TIME – Year A

Matthew 13:1-23

We are now in the discourse subsection of the third stage of the revealing of the kingdom; in this subsection, Jesus uses his favourite method of teaching – parables, of which there are around forty in the gospels. It is a very effective method, particularly because Jesus chooses stories that have characters and situations that were familiar to the mainly unlettered peasants who made up his audiences. Today's parable exemplifies this. His hearers would know all about sowing seed in favourable places for growth.

The parable is easily intelligible, even if we are not farmers or agricultural workers. But the interpretation also needs to be understood. The person sowing is Jesus himself; the seed is his teaching on the kingdom – namely, that God calls us to a new way of living which will be for our good, both on earth and thereafter. If the seed is received gladly by us and taken gladly into our hearts to be cherished, it will flourish and so shall we. If the Good News is heard but not understood, it will vanish without trace; if is not firmly rooted, any trial or opposition will bring it to an early end; if it has to compete with worldly attractions, it will be smothered and unproductive.

Jesus is a realist and wants us to be the same. Many of us have had the experience of hearing the Good News seriously for the first time as adults and wanting to commit ourselves firmly to follow Jesus. We have started to grow – but sadly nothing that lasted came of it. Jesus is well aware of the situation. Despite the present parable, such a failure is not definitive. God's grace will not be denied. The invitation remains to make another effort.

In the middle of today's passage, there are some rather obscure verses (10-15) about those who do not understand (or accept) what Jesus is saying. He is speaking of some of the Jews, specifically some of the religious leaders, and their obdurate refusal to accept his teaching. An angry passage from Isaiah (6:9-10) is adduced as being fulfilled in this instance. But, in the gospel today, we hear that the Good News is 'not revealed to them' and 'from anyone who has not, even what he has will be taken away' (verses 11-12). These are harsh assertions and their meaning is obscure. Both Mark (4:1-20) and Luke (8:4-15) include the parable and also refer to the fate of those who do not accept Jesus' teaching. Exegetes suggest that verse 12 may mean that those who reject the teaching will cling only to the Jewish law - which soon will be obsolete; or (an alternative suggestion) that the words are a later insertion attempting to explain the Jews' lack of acceptance of Jesus.

In a short first reading (Deutero-Isaiah, i.e., later, sixth century BC, Isaiah 55:10-11), God tells us that his word (his teaching? his Son?) will come down and produce what God wants, as rain and snow provide fertile seed that is productive in the earth.

St Paul (Romans 8:18-23) teaches that, since the material world was made for humankind, it shares our destiny after sin was committed. It is deformed but, like us, to be redeemed and glorified. In contemporary Greek philosophy, matter was regarded as evil and the human spirit needed to be freed from it; but Paul asserts that, in Christian philosophy, matter is itself enslaved and awaiting liberation. Is the passage of interest for its ecological significance?

SIXTEENTH SUNDAY IN ORDINARY TIME – Year A

Matthew 13:24-43

Chapter thirteen of Matthew's gospel is exclusively a collection of the parables of Jesus, recollected from various moments of his public life (and probably repeated often as he moved around Galilee). Matthew has collected seven of them for the 'discourse' subsection of this stage of the unfolding of the Good News or, in other words, the development of Christ's teaching as he establishes God's kingdom.

Last week we heard the first of the seven parables in the chapter, the parable of the sower. Of the three parables today, the first is given most explanation, although its meaning is not obscure. It is again about the sowing of seed but, instead of the seed representing the truths Jesus taught, here it is the people who hear the word and accept it; further, instead of the seed sometimes falling in unsuitable places, the problem this time is that the good seed has to thrive in the midst of weeds, sown by an enemy (viz., the devil) who has made his victims become evil. The weeds are to be left until the harvest (viz., the day of judgment).

Again, the imagery would appeal especially to the peasants and country people who came to listen to Jesus. They would follow the story Jesus told, but would they understand the point of the parable? We have already been told (last Sunday) that Jesus did not explain his parables to the crowds who were listening. His reason for not doing so is obscure and the justification offered in the text (a quotation from psalm 77/78:2) is hardly conclusive. It may be that the evangelist was suggesting that Jesus knew that many were not going to become his followers. On the other hand, is it not in the very nature of a parable that it should not require explanation? Later, however, Jesus did explain this parable to a small number of his disciples. The moment in it when the owner decides to leave the weeds where they were until harvest time allows Jesus to tell the disciples that, at the end of the world, the evil people will be 'thrown into the blazing furnace'.

Apart from the fact that there will be evil people, unrepentant sinners, in the Church even until the judgment and that they will be punished, the great lesson of this parable is the need of patient tolerance, both by God and also by us. Tolerance not only because, as wheat takes time to grow, so our time on earth may also seem long; and tolerance also because, like the wheat and the weeds together, we have to live in the world as it is, with both good and evil. But remember that, although real wheat can do nothing to improve the situation, we can – by sharing our faith, offering an example of goodness, showing love and care even to those who oppose us. Moreover, people can change – the evil can become good, we (God forbid) can become evil.

Two other parables of Jesus are mentioned, but more briefly since the allegorical parallels are not added. The mustard seed, almost imperceptible at the start and unnoticed, becomes a large shrub in which birds can shelter. It provides an allegory of the Church, hardly noticed at first but which greatly increases in size and consists of many people.

The parable of the yeast teaches a similar lesson – small and unpretentious at first but with the power to bring about a general and thorough change in everything it reaches.

These two parables are probably not as influential for us as individuals as the first parable can be, but they do show the effect and the value of evangelisation.

The first reading is from the book of Wisdom (12:13.16-19), written in the first century BC to extol the wisdom, justice and solicitude of God. The extract speaks of God's wish to treat us with great kindness and mildness, ready to pardon our sins and so teaching us by example. It is a passage that offers a commentary on the parable of the wheat and the weeds.

St Paul (Romans 8:26-27) consoles us by explaining that, when we find it hard to pray, the Holy Spirit will express our prayer so that we utter it in a way without words but which the Father understands, knowing that the Spirit is praying in and for us. Is Paul here referring to speaking in tongues, a charism which was in use at the time?

SEVENTEENTH SUNDAY IN ORDINARY TIME – Year A

Matthew 13:44-52

This is the third and final Sunday for the seven parables which Matthew narrates in chapter 13 of his gospel. Today, the first two (numbers five and six of the seven) are very brief and told without explanation. It is fairly obvious what the point is in both: that, when a person discovers the riches that are received in becoming a member of God's kingdom through embracing discipleship, the wise decision is to surrender all our other possessions (or at least all those which we need to give up) in order to gain that treasure. The ethics of not reporting the discovery of the treasure to the owner of the field are omitted from the parable's narrative.

It is not always easy to discover the treasure of the kingdom. Those who have found it need to be much more courageous and generous in sharing their faith in Jesus, in evangelising. Again, although in theory the kingdom is the obvious and wise choice when a person has heard of it, we all know how difficult it is in practice to opt for it. Doing so will cost us the surrender of much that we cherish now, particularly in the areas of selfishness and greed. We need the Holy Spirit to give us wisdom and courage. Therefore we need to want the Holy Spirit to do so!

The final parable is given a short explanation which shows that the lesson is similar to the lessons of the parable of the weeds (discussed last Sunday). The explanation speaks of the wicked being consigned to the blazing furnace, a remark that contributed to a literal understanding of the fires of hell.

The gospel passage ends with the crowds whom Jesus was addressing telling him that they had understood all that he had been saying, an assertion that seems at odds with the earlier assumption that they definitely had not (Matthew 13:10-13). A final sentence has Jesus remarking that a scribe who becomes a disciple is doubly blessed, having knowledge of the New Law to add to his familiarity with the Old.

The first reading today (1 Kings 3:5.7-12) has the new king Solomon (970 BC) being offered any gift he would like from God and choosing wisdom, a quality that the finders of the treasure and the pearl in the gospel parables showed that they also possessed.

St Paul (Romans 8:28-30) tells us that those whom God has gifted with love for him have become images of his Son so that the Son can be the eldest brother of these brothers and sisters who, indeed, have been justified and called to share God's glory.

EIGHTEENTH SUNDAY IN ORDINARY TIME – Year A

Matthew 14:13-21

This passage occurs shortly after the beginning of the narrative subsection of the fourth stage in Matthew's gradual development of Jesus' teaching on the kingdom. It is a stage that sees the followers of Jesus forming a community – an embryonic Church.

The event recounted can be seen as prefiguring Christ's gift to us of the Eucharist (especially in the verbs which the evangelist uses to describe the feeding of the multitude: 'took . . . raised his eyes to heaven . . . said the blessing . . . breaking the loaves, he handed them to his disciples'). Indeed, the scene can be considered as also looking forward to the 'paschal banquet' of heaven.

But, leaving aside the symbolic significance, the gospel excerpt illustrates the loving care that Jesus has for people in need. He had gone to a lonely place seeking solitude but, on arrival there, he found a large crowd awaiting him; taking pity on them, 'he healed their sick'. Then, he spent the afternoon and early evening in teaching them.

At that point, there is further thoughtfulness shown to the crowd. He rejected the disciples' advice – 'Send the people away . . . to buy themselves some food' – and took upon himself the duty of feeding them, using the power he possessed in order to provide enough for several thousands from five loaves and two fish. Nor did the people need to eat sparingly; there was plenty for all and a large amount left over. That final detail impresses on us the abundance of the generosity with which Christ looks after the poor and those in need.

The miraculous event cannot but make us think. We live in a world where there is, or easily could be, enough food for all humankind. Yet not only do famines occur but there is also chronic and widespread malnourishment. Even in our own country, we are ashamed that so many people seek the charity of food banks. If people go hungry, that is not just the unfortunate result of the difficulties of worldwide distribution. No, it is the consequence of sinful apathy, selfishness, greed and corruption.

Many people already give with great generosity and self-sacrifice. But the majority of us do not, and the 'haves' especially are guilty of dreadful negligence and downright lack of interest. There is a phrase that speaks of 'self-giving love', a love that costs us inconvenience and even self-sacrifice; an attitude that is the opposite of 'I can't be bothered'. St John Paul II, in his Apostolic Letter *Mane Nobiscum Domine,* makes a statement that remains with me. He asserts that our concern for the victims of such scandals as hunger in a world of so much wealth 'will be the criterion by which the authenticity of our Eucharistic celebrations will be judged' (§28).

In the first reading (Isaiah 55:1-3), God speaks of the everlasting covenant he has made with the Israelites, a covenant that ensures them an abundance of corn, milk, wine and water, and at no cost to them. This messianic promise may have to await fulfilment in eternal life; or at least until the world becomes a much kinder place than it is.

The second reading today is surely one of the most inspiring (and inspired) passages ever written by St Paul (Romans 8:35.37-39). Read it at any time, but especially when feeling sad or depressed or even sinful; or when you seek renewal or increase of faith. I only wish that the lectionary had also given us from verse 31 to verse 39!

NINETEENTH SUNDAY IN ORDINARY TIME – Year A

Matthew 14:22-33

The events in today's gospel come immediately after the feeding of the multitude, narrated last week. Jesus at last finds an opportunity to be alone and to pray. The disciples, probably the apostles, were in their boat crossing the lake when, as often happens on the Sea of Galilee, a sudden storm blew up. Perhaps Jesus had seen his disciples in the boat before it got completely dark or he could see their light when they seemed to be making little progress against the wind. At all events, the gospel tells us that, well on in the night and only a few hours from dawn, Jesus went walking on the water towards the boat.

After a cry of terror from the men because they took Jesus to be a ghost, he calmed their fear and then agreed to Peter's proposal of getting out of the boat and walking across the water to Jesus. Peter falters and then panics, cries to Jesus to save him as he fears he will drown. As Jesus holds him, he says to Peter, 'Man of little faith. Why did you doubt?' They both get into the boat, the wind abates and those in the boat exclaim 'Truly, you are the Son of God'.

Exegetes discuss this event and particularly two aspects. First, it illustrates the prominence given to Peter as the leader of the Twelve and of the disciples and therefore it suggests that the disciples are gradually becoming a community, a nascent Church, with Peter leading. Second, the disciples acclaiming Jesus as the Son of God seems to come too early in the story since the profession of faith at Caesarea Philippi is still in the future (Matthew 16:15-16); so today's event may belong to the days of the risen Lord.

Notwithstanding this reservation, the episode has great significance, as it were a parable in actions rather than words. The boat is the Church, it has a journey to do and is steered by those on board, it encounters dangers and problems and attacks, those on board become fearful, Jesus is at hand to protect and encourage and, if need be, to rescue; Peter leads the group both in action and in words, his faith is essential and must always be strong.

We have all experienced, especially in recent decades, the truth and accuracy of the allegory. Decisions have had to be taken and choices made, the Church has been and is constantly under attack both openly and in more subtle ways, the members have experienced doubt and fear and for a number of reasons. Many have been aware of the presence of Christ with us in these difficult times and have been conscious of the guidance of the Holy Spirit.

Apart from the common and general experiences, each of us can, as an individual, be alive to the situation and play his or her part. We have to use the gifts we have received in order to enrich the Church and share our faith. We have to combat fear (as well as apathy, laziness, feelings of superiority or inferiority) to be good members of the community. We have to know that Jesus is with us and pray confidently for his counsel and help. We have to be faithful to the responsibilities of our baptism.

The first reading (1 Kings 19:9.11-13) tells how the prophet Elijah, when in serious danger and worry, sought the Lord. He found him not in a hurricane, nor in an earthquake nor in a fire, but in a gentle breeze. The Lord will bring calm to our troubled selves (as did Jesus to the disciples when fearful of shipwreck).

St Paul, in chapters 9-11 of the letter to the Romans, and very clearly in today's excerpt (9:1-5), expresses his great sadness that most Jews, his own race and God's chosen people, were refusing to share in the saving plan of God for all the human race. What makes this particularly tragic is that Jesus, God's chosen one to bring the plan to fulfilment, is himself a Jew.

TWENTIETH SUNDAY IN ORDINARY TIME – Year A

Matthew 15:21-28

This passage narrates a rather unusual incident. First, to identify the places: Gennesaret is another name for the Sea of Galilee (sometimes also called Lake Tiberias); Tyre and Sidon are towns on the Mediterranean coast, in an area the south of which was then in Palestine territory (where it seems that the incident occurred) although nowadays both towns are in Lebanon; the Canaanite woman (who is called a Syro-Phoenician in Mark) was of that gentile people who were very unfriendly and belligerent towards the Jews.

Two circumstances require particular notice. The woman is a gentile and it was highly unusual for Jesus to have contact with anyone but Jews. She had come into Palestine territory (and the gentile Roman centurion lived there, in Capernaum: Matthew 8:5-13). Jesus had come to save the whole human race and, where he found faith, he acceded to pleas for help. Of course, this question of admission of the gentiles to baptism and faith caused great controversy in the very early days of the Church, as described in the Acts of the Apostles. We can say that Jesus chose, in the relatively short time he himself had, to limit his work to Palestine and God's chosen people of the Old Law but with every intention that his work should be extended throughout the world by his followers.

The other circumstance is the manner in which Jesus speaks to the woman. First, he seems to ignore her. When he does reply to her request, his words seem brusque and even insulting. It is said that this was normal Middle Eastern dialogue and that her pert retort, which does not accept, but rather rejects, the reason for his initial refusal, indicates as much. Jesus does not maintain his refusal but commends her faith and grants her request. A daughter is cured and a mother's great worry is removed.

The two circumstances that we have considered lead us to think about such circumstances nowadays. The first is straightforward enough – we must not be mean or cruel in our attitude to strangers or foreigners or people different from ourselves. There are laws against racial abuse or discrimination, but it is not only our treatment of others that matters, but also our way of speaking of them and even how we think of them. And since very often the fact of being a stranger or different puts that person in need of help or friendship, there is a duty there for us to keep in mind.

The other circumstance – the ways in which women can be ill-treated or ignored – is still in our day a very live issue. At its worst, women can be enslaved (in all manners of conditions) and that is probably the most extreme abuse to which women are still subjected. But there are many other injustices that occur – inequality, exclusion, marginalisation, trafficking, ill-treatment of various kinds – all the way to discourtesy and rudeness. Women have rights and needs. They are still sometimes denied them; perhaps more often they simply pass unnoticed. Even in the Catholic Church, this is an area that demands our careful observance.

The first reading (Isaiah 56:1.6-7) is an appropriate passage to be with the gospel today. God welcomes all peoples; foreigners are gladly invited to serve and love him.

Paul (Romans 11:13-15.29-32) continues to be saddened by the refusal of most Jews to become disciples of Christ. Perhaps the witness of gentile converts will make his own people jealous and become Christians. Eventually, he concludes, God will show mercy to everyone.

TWENTY-FIRST SUNDAY IN ORDINARY TIME – Year A

Matthew 16:13-20

This is a crucial juncture in the relationship between Jesus and the disciples, in particular between him and the Twelve. 'Who do you say I am?' The question appears in all three synoptic gospels and in each the answer, given by Simon Peter, is 'You are the Christ'; in other words, 'We believe that you are the messiah for whom Israel has been waiting'. Matthew's gospel adds to Peter's reply the words 'the Son of the living God'.

The same evangelist indicates that Jesus continued this solemn moment, first, by naming Simon to be Peter because he was to be the visible rock on which Christ would build his Church (the first occasion on which 'Peter' is used as a person's name); second, by guaranteeing that the Church would never be overthrown by the evil powers of the underworld; and third, by giving Peter the authority to bind and loose both in discipline (whom to admit into, or exclude from, the Church) and in matters of faith (both belief and morals).

The word 'church' in Hebrew is used in the Old Testament to speak of the community of God's chosen people. Christ's adoption of the word to indicate those who were his disciples shows that those who wanted to be in the 'kingdom of God' already formed a community, existing and organised, with a visible leader here on earth.

The Catholic Church teaches that Peter's leadership and authority is transmitted to his successors; this is evident since Jesus clearly wanted his Church to continue after Peter's death. Of course, the precise extent of the Petrine primacy and authority has been much debated and disputed in the centuries since. The First Vatican Council (1870) defined the authority as having infallibility in faith and morals and the Second Vatican Council (1962-65) confirmed and developed that teaching, placing the pope's ministry within the context of the Church. Each pope tends to bring to the exercise of his office his own style, with the result that his ministry may seem sometimes more or sometimes less collegial in character.

Reverting to today's gospel, we obviously wonder how we would answer Jesus' question if he asked it of us. No doubt we would use the same words as Simon Peter used, but would that be enough? Evidently not; like him, we should have to show by our actions that we really meant what the words implied and that they were not just a familiar formula. We recall Jesus' own warning: 'It is not those who say to me "Lord, Lord" who will enter the kingdom of heaven, but the person who does the will of my Father in heaven' (Matthew 7:21). The formula of words must come not just out of custom or education but because we truly believe that he is the Messiah and the Son of God whose instructions we obey, whose values we choose and whose life we copy.

At the end of today's excerpt, Jesus orders the disciples present to keep secret his identity as the messiah. Known as the 'messianic secret', this measure was because most people would presume that the messiah had come to lead the Jews to worldly freedom and prosperity.

The first reading (Isaiah 22:19-23) refers to an event in 705 BC during the reign of King Hezekiah. The king's major-domo, Shebna, has been guilty of corruption. He is replaced by Eliakim and the passage tells of his investiture and the authority he will hold. This secular event bears some resemblance to Christ's choice of Simon Peter.

Paul (Romans 11:33-36), having reflected on God's possible plans for the Jews in the changed conditions of the gentiles' acceptance of Jesus, confesses that God's motives and methods in fulfilling his plans are totally beyond his, Paul's, comprehension. We leave things to the divine wisdom and mercy. (The three questions in the passage are taken from chapter 40 of the prophecy of Isaiah.)

TWENTY-SECOND SUNDAY IN ORDINARY TIME – Year A

Matthew 16:21-27

Last week Peter was the hero, the one Jesus trusted with great responsibility. The gospel indicates that, immediately after the conversation at Caesarea Philippi, Jesus tells the Twelve what awaits him when they go to Jerusalem. Peter's reaction is one of horror and he is severely rebuked by Jesus. He is now the villain, accused of being like Satan, an obstacle to Jesus fulfilling the Father's plan.

In a way, we can feel sorry for Peter because the idea of his beloved Jesus having to suffer as he had anticipated repelled Peter so much that, in his impulsive nature, he felt he had to protest. Objectively, of course, Peter was still thinking of Jesus as a triumphant messiah and not as a servant who would accept all the suffering that he was destined to endure, even to being put to death.

Today's excerpt then informs us that Jesus asks of his followers the same self-renunciation and readiness to accept the burdens that discipleship may bring. The self-renunciation of which Jesus speaks ('let him renounce himself') is not merely abstaining from some optional benefits, but acceptance of the fact that the self is nothing, is of no value, has no right to be considered of importance by a disciple. If we wish to follow Jesus faithfully, we should not be thinking of our own welfare or interests.

Jesus' words in today's excerpt show clearly, if we had not already understood, that being a Christian is to be called to a life lived not on our terms, especially if that would imply only external compliance or selective obedience. Discipleship is costly, not to be lived on the cheap. How do we react to an awareness of this? With grim acceptance? Or regretful refusal? Or, admitting our human frailty, with a generosity that brings fulfilment and joy and love?

The final verse today is, in fact, taken from Jesus' teaching on his second coming and the general judgment but Matthew has placed it in this spot because of its relevance to what Jesus has been saying. In other words, the disciple who accepts the burdens and sufferings which he may have to endure for Jesus' sake will not be overlooked or ignored on the day of judgment.

Both Mark and Luke deal with the apostles' recognition of Jesus as messiah (last week's gospel) and also with the crosses which await Jesus and those who wish to follow him (today's). The references are Mark 8:27-9:1 and Luke 9:18-27. Matthew's account tends to include some details omitted by the others. In particular, Luke does not mention Peter's outburst against the idea of Jesus suffering and the severe rebuke with which Jesus responded.

The first reading has Jeremiah (20:7-9) speaking frankly to God. He has accepted a prophet's mission from God and obediently warned the Israelites of the disasters that awaited them unless they were converted. The result has been 'insult, derision, all day long' from those to whom he had been sent. The appropriateness of this reading for the gospel passage of today is evident.

As Paul nears the end of his letter to the Christians in Rome, he urges them (12:1-2) to behave in a way that is fitting for those who have found faith in God. Only thus will they know how to live and act according to the will of God for them.

TWENTY-THIRD SUNDAY IN ORDINARY TIME – Year A

Matthew 18:15-20

The lectionary omits extracts from chapter 17 of Matthew's gospel (the chapter which concludes the narrative subsection of the stage in which God's kingdom on earth is manifest in a community (church) of the disciples of Christ). Chapter 18 gives us his discourse on this stage; in today's and next week's gospel readings, we have two extracts from that discourse.

Today, Matthew has collected three sayings of Jesus when he was instructing his disciples. The first is in regard to disputes between members of the community (the local church). The steps by which fraternal correction is attempted are laid out but, if all this fails, the offender is to be excommunicated. Most commentators think that this measure is one introduced by the early post-ascension Church; after all, Jesus was known as a friend of sinners and tax collectors. The general tone of Jesus' words about gentiles is very different from 'treat him like a pagan or a tax collector'; these words, in fact, are those used in Jewish communities in regard to stubborn offenders.

In the second instruction, Jesus extends to the community of disciples the authority over matters of doctrine, morals and discipline which he had already given to Simon Peter (Matthew 16:19).

The third saying is an assurance that, when disciples gather in a group and in Jesus' name, he will be with them and the Father will grant them their petitions. Again, the idea of the ecclesial community is present, although it is not necessary for every member to be there. This third teaching of Jesus is one of which most Christians are still very aware. For Catholics, the most obvious occasion on which we meet in Christ's name is the celebration of the Eucharist. So perhaps we need to examine the manner in which we carry out the Lord's command to 'do this in memory of me'.

For example, as members of the celebrating congregation, do we remember that Jesus is present among us throughout the Mass? As those with a ministry to carry out, do we do so with reverence and respect? As presiders, do we, who are priests, celebrate the Eucharist with devotion and in a manner that is exemplary? There are other questions that have to be asked, but they are directed to those in authority. Are the Masses organised and celebrated in a way that allows proper participation? Are those present enabled and encouraged to be active and devout participants? Are the actions visible to all and the words audible to all? Are the words to be spoken intelligible to those who have a reasonable knowledge of English?

The first reading is from the prophecy of Ezekiel (33:7-9). He was in Babylon with the Jewish exiles in the early decades of the sixth century BC. In today's reading, he tells us of God's instruction to him regarding the manner in which he should treat offenders. There is obvious similarity between the excerpt and the first of Jesus' three sayings reported in today's gospel. (Note the use of the address, 'son of man', used later of himself by the prophet Daniel and which became a favourite method by which Jesus spoke of himself.)

St Paul (Romans 13:8-10) reminds us that all our duties to fellow humans can be summed up in the single commandment to 'love your neighbour as yourself'.

TWENTY-FOURTH SUNDAY IN ORDINARY TIME – Year A

Matthew 18:21-35

This is the second of two extracts from Jesus' teaching which Matthew places in the so-called discourse subsection of the stage at which his gospel discloses that God's kingdom being established by Jesus is to be a community (church). Peter asks Jesus a question which allows Jesus to teach that his disciples must always be ready to forgive any and all wrongdoing. To express that our forgiveness is to be absolute and never withheld, Jesus replies to Peter by saying he must pardon 'not seven times but . . .' and here, the different translations say either 'seventy-seven times' or 'seventy times seven times'.

This is followed by the parable of the unforgiving debtor. The parable, as illustrating the virtue of forgiveness even in very serious offences (ten thousand talents is an enormous sum), is relevant at the start. However, a parable urging us always to forgive seems to lose its relevance when, after the forgiven debtor refuses to forgive a very small debt owed to him, the fellow servants report this to the king, their master, who then revokes his forgiveness.

It is best, in these circumstances, not to try to use every detail of the parable as it has reached us, but only to draw the basic lesson which it teaches, namely that our forgiveness should not be refused even when the injury is serious; and, if we do refuse to forgive our debtors, we can hardly expect that God will forgive us our debts. After all, this is the very point which we express in saying the Lord's Prayer.

To forgive is sometimes very difficult and can be doubly so if, by our forgiveness, others are going to be deprived of their rights. For instance, can I, on my own, forgive a debtor what he owes to another person as well as to myself? It is true that we should always forgive someone for an offence or insult or inconvenience suffered. Nevertheless, in some cases and if the debtor is able to do so, we may, and even should, seek restitution. Of course, we must resist all temptation to feelings of hatred or thoughts of vengeance.

Quite often one hears victims of a serious offence, or relatives of the victim, say in very strong terms that they can never forgive the perpetrator. The feeling is understandable, especially at the immediate time of the offence or when the identity of the guilty person becomes known. Expressions such as 'I hope he rots in hell' are not acceptable but in many cases they are said by a grieving person and while being interviewed by the media. On the other hand, there are, from time to time, heroic victims who will publicly say that they forgive the perpetrator. The grace of God is very evident on such occasions, as is the example of Jesus on the cross: 'Father, forgive them . . .'.

The first reading comes from the book of Ecclesiasticus (27:30-28:7), written in the second century BC to encourage Jews to maintain their religious and moral way of life despite the spread of hellenistic values. The sentiments expressed in this passage are admirable and provide an excellent companion piece to today's gospel.

This is the final Sunday (of sixteen successive weeks) of extracts from St Paul's letter to the Romans (14:7-9). He tells us that, through the death and resurrection of Christ, he has become Lord of every one of us, both of those already dead and of those still on earth; all of us belong to him.

TWENTY-FIFTH SUNDAY IN ORDINARY TIME – Year A

Matthew 20:1-16

We have now reached the fifth and final stage of Matthew's chosen way of divulging the establishment and growth of God's kingdom. The stage shows the advance of a visible community of Christ's followers; (remember the parables of the mustard seed and the yeast in chapter 13, sixteenth Sunday). This is the narrative subsection of the stage. The evangelist informs us that Jesus has left Galilee and is in Judea; he still attracts big crowds and heals their sick (19:1-2).

Today's gospel excerpt is the parable of the labourers in the vineyard. It is a surprising tale. We would expect that those who had worked all day would be paid more than those who were hired near the day's end. Yet each worker, no matter how long he had worked, was paid exactly the same amount. The apparently just objections allow the landowner (representing God in the parable) to explain his strange behaviour.

One explanation could be that the first hired men had agreed to the rate offered and so had no reason for objecting. But we can go further than that. This is a parable about God and ourselves when, at the end of the day's work (that is, when we die), the amount we receive (eternal happiness) is not a payment merited and varying by the grade of our virtue or the length of our life on earth. Heaven is not earned but is totally gratuitous and the result of God's love for us; just as our work on earth should be performed out of our love for God.

It may be hard to accept this state of affairs, yet I think that most of us can understand the reasoning. I hope that we have no objection to babies or children who die being the recipients of God's love for them. Nor do we feel resentful when we hear about death-bed conversions; when this happens, the families and relatives rejoice and priests thank God for the privilege of being his instrument.

Of course if we use worldly criteria, the parable seems grossly unfair. And, lurking beneath the surface of the parable, there is the fact that the Jewish people who, since the time of Abraham, had been the recipients of God's favours on earth and, in many cases, had lived virtuous and even scrupulous lives in strict observance of the myriad of laws and regulations, had to witness gentiles (whom they considered pagans) being taught that God loved them too and that they were destined for eternal salvation. This seems to be the implication of the final short sentence of today's gospel.

Throughout his whole ministry and teaching, Jesus proclaimed love of neighbour, care for those in need, disapproval of every kind of injustice. Following that example, the Church, since the final years of the nineteenth century and especially in recent decades, has spoken out on many contemporary social issues and human rights; for instance, on war, violence and the arms trade; on migrants, refugees and asylum seekers; on unemployment, wages and working conditions; on proper provision of health care, food and water, housing and education; on economic, financial and environmental issues. In fact, some object that the Church 'should not interfere in politics'. But politics can involve right and wrong, moral and immoral treatment of people – and here, the Church has a right, and a duty, to speak out. It has the constant example of its founder!

In an extract from Second Isaiah (55:6-9), the prophet proclaims, and God confirms, a call to repentance since God has pity on sinners. His ways, he says, are different from ours. The passage has the same message as the gospel for today, but in more direct language.

We have the first of four readings from Paul's letter to the Philippians (1:20-24.27). Even on earth, Christ is the object of Paul's life. He yearns for death in order to be even nearer to the Lord but, if he is required for the sake of his missionary work to remain here, he acquiesces.

TWENTY-SIXTH SUNDAY IN ORDINARY TIME – Year A

Matthew 21:28-32

Jesus is in Jerusalem, in fact in the precincts of the Temple and he is teaching those who came near to listen. Among them are the religious leaders, suspicious as usual and hostile. He tells them a simple parable: a vineyard owner had two sons; to the father's request to go and work in the vineyard, the first agreed but then did not go; the second refused but then changed his mind and went. To Jesus' question about which had been obedient, the religious leaders had no problem in saying the second. Jesus then makes the point that the leaders are like the first son because they had promised loyalty to God but had then rejected John the Baptist and also Jesus though these two preached God's message; but the very people the leaders despised, who had been disobedient and were excluded from the Temple, had been attracted by John and were now listening to Jesus and on the way to conversion. We are told that the chief priests and scribes realised that Jesus was speaking of them and would have liked to arrest him but, since he was so widely admired, they feared the people's reaction.

This parable can easily be used in our day as well as two thousand years ago; and once again, it is those who are the religious leaders today who have to examine their consciences to decide whether the parable is applicable to them. Perhaps also those who may not be leaders but are generally thought to be fervent should also ponder the parable – just in case.

The parable also has relevance for circumstances which are not strictly religious but which are worth considering. For example, can others trust our words of assurance to them? In business and trade matters, is a guarantee truly what it claims to be? Do we borrow books, tools, money and forget to give them back? Are we liable to make promises, commitments, appointments and then fail to keep them?

We know that we can implicitly trust God. It would be a virtuous habit in us if we could likewise be trusted by God and by others. Dependability and reliability in us show honour and respect both for God and for others.

A passage from Ezekiel (18:25-28) forms the first reading. The teaching is very similar to that of the gospel and provides consolation for a repentant sinner.

Paul, writing to the church in Philippi (2:1-11), urges the Christians there to seek always to be humble and anxious to help others. The supreme example of this, he teaches, is Jesus Christ. Quoting a hymn, Paul reminds us that Jesus accepted a double 'emptying of himself' (*kenosis*) first, by becoming human, and second, by dying on the cross. He willingly accepted these two self-sacrifices for our salvation; and God rewarded him and wanted him to be recognised by all as Lord (*Kyrios*, a divine title).

TWENTY-SEVENTH SUNDAY IN ORDINARY TIME – Year A

Matthew 21:33-43

Immediately following the parable of last Sunday's gospel, Matthew recounts another parable, also addressed to the religious leaders (and it is at the end of this parable that they are said to fear the people's wrath if they were to do as they wished and arrest Jesus).

Today's parable is graphic and, at the end, has a bitter conclusion for the chief priests and scribes. It is usually called the parable of the wicked husbandmen and each detail is to be identified as representing real people and actual things or events. For us now, the identification is fairly evident: God who had carefully cultivated his chosen people; the servants badly treated are the prophets and the son is Jesus whom the faithless Jews put to death outside the city walls; so the previous tenants will be replaced by new ones, pagans/gentiles. The religious leaders seem not to have grasped the lesson of the parable until Jesus shocked them with the explanation.

This parable is so harrowing and grim that it is difficult to apply it to ourselves. The temptation is to see it merely as a just condemnation of conditions at the time of its telling. However, we have to ask the question – could it be true of things nowadays? Of the Church in Europe? In this country? In our diocese or parish? Recent popes have lamented of a world characterised by secularism and relativism, of values that take little note of God's laws. Our Church of baptised Catholics seems to have a very high proportion of the apathetic, the uninterested, the selfish, does it not?

The first reading, taken from one of the early chapters of Isaiah (5:1-7), is a hard-hitting lament by a disappointed owner of a vineyard which has failed to produce its expected fruit. The image of Israel as God's vineyard is first mentioned by Hosea (10:1) and frequently used by Isaiah, Jeremiah and Ezekiel. In today's gospel, the unproductive vineyard is again the basic image, but with some details added.

In the letter to the Philippians (4:6-9), Paul assures the people that God will protect and guide them with his gift of peace. For their part, they are to keep to the paths of virtue and to pray trustingly to God for all their needs.

TWENTY-EIGHTH SUNDAY IN ORDINARY TIME – Year A

Matthew 22:1-14

The parable of the wedding feast is the third parable in succession which Matthew recounts on the subject of the rejection of Jesus by the Jewish people or their leaders. This parable is also found in Luke but not in Mark. However, Luke's version differs from Matthew's in several ways. Exegetes think that Matthew rewrote the original story, adding new elements from another parable. The result can be somewhat confusing, but the basic message is clear. Since Luke's version (14:16-24) is omitted from the Sunday gospels of year C, there is no need to include here a comparison between the two.

Conscious of how hard and routine were the lives of the peasants whom he knew, Jesus was aware how much they enjoyed the occasional experience of a meal with friends. He himself sometimes was invited to such meals. Moreover, he spoke of the happiness with which God wanted to provide them in heaven, and he would therefore describe it in terms of a banquet. The parable of the wedding feast would be an attractive story to tell – and with a very serious point to it.

Again, the meaning of the parable is fairly evident, at least in its first part. God has prepared great happiness for all the invited guests at his Son's triumphant reception in the messianic age. But the guests were not interested and they had their excuses ready. Moreover, some of the guests attacked God's messengers and even killed them. As punishment, the killers were themselves put to death and their town destroyed (possibly an addition after 70 AD, the year of the destruction of Jerusalem by the Roman army). The empty places were filled with all and any who, very unexpectedly, found themselves invited (i.e., gentiles instead of the invited but unwilling Israelites).

The parable then continues with the incident of the guest not properly dressed for a wedding. Apparently those attending weddings were expected to wear a white garment; so the person in question had got into the celebration without being clad in the symbol of God's gift of grace. This part of the parable may have been imported by Matthew from a different source and refer to the end time and the general judgment. However, the final short sentence in the passage belongs to the first part of the excerpt and probably indicates that some Jews had accepted the invitation to become disciples of Jesus.

The lessons that we, in our day, could draw from today's gospel are probably more easily and better taken from one or other (or both) of the preceding two parables.

The prophet Isaiah provides the first reading (25:6-10), an image of the messianic age as a banquet and a time of salvation and great happiness – a very suitable introduction and partner for today's gospel.

In this final extract from his letter to the Philippians (4:12-14.19-20), Paul thanks them for sharing the hardships of his life and ministry, although he says that, even without their support, he would have survived with God's help. He gives thanks that God will fully provide all their needs.

TWENTY-NINTH SUNDAY IN ORDINARY TIME – Year A

Matthew 22:15-21

All three synoptic gospels report this encounter between Jesus and some Pharisees (who opposed the Roman occupiers but did not encourage the use of force against them) and a group of Herodians (supporters of the Romans and dependent on them for their livelihood). In Matthew, the meeting is reported immediately after the three parables (on the previous three Sundays) which spoke of the majority of Jews and their leaders who rejected Jesus' teaching on the kingdom.

The leaders begin the conversation with some pretence of flattery for Jesus, which is followed by the question set to trap him. He will either have to declare his support of the Romans and their occupying forces or he will be seen as an opponent and a rebel. Jesus, however, avoids the dilemma. His answer is noncommittal. If something belongs to the emperor, he says, then give it to him; if it belongs to God, then it is God's. He does not say what belongs to either.

The response which Jesus gives does not conflict with his concern for the poor. His mission is to them; he wants to show his concern for them in their poverty which is due to their being marginalised by those in power (whether Romans or their Jewish supporters). He is anxious that the poor should know God's love for them and the invitation given them to hear of the kingdom which Jesus is inaugurating – a kingdom not like those already in the world, certainly not political and with benefits reserved for certain powerful people. At the same time, Jesus' response does not incriminate him or show him to be a friend or an enemy of the Romans.

The manner in which Jesus dealt with the question that was meant to compromise him is a lesson that is still valid for us. As Catholics, and especially if we hold a responsibility as leaders or spokespersons, what we say on behalf of the Church in matters of public policy should not embrace or favour any political party or economic theory, except in so far as the issue may be one with religious, moral or faith involvement. Our concerns must be for justice and freedom for all, and especially for those without power or influence. In so doing, we shall be following the example given by Jesus himself.

Isaiah (45:1.4-6) is from Deutero-Isaiah (Second Isaiah, sixth century BC). The reading is a message from God, via the prophet, to Cyrus, king of Persia. The Persians had captured Babylon from the Chaldeans and Cyrus decreed that the Jewish slaves should be freed and returned to their own country. God tells Cyrus that he (God) is the one and only deity and that he confers on the king the honour of being called 'anointed' because of his decree freeing God's people. This reading, although not directly like the gospel, does bear some relation to it in the sense that a ruler can also be God's ally and do his will.

The second reading is the first of five from Paul's first letter to the Thessalonians. Paul had been in Thessalonika (today Thessaloniki) in AD 50 and wrote this letter the following year. This passage (1:1-5) brings greetings and an acknowledgement of the people's ready acceptance of the Good News and the resulting graces of the Spirit.

THIRTIETH SUNDAY IN ORDINARY TIME - Year A

Matthew 22:34-40

The central statement of Jewish belief, the profession of faith for Jews, is called the *shema*. It is recited twice daily by the devout and comprises three texts: Deuteronomy 6:4-9 and 11:13-21; and Numbers 15:37-41. In his answer to the Pharisee's question, Jesus quotes the words of Deuteronomy 6:5. He then adds the words of Leviticus 19:18 concerning love of our neighbour, a precept which, although for Jews it does not have the same weight as love of God, Jesus appears to treat as of equal importance.

The Jews had over 600 commandments in their law and they were considered as either 'heavy' or 'light'. Love of neighbour was in the latter category, even although a great number of examples are clearly and explicitly given as to be obeyed. Some examples, in fact, form the first reading of today's Mass (Exodus 22:20-26).

All three synoptic gospels, on the other hand, present love of God and love of neighbour as equally important and even as part of the one great commandment. (By the way, it is interesting to note the variations among the synoptics' account of the incident: who questions Jesus, is the questioning friendly or hostile, does Jesus himself answer or does he challenge his questioner to respond? Cf. Matthew 22:34-40; Mark 12:28-31; Luke 10:25-28).

The equal seriousness of the obligation to love God and to love our neighbour is confirmed, for example, in the letter of James (2:8) and the first letter of John (chapter 4 and especially 4:21). This difference between Jewish teaching and that of Jesus throws light on the Lord's words: 'I give you a new commandment: love one another; just as I have loved you, you also must love one another' (John 13:34-35).

Whether we consider the commandment to love God and neighbour as one great obligation or as two, we have to avoid a tendency to regard explicit love of God as implying love of neighbour, or vice versa. It is our duty to be committed explicitly to the love of both; insufficient to concentrate on one to the exclusion of the other. Moreover, to love God properly implies more than an emotional attraction; it means an absolute desire to do what God wants – and that is the welfare of all creation. This must have been in St Paul's mind (today's second reading) when he urges the Thessalonian Christians to imitate his way of life, and thus that of Christ (1 Thessalonians 1:5-10).

How good it would be, and how pleasing to God, if our time of prayer were not limited to prayer of petition, praying for things, but also expressed our love for God just because God is God. As *The Catechism of the Catholic Church* tells us: adoration 'exalts the greatness of the Lord who made us and the almighty power of the Saviour who sets us free from evil . . . adoration of the thrice-holy and sovereign God of love blends with humility and gives assurance to our supplications'; and again, 'praise is the form of prayer that recognises most immediately that God is God . . . praise embraces the other forms of prayer and carries them towards him who is its source and goal' (CCC 2628 and 2639).

Brief comments on the first reading (Exodus 22:20-26) and second reading (1 Thessalonians 1:5-10) are today incorporated in the gospel reflection above.

THIRTY-FIRST SUNDAY IN ORDINARY TIME – Year A

Matthew 23:1-12

'You are all brothers', says Jesus; 'the greatest among you must be your servant; anyone who exalts himself will be humbled'. These are strong words, primarily warning his followers against the behaviour of the scribes and Pharisees of his day who, by the titles they used, regarded themselves as superior to 'ordinary' people and wanted that superiority to be recognised by being called *Rabbi* (master or teacher). Such claims to superiority showed arrogance, compounded by the fact that the conduct of the leaders was often sheer hypocrisy. Jesus' criticism was perhaps 'sharpened' by the evangelist if, in his time, convert Christians were being harassed by the Jewish religious leaders.

This gospel passage is not merely a criticism of the Jewish religious leaders' behaviour, but an instruction that the followers of Jesus should not copy them. They are not to allow themselves to be addressed by titles of honour like 'Master', 'Father' and 'Teacher'. 'You are all brothers', says Jesus; to which we should nowadays rightly add the words 'and sisters'.

How are we to respond to these commands of Jesus? I am afraid that we limit ourselves to eschewing (or claiming to eschew) arrogance and hypocrisy. That is at least something to attempt, although we, and the reference here is to those of us who are clergy, do not always succeed even in that. Phylacteries and tassels are not worn, but vestments are – and so also are distinctive non-liturgical apparel. And places of honour, front seats and obsequious greetings?

The reforms of the Constitution on the Sacred Liturgy of the Second Vatican Council and other documents have done away with many of the liturgical rites and ceremonies which used to clutter the celebration of Mass. Those that remain can be justified as appropriate ways of honouring the sacred nature of the rites of Mass; the others which have been discarded often seemed to exist to enhance the dignity of the priest or to have little point. 'The rites are to be simplified . . . elements which, with the passage of time, came to be duplicated, or were added with but little advantage, are now to be discarded', the Council decreed (no. 50). Some of the vestments worn by the priest are now simpler (albs, stoles and chasubles), maniples have gone, while amices and cinctures are used only if necessary. Distinctive non-liturgical apparel is recommended as a witness to the vocation and work of a priest or deacon and not to attract preferential treatment or 'obsequious greetings'.

The titles (master, father, teacher), which Jesus disliked, can perhaps be justified since nowadays they are in common usage and by no means restricted to members of the clergy, even less to enhancing their status or dignity. But it is significant that Pope Francis has asked that the award to the clergy of honorific titles should cease. On a personal note, I am glad that hardly at all do I hear myself addressed as 'My Lord', 'Your Lordship' or 'Your Excellency'. How to address people can be a tricky subject for both the addresser and the addressee, the former often solving the problem by abstaining from the use of any title.

In the first reading today, God, through the prophet Malachi (1:14-2:2.8-10), addresses the Jewish priests as 'contemptible and vile in the eyes of the whole people' because of their neglect of the covenant, their false teaching and their favouritism in administration. No wonder Jesus had hard words for those men. May we not deserve the same!

The contrast with St Paul's total commitment to those he served (the second reading - 1 Thessalonians 2:7-9.13) is stark and dramatic. He is imitating Jesus and providing a challenge for us all.

THIRTY-SECOND SUNDAY IN ORDINARY TIME – Year A

Matthew 25:1-13

The parable of the bridesmaids gives us some idea of wedding customs in Palestine in the time of our Lord. Jesus illustrates the teaching he wants to give by reminding his listeners of what they had seen when a wedding was to be held in their villages. A number of girls and young women (twenty suggests a rather splendid affair) awaited the bridegroom – at night – to accompany him to the house of his bride-to-be. (Knowledge of details of Jewish weddings in those times is not great but it is thought that the actual rite of marriage lay in the bridegroom taking the bride from her father's house to his.)

The point of the parable, of course, is to illustrate the similarity of the bridesmaids waiting for the bridegroom with Christ's followers waiting for his second coming.

The time of arrival in each case is unknown but Jesus wants us to learn how important it is for us to be ready whenever he does come. Perhaps we can extend the parallel by suggesting that our equivalent of having sufficient 'oil in their lamps' is a life of good deeds and which, in fact, we cannot borrow from others. The faith that we confess in Jesus Christ must have its impact on the way we live.

It is interesting to remember that eternal life, to which Jesus will take us when he arrives, is described in the Apocalypse as the 'wedding feast of the Lamb' of God. Further, our celebration of the Eucharist is a pledge and foretaste of heaven, a point of which we are reminded when the priest, at Holy Communion, proclaims 'Blessed are those who are called to the supper of the Lamb'.

The reading from the book of Wisdom in today's first reading (6:12-16) is appropriate for the gospel. The wise bridesmaids were aware of wisdom's value; for the others, their experience of that truth was learned too late.

St Paul, in the second reading today (1 Thessalonians 4:13-18), reassures his friends that, whether they are alive or have already 'died in Christ' when the Lord arrives, they will (arise if already dead and) be taken into eternal happiness. Provided, we presume, that they were wise, not foolish.

THIRTY-THIRD SUNDAY IN ORDINARY TIME - Year A

Matthew 25:14-30

The gospel passage is Matthew's report of Jesus telling the disciples another parable, the parable of the talents. It is not a difficult parable to explain. Fortuitously, the word 'talent' has a very convenient double meaning.

Each of us is given gifts by God in order to enable us to take an active part in the mission of Jesus. Some gifts are given to us all, but we also receive gifts that not everyone receives. Hence, the different number of talents that each servant in the parable receives. The crucial words of the parable are in verse 25, when the third servant (who had been entrusted with only one talent), in explaining that he did not use the talent profitably, confesses 'I was afraid'.

These words reveal that the servant was ruled by fear. Neither love for his master nor a desire to further the master's plans influenced his behaviour. If we 'translate' this into the meaning of the parable, Jesus wants us to love him and not to fear him. Moreover, he expects that our love for him will impel us to use the gifts we have been given to advance his mission of establishing God's kingdom.

In Jesus' day, money could be invested in banks or with moneylenders. Jews were required by religious law not to lend or borrow in a way that would be punitive, especially if the person who suffered was poor or otherwise in need. Bankers today have no reason to presume that Jesus admires some of their questionable practices; nor is he recommending rampant capitalism.

A talent was the largest coin that existed then in Palestine. It is impossible to give an accurate estimate of its value today, but it was the equivalent of 6000 drachmas and a drachma was a typical day's wage for a workman. Since the disciples were peasants, it is unlikely that many of them (except perhaps Matthew and a few others) had any accurate notion of a talent's value or of financial investment. They would simply be aware that, in the parable, the master was trusting the servants with objects of great worth and therefore God's gifts entrusted to us are similarly valuable.

In the parable, Jesus gives us no idea of when the *parousia* will take place. However, there will, at some time, be a judgment and a reckoning. And it is clear that gifts received grow with use and wither if unused. So to discover what special gifts we have been given, we should experiment (and not be afraid of failure!). Note that Jesus condemns not the misuse of gifts (which is clearly wrong), but their non-use.

The first reading, some verses from the final chapter of the book of Proverbs (31:10-13.19-20.30-31), is a paean of praise for 'a perfect wife'. The connection of this reading with today's gospel is somewhat vague and tenuous. It perhaps tells us something of the busy life led by a conscientious Jewish wife at some pre-Christian time. Nowadays, the praise heaped upon the perfect wife can seem very patronising and therefore displeasing to those whom it seeks to commend.

In the second reading, Paul, in his first letter to the Thessalonians (5:1-6), also gives no information about the end times, simply declaring that we must always be ready for 'the Day of the Lord', reading the signs of the times and being vigilant and prepared.

LAST SUNDAY IN ORDINARY TIME – Year A
OUR LORD JESUS CHRIST, KING OF THE UNIVERSE

Matthew 25:31-46

The imagined scene of the universal judgment which Matthew's gospel presents shows Jesus using, as the decisive criterion of our fitness for eternal life, our treatment of those who suffered in this life – have we helped them or ignored them? This shows that the two great commandments are, in fact, inseparable. Furthermore, he presents himself as identified with the poor and those in need. When we show compassion for such people, we are showing compassion to him. Nor is this surprising. Jesus himself knew and practised poverty throughout his life; he constantly saw how the poor were treated in the Palestine of his day – very often those who were comfortable and who could have shown concern for the needy simply passed by and did not help.

So in a real sense, we are on trial now and every day, not just on the last day and the general judgment. It is now that we help or turn away from those who need us; it is now that we opt for Jesus or not. The verdict will come later, delivered by 'the King', 'the Son of Man'. We are providing the evidence now. Moreover, keep in mind that, although unmentioned in Matthew's depiction of the judgment, our relationship with God, especially our faith as well as our love for God, will also be judged. The punishment for those found guilty is described as 'eternal fire' (verse 41), a term taken from a common description of the Valley of Hinnom (or Gehenna), a grim site of constant fire; there, just south of the city walls of Jerusalem, corpses and, later, refuse and rubbish were burnt. It provided an image or metaphor of the dreaded punishment of being excluded from the kingdom of God.

In the Old Testament God is constantly portrayed with royal attributes and as our supreme ruler. The passage chosen for the first reading today, from the prophet Ezekiel (34:11-12.15-17), depicts God as our shepherd, keeping us in view, feeding us, guiding us as well as caring for us, especially when we are lost, wounded or weak. Then, at the end of the passage, God tells us that he will also be our judge.

A question can arise in our minds: if Jesus is our king, is God the Father also/still our king? Yet, we remember that, although the Father and the Son are distinct Persons, they are not two Gods and therefore not two kings. The divinity is a mystery beyond comprehension; and so is the kingship. Note that, in the second reading appointed for today, St Paul (1 Corinthians 15:20-26.28), after extolling Christ for having brought us all to life through his own resurrection, teaches us that he must be king until all his enemies are vanquished and then he will hand over the kingdom to God the Father. This, of course, does not mean a downgrading of the perfections that Jesus has; he is still king (in our analogical language) and the 'subjection of the Son to the Father' (verse 28) is a reference to the homage that the Son, divine and human, gives the Father.

The words which the preface of today's Mass uses to express the kingship of God are interesting: 'so that . . . making all things subject to his (Christ's) rule, he (Christ) might present to the immensity of your (the Father's) majesty an eternal and universal kingdom.' Remember that, in the prayer that Jesus taught us, we address the Father: 'Your kingdom come'; while, during his trial before Pilate, Jesus asserted 'Yes, I am a king'. . . but 'mine is not a kingdom of this world'. We are considering here the most profound of all mysteries, totally beyond our understanding – the mystery of the inner life of God, three Persons, one in nature, equal in majesty. That is all that we can say.

Brief comments on the first reading (Ezekiel 34:11-12.15-17) and second reading (1 Corinthians 15:20-26.28) are today incorporated in the gospel reflection above.

The Seasons and Ordinary Time of Year B

Advent and Christmas

FIRST SUNDAY OF ADVENT – Year B

Mark 13:33-37

Since the word 'Advent' implies that someone is coming, it also implies that others are waiting for that someone to arrive, and with a sense of expectancy for that to take place. Because the season of Advent starts between three and four weeks before Christmas, the natural conclusion is that the arrival for which we are waiting is the birth of Jesus in Bethlehem. However, in the liturgy texts and Scripture readings for Advent, that event only gradually begins to be considered. In the readings for today, the emphasis is very definitely on waiting for the second coming of Jesus.

A few days before his arrest, trial, passion and death, Mark's gospel today tells us that Jesus along with four of the apostles (Peter, James, John and Andrew) was sitting on the Mount of Olives, looking across the Kedron Valley to the walled city of Jerusalem and its most prominent feature, the Temple. He was speaking to them about the end of the world as we know it, the fearful events and dangers that would occur and then the coming of 'the Son of Man' (as Jesus referred to himself when speaking of solemn occasions) in great majesty to judge every human being. These events are sometimes collected and given the name *parousia*, a Greek word meaning 'arrival' or 'presence'. The final part of this eschatological discourse forms today's gospel.

In the excerpt for today's Mass, Jesus is reported to have laid particular importance on our taking great care to 'stay awake' since we do not know the time of his second coming and we must not be caught unprepared. Scripture scholars speak of the context in which Mark's gospel came to be written, probably sometime in the decade of the 60s AD. Between the Lord's ascension and the writing of the gospel, the early generations of Christians had, at first, expected that the second coming was imminent. Then, when it did not happen, there was a tendency to put it out of their thoughts, to cease to be alert to the possibility of it catching them unawares; hence, the stress that Mark uses in quoting Jesus' warning to 'stay awake'.

No matter the exact reasons for the emphasis attributed to Jesus, the question is also relevant for us – probably not in the sense of an imminent second coming but because we all have to face death and judgment as individuals, and death can easily occur unexpectedly. So, even if we are unlikely to be still alive at the *parousia*, the words of Jesus still retain their relevance for each of us. These matters have to be given serious and regular consideration, have they not?

The first reading gives us some verses from Isaiah (63:16-17; 64:1.3-8). They come from chapters towards the end of the prophecy, therefore written not in the eighth century BC (as chapters 1-39 were) but probably two centuries later by a follower or imitator of Isaiah. Israel has been sinful and corrupt and has abandoned God and been taken into exile in Babylon. The extract pleads with God to return – 'tear the heavens open and come down' – and save his people. So this passage can be seen as seeking God not as judge but as saviour (and therefore first coming rather than second) but without giving any hint of how that would take place.

In the letter to the Corinthians (1 Corinthians 1:3-9), Paul rejoices that, due to God's graces which they have received through Jesus Christ, they will remain strong in virtue as they await the second coming.

SECOND SUNDAY OF ADVENT – Year B

Mark 1:1-8

As last Sunday, the gospel is from St Mark but, whereas last week the extract came from the end of Christ's public ministry and immediately before the account of the Holy Week events, today's passage is from the very beginning of the first chapter. Mark opens with a very brief but comprehensive summary of his gospel, almost like the headline of a newspaper. But then he proceeds to speak first about John the Baptist.

For this, he opens with two quotations, one from the prophecy of Malachi (3:1) without acknowledging its provenance and another from the prophecy of Isaiah (40:3) which, in fact, is a verse in today's first reading. John the Baptist tells the people that someone else will come who is much more important than he is; he says that his (John's) baptism is with water and for repentance while the other will offer baptism of the Holy Spirit. John the Baptist was living in a very austere manner and in the Judean wilderness, beside the Jordan. The location is not specified but it is thought to be east of Jericho and a few miles north of the river's entry into the Dead Sea. The text states that large crowds were going to John for baptism.

We tend to expect that the Scripture readings for the liturgy of Advent will be preparing us to celebrate the feast of Christmas. However, in the first three Sundays there is little that is directly on the human birth of Jesus. The gospels go into detail about John the Baptist (who was preparing the people for the adult public ministry of Jesus) while the first readings look forward, from several centuries beforehand, to the messiah (but usually in terms of triumph and prosperity) while the second readings warn us about being ready for the second coming of Christ (called the *parousia*). All of this, plus the fact that, in non-liturgical life, the celebration of Christmas with parties, carols, Yuletide decorations in shops, houses and streets, has already been under way for several weeks, makes a realistic liturgical or devotional preparation for the feast very difficult.

Perhaps we should widen our horizons and see Advent as a call to prepare for the various comings of Christ, not only those which are commemorated in the liturgy, especially in the readings, but also his coming to be our judge when we die. In that respect, there is advice in today's gospel in the way that crowds took the trouble to go to the desert, miles distant from Jerusalem and from all the other Judean towns and villages, far and near, seeking the graces of repentance and conversion. That detail reminds us that such graces cannot be seriously sought in a speedy and distracted manner but require a certain amount of thought, prayer and time and therefore a certain period of singlemindedness, free of interruption and distraction.

The first reading is from the start of Second Isaiah (Isaiah 40:1-5.9-11), written in the sixth century BC at the end of the Jews' period of exile. From its hopeful themes and promises of a saviour-messiah, Second Isaiah is often called the 'Book of the Consolation of Israel'. Today's passage, from the opening chapter, well illustrates its character and style. A curious point is that, in the first reading of today's Mass, the third verse uses the Hebrew version: 'A voice cries, "Prepare in the wilderness..."' but, when the same verse is quoted in the gospel, it is the Greek translation that provides the text: 'A voice cries in the wilderness: prepare...'. In the former version, it is God addressing Isaiah; in the latter, in Mark's gospel (and also John 1:23), it becomes John the Baptist crying in the wilderness.

In the second reading (2 Peter 3:8-14), the author is coping with the widespread disappointment that the second coming, expected to be imminent, has not yet happened. He counsels continuing vigilance.

THIRD SUNDAY OF ADVENT – Year B

John 1:6-8.19-28

The first three verses of today's gospel interrupt John the Evangelist's introduction of the Word of God, truly God but also now human, Jesus Christ. The interruption tells us that John the Baptist, though sent by God, was not the light itself but was to be a witness 'to speak for the light'.

In the second half of today's reading, priests and Levites came from Jerusalem to ask John the Baptist who he was. He denies that he is the Christ/messiah, neither is he Elijah (whom the Jews expected to reappear on earth) nor 'the prophet' (perhaps the questioners meant Moses or just 'a prophet'); but, using the Greek version of the verse in Isaiah (40:3), he asserts that he is 'a voice . . . in the wilderness' preparing a way for the Lord, as the prophet foretold. (The Hebrew version reads that a voice is calling for a way to be prepared in the wilderness; which indicates that the voice is God's, not the Baptist's.)

The questioning continues, but this time on behalf of Pharisees; perhaps this is on another occasion because normally Pharisees did not work closely with priests and Levites. The specific reason for the questions now is because of John's custom of baptising; rites of baptism were practised at the time by various religious groups and communities in Israel. John's answer does not explain why he was baptising but takes the opportunity to indicate that he is preparing the way for someone else, more important than he is.

John does not identify this person. In fact he declares that the person is present among them but 'unknown to you'. This arouses a thought about our own situation. We know about Jesus, but do we know him? We should consider this question seriously. During the Year of Faith (2012-13), Pope Benedict wrote a prayer which was widely used and in which I remember that we prayed to Jesus that 'the men and women of our time will hear of you, will believe in you and will come to the beauty of knowing you'. I think I can claim to have taken the first two steps in my own life, but the third? The question troubles me because I want to know Jesus and to be able to speak to others about my friendship with him. Such a desire is one which we all have, I am sure.

Here are my own suggestions on a way of getting to know Jesus: first, we should talk to him, or better, talk with him in prayer; then we should discover the kind of person he is (most of all by reading the gospels); so we get to like him (he becomes a friend); and finally we discover that our love for each other is mutual because we know each other (but the initiative has been his).

It is perhaps worth noting that, although the readings today do not refer directly to the birth of Jesus in Bethlehem, the collect of the Mass does (for the first time in Advent). Another point to mention. When Jesus says that John the Baptist 'is the Elijah who was to return' (Matthew 11:14; also 17:9-13), he is speaking figuratively and not in an actual physical sense.

The first reading is part of the 'Book of the Consolation of Israel' by Deutero-Isaiah (61:1-2.10-11), written when the Jews were soon to return, or had already returned, from exile in Babylon. It is a passage full of rejoicing for the kindness and care of the Lord for his chosen people. It was the first part of today's reading (60:1-2) that Jesus read to the people in the synagogue at Nazareth and then told them that the messianic figure of whom the passage speaks was himself (Luke 4:16-21). The second part of today's reading speaks of the joyful exultation that God's gifts bring us, a note that is in keeping with the theme of joy that pervades the liturgy this day.

Paul strikes the same note (1 Thessalonians 5:16-24) when he calls us to 'be happy at all times', gratefully rejoicing in all God's gifts. The reading also contains Paul's hope that his readers may 'be kept safe and blameless' for the second coming (but without indicating that it may be soon).

FOURTH SUNDAY OF ADVENT – Year B

Luke 1:26-38

At last our patience in being rewarded! Until now, the Advent gospels have been speaking about various 'advents' of Jesus – his second coming, his appearance to start his adult mission. Now, in this final Sunday the gospel tells of his human conception from which will come his birth in human nature, the incarnation leading to the nativity.

In those days, the calendar dates of events did not seem to matter; or at least, they do not seem to have been recorded for yearly observance thereafter. We celebrate Christ's conception on 25th March because we celebrate his birth on 25th December. We do not know the date of the Lord's birth but there is a credible theory that 25th December was chosen because, 21st December being the winter solstice, 25th was at the start of the annual daily increase in the length of time between sunrise and sunset and therefore was an appropriate day to celebrate (when annual celebration was inaugurated) the birth of 'the

Light of the World'. Since, at the time when the date was chosen, there were no Christians in the southern hemisphere, the idea of a midsummer Christmas never occurred to anyone.

Luke is the only evangelist to give us an account of the incarnation. It is noticeable that he also narrates the story of the incarnation of John the Baptist (1:5-25), as if he were urging us to compare the two. In both, the archangel Gabriel was God's messenger to give the very unexpected news to the parents-to-be. But there is a clear contrast between the two events. First, in the locations of the announcements, one in the city of Jerusalem and in the sacred precincts of the Temple, the other in an obscure and even disreputable village far away from the holy city, in the north of Palestine. Then again, in John's case, the parents are elderly and infertile but of good reputation and considerable status since the husband was a priest and both 'scrupulously observed all the commandments' (Luke 1:6); in Jesus' case, the mother-to-be is a young and unknown peasant and, although betrothed and therefore considered married, she conceives not in the normal manner but through the miraculous intervention of the Holy Spirit. The contrast also is seen in the circumstances of the babies' births, John's taking place at home (although no details are given, the neighbours and relations rejoiced with the parents), and Jesus' in the strange and impoverished circumstances which are described and which we know so well, conditions which remind us of the tent in which God's presence dwelt in the time of King David (see first reading today).

This Sunday, given the choice of the gospel passage, is an occasion for us to grow in admiration and love for Mary. Particularly, I like to think about her courage in accepting the angel's message, her trust in God since she was faced with the completely unknown as well as the danger of ridicule, and her holiness as the one person in history selected by God to bear his Son to human birth. This can be a day on which we say the *Hail Mary* with great admiration and gratitude.

The first reading (2 Samuel 7:1-5.8-12.14.16) tells of a period in the life of King David (late eleventh-early tenth centuries BC), from which two points may be noted. First, since the ark of the covenant was kept in a tent, David's offer to build a proper dwelling – a temple – for God's presence is refused; and second, God nevertheless assures the king that his royal line will continue through his descendants (among whom is Jesus).

Paul, ending his letter to the Christian community in Rome (16:25-27), thanks God that the gentiles have remained faithful to the great mystery, hitherto secret but which he made known, that Jesus came to save not only the Jews but the entire human race.

THE NATIVITY OF OUR LORD – Years ABC

Luke 2:1-14	**Mass during the night**
Luke 2:15-20	**Dawn Mass**
John 1:1-18	**Mass during the day**

All Scripture readings are common to years A, B and C. The notes are at year A.

THE HOLY FAMILY OF JESUS, MARY AND JOSEPH – Year B

Luke 2:22-40

Mark has no mention of the early years of the Lord's life and so, for this feast of the Holy Family, we use Luke, even in year B. His narrative is fairly detailed so that a number of points can be made.

The Holy Family were punctilious in observing the Mosaic law. To conform to the law, they went to the Temple (strictly, only for Mary) 'to be purified'. The law decreed (Leviticus 12:2-4) that, after the birth of a boy, the mother was ritually (not morally) unclean and had to wait forty days before she was purified. The reasoning was that loss of blood meant loss of vitality so, to restore the loss, ritual reunion with God, the source of life, was needed. At the same time, the infant was to be presented to God (Exodus 13:11-16) and the parents had to make an offering to God. The offering for poor people who could not afford a lamb was two pigeons or turtledoves, one for a holocaust of adoration, the other for a sin offering (Leviticus 12:6-8).

The devout man Simeon had been promised by the Holy Spirit that he would see the messiah before he died and thus the Spirit induced him to go to the Temple when Jesus was brought there. In the canticle *Nunc dimittis* (now recited every night during Compline), Simeon thanks God for the favour promised and now fulfilled and for the messiah 'for all nations to see' and 'a light to enlighten the pagans' (= gentiles; a phrase quoting Isaiah 49:6). Simeon also foretells that Jesus will be both openly accepted and openly rejected by many in Israel and that Mary will also experience suffering; how and when this last is to occur is left unsaid – mainly perhaps as she shares in her son's suffering and thus becomes an exemplar for all of his disciples.

The widow Anna, who daily spent long hours in the Temple, also saw Jesus and praised God, and she told other devout people who awaited the messiah of what she had witnessed.

The extract ends, informing us that the Holy Family then returned to Nazareth and Jesus grew up there, with God's favour on him and filled with wisdom.

It is salutary to recall that we are celebrating the feast of the Holy Family and that the liturgical prayers present that family as a model for our families. The Holy Family is so unique that the call to imitate can sound unrealistic; but at least we can try to imitate some aspects and qualities of their lives as well as to pray for their help.

Families nowadays can be the scene of so much suffering – marriages that do not last or where one partner is the victim of the other's cruelty; or in which the children are rebellious, out of control, in trouble with the law, or using drugs. In other cases, one partner (usually the father) has gone and a stranger has taken his (or her) place.

Unfortunately, complete family breakdowns occur and the children especially are caused to suffer and are exposed to many kinds of danger.

This is not the place to go into details nor to ask what can be done to remedy (or, better, prevent) these tragic situations. But, in addition to anything that public authorities, the extended family or those directly involved may attempt, we should all include the hope of successful and happy family life as a prominent intention in our prayers.

The lectionary provides alternative first and second readings.

For the first reading, an extract from the book of Ecclesiasticus (3:2-6.12-14) provides the first option. It was written early in the second century BC by a Jew named Ben Sira. The reading urges children to obey their parents and to treat them always with respect.

The alternative first reading is from Genesis (15:1-6; 21:1-3). God loves Abram and his wife Sarah. They are childless and do not expect to have a son and heir, but God provides and Sarah conceives and bears a son, Isaac, who will provide Abraham (God changes his name, 17:5) with a line of descendants.

The first option for the second reading is Paul's letter to the Colossians (3:12-21). The apostle urges his Christian readers to excel in the virtue of love, especially in their dealings with one another. The final verses have a few words of advice to wives, husbands and children about their relations with each other.

The alternative second reading is the letter to the Hebrews (11:8.11-12.17-19). The extract, in showing the necessity of our having faith in Christ's work for our salvation, recalls various ways in which Abraham, chosen by God, showed that he had faith. One example cited is the faith that Abraham showed in believing that indeed God would provide him and his wife with an heir.

SOLEMNITY OF MARY, MOTHER OF GOD – Years ABC

Luke 2:16-21

All Scripture readings are common to years A, B and C. The notes are at year A.

SECOND SUNDAY AFTER THE NATIVITY – Years ABC

John 1:1-18

All Scripture readings are common to years A, B and C. The notes are at year A.

THE EPIPHANY OF THE LORD – Years ABC

Matthew 2:1-12

All Scripture readings are common to years A, B and C. The notes are at year A.

THE BAPTISM OF THE LORD – Year B

Mark 1:7-11

That Jesus, the perfectly holy one, should seek baptism and from an 'inferior' is not only puzzling for us, but was also for John the Baptist himself. The best we can do is to suggest a few reasons. Throughout his public life, Jesus showed great humility and a desire to identify as much as possible with those whom he had come to serve; therefore his seeking to be baptised was in conformity with these two aims. Also, his baptism was an element in his epiphany, his being presented as sent by the Father and with the Holy Spirit dwelling within him; although, somewhat perversely but in keeping with his desire to preserve from the people's knowledge the kingly messianic identity of Jesus (the so-called 'messianic secret'), Mark indicates that only Jesus himself, and not the people there, were aware of the Father's voice and the Spirit's descent.

John the Baptist, although he seems to be largely unfamiliar with Jesus in spite of the relationship of their mothers, nevertheless knows that he is someone exceptional, that in fact it is he (John) who should be subservient to Jesus, and that, while he baptises with water, Jesus 'will baptise you with the Holy Spirit' (verse 8).

Since the baptism that Jesus will offer also uses water, what is the meaning of this statement of the Baptist? To solve this question, we need to recall the effects in us who have received the baptism that Jesus instituted. It removes our sins, brings us into friendship and reconciliation with God, confers a share in Christ's threefold role of priest, prophet and king, gives us the gifts needed to be the active members of the Church that God wishes us to be, and enables us to be fit for the Holy Spirit (and indeed the Trinity) to dwell in us. John's baptism was the occasion for repentant sinners to receive God's forgiveness but it did not confer a share in Christ's mission, nor the presence of the Spirit with gifts. Hence the statement that the baptism of Jesus, and by implication not that of John, confers the Spirit on the recipients. The assertion has particular relevance because we are told that it was at this point that the Spirit descended on Jesus.

This feast is an occasion for being reminded that we are baptised with the baptism of Christ, that we have received the Spirit and gifts with a lifelong commission to be active in the Church and in the community to which we belong, so that we may share, in whatever way God calls us, in helping to build the kingdom. It is also a day on which parents, godparents and the parish community should recall their responsibility for helping those in their care to fulfil the trust placed in them.

It is remarkable how much stress the early Church placed on the presence of the Holy Spirit in its midst. Perhaps we notice that emphasis because nowadays we tend to overlook that presence or, at least, afford it less prominence than we ought. The point has also been made that, if we were to be more aware of the Spirit's activity, we would realise that that activity is not restricted within the lives of those whom we consider 'good

Catholics'. It is argued that, if we were less censorious of those whom we consider different and even errant, we should all benefit by allowing the presence and effect of the Holy Spirit to be more recognised in our world.

In years B and C, there are, in addition to those Scripture texts appointed for all three years, alternative first readings, psalms and second readings for this feast. Here, therefore, are brief notes on both choices of first and second readings for today.

Isaiah 42:1-4.6-7 is part of the first 'Song of the Servant of the Lord', a prophecy, clearly messianic, about a person whom God will appoint 'as covenant of the people and light of the nations', sent to bring justice and freedom to the world.

The alternative first reading is Isaiah 55:1-11, which comes at the end of the 'Book of the Consolation of Israel'. It is a call to Israel (and indeed to others also) to come back to the Lord, to give up their sinful ways and enjoy the benefits that the Lord provides. Again, the messianic character of the reading is apparent.

The second reading can be Acts 10:34-38 where Peter, speaking to a household of gentiles, declares that, though Jesus was sent in the first place to the Jews, God has no favourites and people of any and all nations can be saved. Having told the family about Jesus and his work of salvation he then baptises its members.

Or the alternative second reading is 1 John 5:1-9 in which John the Evangelist teaches that faith in Jesus Christ, loving God and keeping his commandments will ensure that we are children of God. For faith in Christ the Son of God, there are three witnesses: the Spirit, the water and the blood. The blood and water from Jesus' side on the cross were the evidence for those who were on Calvary; but they are also witnesses now for all Christians since water is the type or symbol of baptism and blood the symbol of Christ's saving death. They, and the gift of the Spirit, are the components of the new life in Christ.

Lent and Easter

ASH WEDNESDAY – Years ABC

Matthew 6:1-6.16-18

All Scripture readings are common to years A, B and C. The notes are at year A.

FIRST SUNDAY OF LENT – Year B

Mark 1:12-15

Mark's account of the forty days which Jesus spent in the desert is extremely brief. Unlike Matthew and Luke, he gives no details of the temptations which Jesus endured. However, even in the few words we have, there are several points to note.

Jesus was driven out into the wilderness by the Holy Spirit; he did not go there of his own initiative. The wilderness is an insecure and dangerous place, indicating that during his public ministry Jesus will face opposition and hostility. Yet the wilderness is also the best place to be aware of the voice of God since it is free of all the distractions of ordinary life among other people.

Mark's remark that, in the desert, Jesus was with savage beasts and that, by contrast, angels were also with him suggests that his time there was a symbolic preparation for the days ahead when he would have to endure those who wanted to destroy him but would be assured of God's presence and guidance.

The contrast which Jesus experienced in the desert serves also as a symbol of the contrasting experiences that befall us, as disciples of Jesus, during our life on earth. And indeed the same is true of the Church itself, Christ's mystical body. We must not forget, however, that the two opposites are not to be thought of as equally powerful. God's caring providence for the Church and for each individual member will always prevail, provided that we ask for it and show ourselves willing to cooperate. Lent is the time to seek the graces that God has for us and, in imitation of Jesus, to resist and repel the wiles of Satan.

In year B, due to the brevity of Mark's account of the days in the desert, the lectionary adds his description of the opening of Jesus' public ministry in Galilee. That description, in fact, provides a summary of his ministry and its purpose – to announce the establishment of God's kingdom and to call us to repentance and faith. It is this divine summons that we heard when receiving the penitential ashes last Wednesday.

In the first reading today, from the book of Genesis (9:8-15), God establishes a covenant with Noah after the flood. This solemn pledge, whose sign is to be the rainbow, is for 'every living creature of every kind', whereas later covenants in the Old Law were to be between God and his chosen people of Israel.

The second reading (1 Peter 3:18-22) has, as its main purpose, to reassure the early Christians who were enduring hostility and even persecution. Jesus was innocent, but he was put to death and then rose again. They, though innocent, are suffering but will be saved through their baptism (just as Noah was saved through the Flood) and will enjoy eternal life. The passage also contains reference to Jesus preaching to spirits who were in prison and who had refused to believe. The allusion is very unclear. Some scholars suggest that it refers to Jesus, between his death and resurrection, 'descending into hell' (as in the Apostles' Creed) but others are very doubtful.

SECOND SUNDAY OF LENT – Year B

Mark 9:2-10

The second Sunday of Lent is the day on which we read of the Lord's transfiguration. It is a suitable choice of gospel since the synoptics indicate that the event took place as Jesus, having preached and healed all over Galilee, was on his way south with his disciples to Judea, Jerusalem and his passion, death and resurrection. This year, we listen to Mark's account.

The transfiguration of Jesus shows us the unique place that he holds in the divine plan of salvation for the human race. Jesus leads the three apostles 'up a high mountain' (not named but probably Mount Tabor). Why only three and why those three? We do not know but can only surmise. Perhaps they were seen as the leaders of the Twelve or perhaps they were still confused about the identity and mission of Jesus – Peter had been horrified at the prospect of Jesus being put to death; John and James had been anxious about their own future, with ambitions that they should be favoured above the others.

The details of the transfiguration are significant in regard to Jesus' identity and mission. So why Moses and Elijah? The Jews saw the Scriptures as having two sections, which they called the Law and the Prophets. The two men stand as representing these two parts, Moses to whom God gave the commandments and Elijah the great prophet. When God wanted to be in touch with Moses who had been given a mission to fulfil, the encounter took place on a mountain. But Jesus is more than a second Moses – it is he, neither Moses nor Elijah, who is transfigured. A voice from God refers to Jesus and speaks in very clear terms: 'my Son, the Beloved; listen to him'. The event enables us to appreciate the unique position in God's saving plan which Jesus holds among his followers (and still does). In addition, his path to fulfilment involved great suffering inflicted by those opposed to him, suffering even to death. Can we expect to be his disciples but be unwilling to accept whatever suffering may, in God's will, come our way?

The transfiguration, occurring as it did when Jesus and his close disciples were on their way to Jerusalem and Calvary, certainly provided reassurance to them that he was fulfilling the will of the Father in making that journey. Above all, the transfiguration would be effective for Jesus as he heroically turned his steps to the grim destiny which he foresaw awaited him. For us, the transfiguration provides a paradigm for us to act in the same way when we are unsure or anxious or fearful of the consequences of an important decision that we have made. For example, events or moments such as a retreat, a pilgrimage, a Mass celebrated devoutly, even a fervent prayer can give us the reassurance that we are carrying out God's will and therefore can allay our fears or doubts.

The first reading (Genesis 22:1-2.9-13.15-18) is the story of Abraham's obedience to God even if it meant the sacrificial death of his beloved son Isaac. That sacrifice was stopped at the last moment by God's decision and a ram was substituted as victim. But God rewarded Abraham for his heroic fidelity and obedience. The link with the gospel passage is obvious, though in the latter case the beloved Son was sacrificed – and for us.

St Paul, writing to the Romans (8:31-34), reassures us of the unlimited generosity of the love for us shown by the Father and Son; the former 'gave up' the latter for our benefit.

THIRD SUNDAY OF LENT - Year B

Even in years B and C, the Scripture readings of year A can be used on the third, fourth and fifth Sundays of Lent, if preferred in place of those appointed to be read. If there are to be baptisms at the Easter Vigil, the year A readings should always be used on the three Sundays.

John 2:13-25

All four evangelists describe the scene in which Jesus drives the money changers and those selling animals out of the Temple in Jerusalem. But, whereas the synoptics suggest that the incident occurred only a few days before Jesus was arrested, John's gospel (today) places it at the start of his public ministry. Chronology was not uppermost in the evangelists' intentions but the variation allows us to mention a detail that can confuse us. The synoptics give the impression that Jesus made only one visit to Jerusalem during his public ministry and that was at the end of his Galilean labours and immediately preceding his arrest. John, on the other hand, has Jesus in Jerusalem several times during those two to three years. Most scholars consider it likely that John's information is more accurate chronologically since the synoptics tended to use other criteria when assembling their material for presentation.

John's account is the only one that is followed by a confrontation with those who had witnessed Jesus' angry reaction to the use of the temple precincts for buying and selling. The opportunity of changing money and buying animals for sacrifice was a great convenience for pilgrims, but it should have been available outside the sacred area. Jesus rejects the protests which demanded to know by what right he had acted as he did, but his words about being able to 'raise up this sanctuary in three days' if it were destroyed seemed incredible and nonsensical to his accusers. The evangelist explains that 'he was speaking of the sanctuary that was his body' and that, after his resurrection, his disciples recalled his words.

John wrote his gospel towards the end of the first century, long after Christ rose from the dead and some years after the destruction of the Temple during the failed revolt against the Romans in AD 70. Although for Jews who had not become Christians, the loss of the Temple meant that they no longer had the presence of God in their midst or at least located on earth, for Christians God is to be found in Jesus and, though no longer visible, he remains truly with us. Reflecting, therefore, on the event in today's gospel passage reminds us of this truth and the need for us to be aware of that divine presence, with us always but in a special way when we celebrate the Eucharist.

The final three verses of today's reading tell us that Jesus was realistic about those who declared their belief in him. Faith to be lasting has to be based not just on having witnessed miracles but requires also a conviction about the person performing the miracles.

The first reading, from the book of Exodus (20:1-17), presents, without context, the ten commandments. They are also listed, this time with some context, in the book of Deuteronomy (5:6-22). They are the basic elements of 'the Law' of the old covenant between God and humanity. They retain their validity in the new covenant, upheld by Jesus who adds 'evangelical counsels', primarily the beatitudes. St Paul's rejection of the law refers not to the ten commandments but to prohibitions and orders added by human authorities.

In the second reading (1 Corinthians 1:22-25), Paul maintains that faith in a crucified Christ is not an insurmountable obstacle or madness but the power and wisdom of God.

FOURTH SUNDAY OF LENT – Year B

John 3:14-21

In the third chapter of his gospel, John tells the story of the meeting between Jesus and Nicodemus, who came seeking to have the basis of Jesus' teaching about God's plan for our salvation explained to him. In the portion of Jesus' explanation that is used as today's gospel passage, the fundamental truth is in the sentence, 'God loved the world so much . . . may have eternal life' (verse 16). It is preceded by a statement of how God offers us eternal life, namely that 'the Son of Man must be lifted up' (verse 13). Jesus is quoted using the phrase about 'the son of Man being lifted up' twice more in John's gospel (8:28 and 12:32-34).

Just as the Israelites in the desert were saved (from death by a plague of serpents) by Moses raising up a bronze serpent on which the people were to gaze (Numbers 21:4-9), so we can be saved by looking with faith at Christ, raised up on the cross in anticipation of his definitive exaltation at his resurrection and ascension. So God's love for us is a saving love brought about through his gift to us of Jesus, the Son of Man.

It follows that the Church's principal duty, instructed by Christ, is to remember and proclaim the love of God for everyone. It is a love that does not condemn but saves; the Church must express that love in the same manner and call us to conversion, not by condemning but in a positive manner. The same positive message of God's love for us should be the theme of each one of us when, as individuals, we seek to tell people about God and his plan of salvation.

The passage ends by transferring the focus of the teaching from God's loving plan to our response. 'On these grounds is sentence pronounced' (verse 19). Our choice is either to live in the light which has come to us through Christ or to remain hidden in the darkness of evil. It is to enable us to make the correct choice that, during Lent, we seek the grace of conversion (*metanoia*) through prayer, fasting and almsgiving.

The first reading is from the second book of Chronicles (36:14-16.19-23). It tells of the sinful corruption of the Jews, punished by God allowing the Temple and Jerusalem to be destroyed and the people carried off to slavery in Babylon. Eventually, the Persians capture Babylon and King Cyrus fulfils God's will that the Jews should be released and returned to their homeland.

St Paul, writing to the Ephesians (2:4-10), expresses the same truths about God's love for us as are found in today's gospel (verse 16).

FIFTH SUNDAY OF LENT – Year B

John 12:20-30

It is the week leading to the feast of the Passover and also to Christ's death. Today's gospel passage opens with a group of visitors (perhaps converts to Judaism) asking one of the apostles if they can be allowed to see Jesus. The response comes at the end of the extract – yes, when he is 'lifted up', he will draw everyone to himself. The expression 'lifted up' is used in John's gospel and indicates 'glorified', referring to Jesus lifted up on the cross and also lifted up at his resurrection and ascension.

This extract, therefore, is a report of Jesus putting his thoughts into words regarding his approaching passion and death, their purpose and their effect on those who are his disciples. He says that his death will be part of his glorification and that, through it, the purpose of his life will be achieved. His true disciples will have to follow him and be with him. Jesus then shows his anguish in thinking about the coming ordeal but he also declares his determination to carry out his Father's will. Thus the Father also will be glorified, a fact confirmed by the Father's voice which Jesus tells the people was itself a divine reassurance given for their sake.

Some of the expressions used by Jesus today require explanation. Exegetes in general offer the following comments. The crucified and risen Jesus 'will draw everyone to himself' in the sense that the great mystery of God's infinite love for us, even to accepting the death of his Son as proof of that love, will become known. To 'follow Jesus and be with him' means to try to be like him, to imitate him, believe and proclaim what he taught, follow his way of life, and accept the consequences as he did. We shall serve him by our determination to do the work that he was doing, to make known the love of God for every human being, to build the kingdom of God. To reach that level of discipleship, we have to discover the overwhelming love of God for humankind, a love shown above all in the death and resurrection of Jesus, his Son.

To sacrifice himself was not easy for Jesus. It is not easy for us. We are asked to be selfless, to be willing to accept hardship and suffering and even rejection and apparent failure, and finally to accept the inevitability of death. As for Jesus, so for us – not only on earth, but with the assurance that eternal life in God's love awaits us.

The prophet Jeremiah had the frequent duty, as he spoke in God's name, of saying some very hard things to the Jewish people. But in today's first reading (31:31-34), he delivers God's promise to his people that there will be a time of forgiveness, reconciliation and peace. We know that this pledge will be realised with the coming of the messiah.

The letter to the Hebrews was sent to Jewish converts experiencing hostility. The extract (5:7-9) encourages them by reminding them that Jesus himself, who has brought us salvation, had to endure suffering also as he obeyed the Father's will.

PALM SUNDAY OF THE PASSION OF THE LORD – Year B

Mark 11:1-10
Mark 14:1-15:47

Fuller reflections on the gospel passages for today have already been provided at the corresponding Sunday of year A. Here, only a few remarks about Mark's accounts are added.

Mark's narration of the Lord's triumphal entry to Jerusalem on Palm Sunday is very similar to Matthew's, which clearly relies on the earlier account by Mark. In Mark's version, there is only one animal provided for Jesus; the two disciples sent to bring it to Jesus are challenged by some bystanders but allowed to proceed; and the shouts of the welcoming crowd are slightly different.

The general impression, when reading the four evangelists' accounts of the events that occurred between the Last Supper and the burial of Jesus, is of their similarity to one another. Certainly the basic facts are present in each account and they tell the same story and provide the same lessons for us to ponder. However, when the accounts are closely examined, there are a great many differences in the details – some details are to be found in all four accounts, others are in some but omitted in others. Moreover, these differences are not simply whether details are included or omitted in any one account, but the differences can produce clashes or contradictions from one gospel to another which cannot be reconciled. In other words, there must be, in some of the gospels, inaccuracies among the details of the narratives. One example which illustrates this point is to be found in Peter's denials: the times at which they occurred and the intervals between them differ in all four accounts. But the basic and essential facts, the truths necessary for the believer or the possible believer, are available for us to learn and thence to grow in faith and love.

The gospel of Mark is the earliest of the four accounts of the Last Supper, Gethsemane, and the trial, passion, death and resurrection of Jesus. The account is stark and unadorned with extraneous details. It emphasises the loneliness and cruel degradation through which Jesus had to pass. Mark's description of Jesus' ordeal as he prayed in Gethsemane stresses more than in the other gospels the terror and sadness he went through. Only Mark reports Jesus' use, during his agony, of the Aramaic word '*abba*'. The innocence of Jesus is, of course, emphasised and so also is the fact that it was in God's salvific plan that his Son should suffer and die. This is confirmed by the citation of a number of Old Testament texts which were being fulfilled.

Today the same first and second readings are used for years A, B and C. Brief notes are given at the appropriate Sunday of year A.

THURSDAY OF THE LORD'S SUPPER – Years ABC

John 13:1-15

All Scripture readings are common to years A, B and C. The notes are at year A.

FRIDAY OF THE PASSION OF THE LORD – Years ABC

John 18:1-19:42

All Scripture readings are common to years A, B and C. The notes are at year A.

THE EASTER VIGIL – Year B

Mark 16:1-7

The notes are at year A.

EASTER SUNDAY – Years ABC

John 20:1-9

All Scripture readings are common to years A, B and C. The notes are at year A.

SECOND SUNDAY OF EASTER – Year B

John 20:19-31

The gospel reading is the same as for the corresponding Sunday of year A. The notes are at year A.

During the Easter season the first readings are from the Acts of the Apostles. Today (Acts 4:32-35) we hear of the first generation of Christians and how they lived as a community, sharing all their worldly wealth and possessions.

The second reading is from the first letter of John (5:1-6). Anyone who believes that Jesus is the Son of God and our saviour is an adopted child of God and one who loves God and all others in God's adopted family. To love God is to keep his commandments. It is by our faith that we overcome the world, a faith founded on three witnesses – water and blood which came from Christ's side but which for us now symbolise baptism and the death and resurrection of Christ, and (the third witness) the Spirit of truth.

THIRD SUNDAY OF EASTER – Year B

Luke 24:35-48

In the corresponding Sunday last year, we heard the story of our Lord's appearance to the disciples on the road to Emmaus. The account ended with them hurrying back to Jerusalem to tell the disciples the wonderful news that Jesus was risen and alive. That ending is repeated at the start of this year's continuation of the narrative. The discussion must have been animated and excited – and then the very subject of their conversation appears among them. They are surprised, to put it mildly – the gospel says they were alarmed and frightened. Jesus has to try and calm them. He assures them that it is truly the Jesus they knew, showing them his hands and feet and inviting them to touch them to convince themselves that it was not a ghost who had come into the room but himself, body and all. To end all their doubts, he eats a piece of fish which they give him. The evangelist describes their reaction now – incredulous, dumbfounded and immensely joyful. The emphasis on evidence, here and elsewhere, of Christ's bodily resurrection may also be made to allay the scepticism of some early gentile converts.

Let us pause here to reflect on the difficulty which those disciples experienced in believing that what they saw was truly Jesus. A similar difficulty can trouble us – to believe that Jesus Christ truly rose from the dead and is alive. Ultimately, we reach that belief through the gift of faith awakened in us by God, and accompanied with a great peace and joy. The gospel account today of the disciples' doubts and confusion can be a consoling one for us, and also for those whom we may be helping to come to faith. Faith may come suddenly but more often it is gradual. But we should always have our minds open to faith and our hearts with the desire to be able to believe. We trust Jesus to bring us to accept his gift so that we can become his witnesses of today. Pope Francis' Apostolic Exhortation *Evangelii Gaudium (The Joy of the Gospel)* is helpful in this most basic and essential element in our lives of faith. I found paragraphs 160-168 particularly important in this respect.

The narrative of today's gospel passage continues. Jesus tells the disciples that all the messianic prophecies and expectations found in the Old Testament had been fulfilled – that the messiah would suffer, die and rise again. He had done this and now people throughout the world had to be brought to faith. They had to know that, with the gift of repentance and as a result of Jesus' death and resurrection, their sins would be forgiven. All four gospels include this instruction on the apostolic mission that had to be undertaken, but they do not agree on the place and circumstances when it was given to the disciples by Jesus. The duty and privilege that we have been given to evangelise is not an easy one to fulfil. Our attempts can meet with hostility and, more often, with apathy. We feel inadequate, ill-prepared, not sufficiently knowledgeable. We can sometimes feel guilt, that we should be more courageous, less fearful of embarrassment or ridicule. It's a tough subject to ponder but, at least, we can evangelise by trying always to give good example.

In today's first reading (Acts 3:13-15.17-19), Peter, having received the Holy Spirit and having healed a cripple, is out in the streets of Jerusalem, evangelising, fulfilling the mission given him by Jesus.

John's first letter (2:1-5) teaches us that we show that we know God by obeying his decrees. However, if we disobey and fall into sin, Jesus, who gave his life for our salvation, will obtain our forgiveness from the Father.

FOURTH SUNDAY OF EASTER – Year B

John 10:11-18

The image of the shepherd of the flock is one that God applies to himself in the Old Testament, especially in the prophecy of Ezekiel. Further, God condemns the religious leaders of Israel who have neglected their duty of shepherding the people in his name and promises that he will 'raise up one shepherd . . . and he will pasture them' (Ezekiel 34:23). It is in fulfilment of this prophecy that, in today's gospel, Jesus claims to be 'the Good Shepherd'. At the beginning of chapter 10 of John's gospel, he describes himself as 'the gate of the sheepfold' (Fourth Sunday of Easter, year A). The use of both metaphors, sheepfold gate and shepherd, is because Jesus fulfils both functions, permitting entry to those who have the right intention but denying entry to robbers, and then caring for the flock.

Picturing Jesus as the Good Shepherd is a favourite image with Christians and has been since very early days. One of the earliest depictions of Jesus on the walls of the Roman catacombs is of the Good Shepherd carrying a lost or injured sheep on his shoulders. The metaphor speaks of tenderness, dedication, love even to a willingness to give his life for the sheep. Not only is the image a very attractive one for all Christians but it is also a lesson for those who, through the sacrament of holy orders, have been given a share in the work of the Good Shepherd. Today we pray especially for them, not only that there will always be those who hear Christ's invitation and courageously respond to it (an urgent need nowadays in many places, including our own country) but also that those who are ordained and consecrated to be shepherds in the Church will carry out their responsibilities with the same conscientious dedication and loving kindness which Jesus himself unfailingly showed.

Jesus also looks forward to there being 'only one flock and one shepherd' (verse 16), a reference to Ezekiel's prophecy (37:22-24) and a declaration that induces us to be aware that there are, unfortunately, many divisions among Christians and that we are called to pray and work for the hope and intention that the unity of Christians will become a reality. In addition, we have to pray for ourselves who belong to the Catholic Church that those of us who have drifted from being active will rediscover the desire and the means to return and that those who are active in our communities will live and work in harmony, avoiding all hurtful behaviour and lack of charity.

The first reading (Acts 4:8-12) tells of Peter and John, arraigned before the Sanhedrin because of their preaching about the risen Christ and their cure of a cripple. Peter declares that he cured the cripple in the name of the risen Lord and that the same Christ is the only saviour of humankind.

In his first letter, St John (3:1-2) teaches that God, in his love, has adopted us as his children and that we are destined to see God as he is and become like him.

FIFTH SUNDAY OF EASTER – Year B

John 15:1-8

Jesus, the Good Shepherd, uses another and very different metaphor in this week's gospel extract. He calls himself a vine, with his Father the vinedresser, the one with the task of caring for the vine and cultivating it so that it will be fruitful. Work in a vineyard involves quite a variety of tasks to be done but probably the most important is the annual pruning. If this is neglected, the vine gradually grows wild and the grapes become less and less useful. The pruning of a branch of the vine that is Christ is a necessary operation but a painful one for the branch, that is, for the person 'pruned'. Jesus says that the pruning process results from 'the word that I have spoken to you', a phrase meaning all that Christ has revealed to us about God's plan of salvation for us. That teaching imposes some rules upon our conduct and, if we observe them, it is a 'pruning' process.

A vine produces fruit and so Jesus assumes that discipleship involves a life of activity, of bearing the fruit that is good works. It is totally essential that, for this, we remain as branches attached to the vine. If a branch ceases to bear fruit, it will be cut off; and, in that state, it cannot produce anything but will be thrown away and will wither. The alternatives give us a stark choice for, since we are human branches, it is we who make the choice. The passage ends with Jesus promising that, if we choose the alternative he asks of us, we shall be his disciples, we shall receive all that we ask or require, and the fruit that we produce will redound to the glory of the one ultimately responsible, the vinedresser, God the Father.

Remaining in Jesus as branches on the vine is crucial. We must, as individuals and in our communities, focus our attention on the teaching, example and person of Jesus. We must be animated by the Holy Spirit and working, as Christ worked, to make the world more just, more peaceful, more aware of God's love and his plan of salvation.

Three years after his conversion, Saul/Paul went to Jerusalem (Acts 9:26-31). His arrival aroused suspicion among the disciples and, when that problem seemed to have been solved, his fearless preaching caused some who heard him to threaten to kill him. So he was sent away, to Tarsus, his native city. Thereafter the Christians in Palestine were left in peace.

In the second reading (1 John 3:18-24) we are told that if our consciences are clear regarding keeping the commandments, we need not fear God's wrath.

SIXTH SUNDAY OF EASTER – Year B

John 15:9-17

Today's gospel excerpt starts where last week's left off, although the metaphor of the vine is not continued. This extract from the discourse of Jesus to the Twelve at the Last Supper provides some basic teaching on the nature of discipleship.

First, Jesus reminds the disciples that, as he is loved by the Father and lives in that love, so he loves them and wants them to live in his love. That is fundamental. It is the basis of our obedience to the commandments we have received from God and the further expectations taught by Jesus; it is what sustains us despite the difficulties and frailties that we experience. We express that love, says Jesus, by keeping the commandments, above all the commandment of love of our neighbours, of loving one another even, if need be, to the extent of being ready to give our lives for others. This crucial commandment, Jesus says, will allow us to share in the joy he has in loving us and giving his life for us.

The second truth which Jesus teaches is that he sees us not as servants but as friends. Although being a servant or even a slave was not seen as a degrading state, it did not imply the mutual love and trust that being a friend did and does. It is Jesus who chooses us. He shares with us all the knowledge that he has been given by his Father, and he dedicates us to continue the work that he was sent to inaugurate. Thus, if we are faithful to him, his Father will provide us with whatever we ask in the name of his Son. This teaching of Jesus, when we put it into practice, will give us, and our active discipleship, a joy and enthusiasm that will be the opposite of a religious life that is sad and grim and full of regrets and complaints. That joy and enthusiasm should be communicated to others in the hope that the communities to which we belong, including our parishes, will be characterised by the same joy and enthusiasm. Can you imagine that?

<small>The first reading (Acts 10:25-26.34-35.44-48) relates the moment when Peter, and therefore the Church, realised that Jesus had come to bring salvation to gentiles as well as to Jews. Peter's discovery leads to immediate action.</small>

<small>St John's first letter (4:7-10) tells us that we know God's love for us because he sent his Son to be our saviour. It is God from whom we come and who loves us. As a result, we can and should love one another.</small>

THE ASCENSION OF THE LORD – Year B

Mark 16:15-20

For this feast, the principal text must be from the first chapter of the Acts of the Apostles (1:1-11). That report forms the first reading in all three years, A, B and C. The synoptic gospels also refer to the event and the three references form the gospels of the three years.

With regard to the date and place of the ascension, the gospels and the Acts of the Apostles offer differing accounts which suggest that the details given are presented for symbolic reasons or to show fulfilment of Old Testament prophecy, and not with the intention of providing factual information. The place named varies between Galilee and the Mount of Olives, near Jerusalem; and the time or date depends on whether Jesus is reckoned to have returned at once to the Father after he rose glorified (though able, when he wished, to be present to the apostles in the glorified state which made him difficult to recognise) or if it is supposed that there was a gap of some (forty?) days between the resurrection and the ascension.

Mark's gospel for this feast comes at the very end of his gospel. However, the full conclusion (16:9-20 and therefore including today's passage) has its problems. It is fairly certain that it is a later addition by an unknown person (possibly by Mark himself, but this is very unlikely). It may have been composed because the original conclusion was lost. The style of the present conclusion is different from the rest of the gospel and it gives the impression of a somewhat makeshift attempt to provide a fitting end to the story.

Today's passage has Jesus appearing to 'the Eleven' as they were at a meal together. He reproaches them because of their reluctance to believe that he had risen and then instructs them to preach the Good News throughout the world. Those who believe and are baptised will be saved and will confirm this by having power to heal and to perform some extraordinary actions. The gospel then merely states that, 'the Lord Jesus, after he had spoken to them, was taken up into heaven'.

A few comments may be added. The impression is given that the appearance of the risen Christ which the gospel reports was the one that occurred on the day of the resurrection (John 20:19-23) and that the ascension took place on the same day. The use of the title 'Lord Jesus' implies Christ's divinity, as also does the statement that 'the Lord' was working with the apostles as they fulfilled his instructions. This last point about Christ's presence in the Church with his disciples is not just something random which Jesus said to his apostles but it should be firmly believed by us and be a permanent source of reassurance. The Church, whether universal or local, wherever his disciples are, has Jesus alive in its community, teaching us how to live in imitation of his life on earth, healing, forgiving, welcoming. And where the glorified Jesus is, there also are the Father and the Spirit. The life and activities of the Church provide a constant testimony of the presence of Christ.

For today's second reading, there are two options, both from Paul's letter to the Ephesians.

In the first option (1:17-23), St Paul prays that God may give us a vivid awareness of the inheritance that awaits us as a result of what God did to save us through raising Jesus from the dead and investing him with all authority as head of the Church, his body.

In the alternative reading (4:1-13), St Paul pleads that, through our selflessness, we should do all we can to preserve the unity of Christ's body (the Church). He explains that Christ distributed different gifts to various people to build up the body of the Church before he 'rose higher than all the heavens to fill all things'.

SEVENTH SUNDAY OF EASTER – Year B

John 17:11-19

The seventeenth chapter of John's gospel is devoted completely to the 'priestly prayer' which Christ offered after his discourse at the Last Supper. On the eve of his passion and death, Jesus offers himself and intercedes for his disciples. The twenty-six verses are distributed among the three years, A, B and C, on this seventh Sunday of Easter.

This middle third is entirely devoted to prayer for his disciples, and especially for those first followers who were soon to lose his visible presence and therefore needed divine guidance. They must remain united and their model is the unity of Father and Son. Jesus asks the Father to keep them 'true to your name', meaning that they should continue to believe and teach what Jesus revealed to them about the Father's nature and plans. The reference to Judas' treachery fulfilling the Scriptures is an allusion to psalm 40/41:9 ('Even my friend, in whom I trusted, who ate my bread, has turned against me').

Jesus prays that the Father will protect them in a world that is sometimes hostile. They are to be in the world, not removed from it, though not of the world. 'Consecrate them in the truth; your word is truth' is a somewhat obscure or difficult expression. As the priests of the Old Law were consecrated or set apart, so also the priests of the New Law will be set apart, but in a more personal and profound way. They will be made holy by God's word which is not only the divine nature but also refers to the Word, Jesus himself who is 'full of grace and truth' (John 1:14). Perhaps it is also helpful to recall the words of Jesus to the Samaritan woman: 'true worshippers will worship the Father in spirit and truth' (John 4:23), where 'spirit' is that which makes the new worship acceptable to God and 'truth' is God's truth, revealed through Jesus.

Although these pleas of Jesus are directly concerned with the disciples who were at the Last Supper and were very soon to be left without the protection and guidance of the visible Jesus to which they had become accustomed, it is certain that the prayer continues to our day. We also cannot continue the mission of Jesus without the help of God. To be accurate, it is not that God helps us but that we are helping God in pursuing the divine plan which Jesus inaugurated and bequeathed to us to continue.

The first reading (Acts 1:15-17.20-26) is a description of the process of choosing, in place of Judas, a replacement 'to be listed as one of the twelve apostles'.

In this week's second reading, St John (1 John 4:11-16) speaks of the importance of our love for one another. If we do this, God the Father will live in us and we in God, we shall have the Spirit dwelling in us and know that Jesus is God's Son.

PENTECOST SUNDAY – Year B

John 20:19-23 or
John 15:26-27; 16:12-15

In the Acts of the Apostles (2:1-11), Luke gives us a description of Pentecost and the coming of the Holy Spirit on the apostles, a description with which we are familiar. It strikes us at first as something of a surprise when we realise that, in one of the options for today's gospel reading, John indicates that the Holy Spirit was given to the apostles on Easter – and he, John, was there! There is apparently a conflict here due principally to the fact that the human authors of the Scriptures were intending to teach the actual mysterious events themselves and not the accurate chronology. When Jesus rose from the dead, it is clear that he lived a different and glorified human existence (the apostles had difficulty in recognising him, he was able to appear and disappear without being seen to make his way in the normal manner, nor was he constantly in the apostles' presence). The conclusion is that, when he rose he also returned to the Father, and that the 'forty days' is not the period before he went to the Father but the period during which he made appearances to the apostles (as well as being with the Father). When he was with the Father, they could together send the Holy Spirit on the nascent Church. Perhaps, then, it may be that, in imitation of the two Jewish feasts of Passover and Pentecost, the early Christians did the same in their (separate) liturgical observances of the resurrection and the coming of the Spirit. Our custom, therefore, of having separate liturgical observance of resurrection, ascension and descent of the Spirit gives us the advantage of being able to reflect more carefully on the meaning of each mystery.

A choice of gospels is offered today. In the first option (John 20:19-23, used in Year A and an option in year B), we hear that Jesus came to the disciples on Easter Sunday evening and, of course, they were overjoyed. His next words are important. He gives them the same mission as the Father had given him – to reach out to those in need, to bring forgiveness and freedom to those who are oppressed by sin or injustice, to give them the new life of the sacraments – and he shows the wounds of his crucified body to show that the task requires total and unconditional commitment. Since he is very aware of their weakness and inexperience and that he will no longer be visibly present with them to lead, he confers on them the Holy Spirit, the Paraclete, the Advocate, literally to be their inspiration in fulfilling their mission even to death.

The gospel links the words of Jesus conferring the Spirit to his giving the Church the power to forgive sin in his name. While this particular privilege is exercised only by those who have a share in Christ's ministerial priesthood, the same Spirit is given to us all in baptism and confirmation in order that we take our share in continuing the mission of Christ and doing so in countless ways.

Prayer addressed to the Holy Spirit is not common in the Church's liturgy, but it does occur, perhaps most notably in the so called sequence (*Veni, Sancte Spiritus*) at Mass on

Pentecost Sunday and in various other hymns. Best known of these are *Veni, Creator Spiritus* and, in English, *Come, Holy Ghost, Creator, come*. And the conclusion of the collect prayers at Mass, although addressed to the Father and through the Son, ends with a profession of faith 'in the unity of the Holy Spirit'. With justification, the *Catechism of the Catholic Church* (§ 687) speaks of the Spirit as the self-effacing person of the Trinity, acting quietly to produce the required effects. For example, at Mass, we pray to the Father (at the epiclesis of Eucharistic Prayer II): 'Make holy these gifts, we pray, by sending down the Holy Spirit upon them like the dewfall . . .' Perhaps the Spirit's modesty was the reason for the farcical situation which Paul discovered when he visited Ephesus (Acts 19:1-2).

Given our awareness of the essential work of the Holy Spirit in the Church, it would be no bad thing if our prayers were more frequently said directly to the Spirit. For example, prayer that we be more alive to the presence of Jesus among us, more courageous in following his example, more open to accepting change when it is needed. We might also seek the Spirit's help in being constantly reminded of the teaching and message of Jesus so that our witness does not become routine, uninspired and uninspiring, but rather that the gospel we proclaim is genuine good news for a vibrant community of disciples. And what about the mission of Jesus, now committed to us to continue, the mission of building the kingdom of God, a kingdom of justice and peace, of a more caring world in which, sadly, unfairness and greed and violence are still so evident, of a world of generous love for others and especially for those in need? For many of us, the work of the Spirit in the Church and in ourselves remains in the background, even forgotten. So, 'Come, Holy Spirit' into our thoughts and prayers; make us gratefully aware of your loving presence in our midst.

The alternative gospel passage (John 15:26-27; 16:12-15) comes from the discourse of Jesus at the Last Supper. He is speaking of 'the Spirit of truth' and 'the Advocate' who will come to the disciples and will be his witness (as they also will be his witnesses). Jesus has more that he would like them to know but since it would be 'too much now', the Spirit will enable them in due course to know 'the complete truth'. In giving them this knowledge, the Spirit will be glorifying Christ because the truth he communicates will be from Christ, since the Father shares all he has, including the truth, with his Son.

Jesus' declaration that both the Spirit and the disciples will be his witnesses means that the Spirit will enable the disciples to fulfil that responsibility according to Jesus' wishes. They, after all, are the Church and the Spirit is 'the soul' of the Church. In verse 13 of chapter 16, Jesus says that the Spirit will inform the disciples of 'the things to come'. This refers in particular to the full meaning of Christ's forthcoming death and resurrection since he is speaking, at that moment, before the two events.

St John uses the word 'Paraclete' of the Holy Spirit. It is a word with a variety of meanings – advocate and defender in the legal sense; also counsellor, encourager, comforter - which help us to form a better knowledge of the activities of the Spirit. To the

Holy Spirit's action is also traditionally attributed the gifts which we receive both as the community of the church and as individuals; for example (and especially) the gifts of faith and of holiness.

The first reading (Acts 2:1-11) is Luke's familiar account, beginning with 'When Pentecost day came round' and providing a graphic description of the coming of the Holy Spirit and of the galvanic effect it had on the apostles and their preaching.

For the second reading, two options are given. An extract from the first letter of St Paul to the Corinthians (12:3-7.12-13) is the first alternative. He explains the work of the Spirit, both in the great variety of gifts conferred to different people and in the unity of the multitude of people who receive the gifts, all of whom are united in the (mystical) Body of Christ, all baptised in the one Spirit and recipients of that Spirit.

In the second option (Galatians 5:16-25), Paul urges us to be guided by the Spirit in our behaviour. If we are, we shall enjoy a life of lawful and meritorious conduct. If, however, self-indulgence is our guide, the result will be all kinds of reprehensible conduct.

THE MOST HOLY TRINITY – Year B

Matthew 28:16-20

The gospel passage chosen for this feast in year B is the conclusion of Matthew's gospel and also the only mention in this gospel of an appearance of Christ following the resurrection and his appearance to the women who had gone to his tomb on Easter Sunday morning. The place is a mountain in Galilee, though which mountain is not disclosed; it is enough that important moments take place on mountains. The apostles, eleven of them, venerate Jesus, although (as in other post-resurrection appearances) there is some initial hesitation.

The gospel closes with Jesus commissioning the apostles, giving them the authority to continue his work. The words with which this is expressed reflect the practice of the early Church in fulfilling the commission. They are to teach all nations and they are to baptise in the name of the three Persons of the Trinity. The expression 'in the name of' means that the one baptised now belongs to the Father, Son and Holy Spirit. Having received the teaching that enables faith to be received as God's gift, the person baptised enters a new way of life. Finally, in today's reading, Jesus promises that he will be present in and with the Church for ever (a truth which Paul greatly develops in his letters to the churches).

The Blessed Trinity – three Persons in one God – is so totally mysterious that it is quite beyond our ability to understand. Because it is incomprehensible, the danger is that we may ignore the truth as being of little obvious relevance to our lives or to our personal faith. Therefore, we need to reflect on what we know of each person in order that we recapture an awareness of their closeness to us and the love for us of Father, Son and Spirit. That will enable us to respond properly to the God who created us, who died for us and who sanctifies us.

The Father not only made us but also keeps us in being throughout our existence. Jesus called him Father and taught us to do the same because, although the Son is the only 'begotten' of the Father, we are his sons and daughters by adoption. He loves us in all circumstances, forgives us when we ask, and awaits us to be with him for ever.

The Son, become man, is God's greatest gift to the world. He re-established God's reign on earth, teaching us how to live at peace and in love with God and among ourselves. He accepted the agony and humiliation of a violent death as a result of our sinfulness, but left us a memorial of that work of salvation. He told us that to know him is to know the Father. He revealed God as tender, understanding, approachable. He gives us a share in his threefold mission as priest, prophet and king.

The Spirit has been given to dwell in and with us. He is the source and preserver of all the good qualities and gifts that we have. He is the advocate who guides us in every moment, never more than in a crisis; our inspiration who wants to make us holy; our comforter in adversity, suffering and grief.

The sign of the cross can be a powerful and public witness of our faith in God's saving love. But it is also 'the sign of the Trinity', a reminder for us, as we say the accompanying words with gratitude, that we are baptised in the name of, and as belonging to, Father, Son and Spirit. So be it. Amen.

In the first reading (Deuteronomy 4:32-34.39-40), written prior to the revelation of the three Persons in God, Moses teaches the Jews, in the desert and fleeing from slavery, of the oneness and majesty of God and of God's caring sovereignty for his people.

In the letter to the Romans (8:14-17), Paul expresses the Church's belief in the triune God. The Spirit enables us to be adopted as the Father's sons and daughters and therefore to be coheirs with Christ, participating in our own way in his sufferings and so in his glory.

THE MOST HOLY BODY AND BLOOD OF CHRIST – Year B

Mark 14:12-16.22-26

Year B is the only one of the three that, for this feast, has a narrative of the institution of the Eucharist as its chosen gospel reading. In fact, the first part of the reading reports the preparations for the Passover meal; the latter part describes the crucial moments of the Last Supper. The five verses omitted between the two parts of the reading contain the account of Jesus foretelling the treachery of Judas.

With regard to the verses recounting the preparations for the meal, scholars mention that the opening words are inaccurate since the Passover lambs were killed on the day before the 'first day of unleavened bread'; also, although the preparations are for a Passover meal, Mark makes no mention of any of the elements of such a meal. Jesus shows his foreknowledge as he instructs the two disciples on the details of the preparations to be made, especially about the man they were to meet and the place where the meal would take place.

At the meal, we have only a description of the Eucharistic part. All four New Testament accounts (Paul, Mark, Matthew and Luke) of the consecration of the bread (perhaps at the beginning of the meal) have the same words: 'For this is my body'. By the word 'is' alone, the statement can mean either 'really' or 'figuratively'. The Catholic tradition has always been for the former, aided by other texts (for example, 1 Corinthians 11:23-32) and confirmed by the authoritative decree of the Council of Trent.

The wine which is consecrated is probably the third cup, after the main course. The blood is understood to be shed as a covenant, bringing the consequent covenant blessings that were prefigured in the Sinai sacrifice and covenant (Exodus 24:8). 'Poured out for many' – 'many' in the sense of a multitude, without any implied restriction. The passage ends with an allusion by Jesus to the next time he will drink wine, thus giving the Eucharist an eschatological connection and an expression of hope of eternal life.

In the Scripture passages chosen for this feast in year B, the notion of covenant is prominent in all three readings. The covenant which God made with the Jews while they were on their journey from slavery in Egypt to the promised land (first reading) is recalled by the author of the letter to the Hebrews (second reading), who declares it to be superseded by the covenant between God and the whole of humanity, solemnised on Calvary and re-presented in the Eucharist (gospel reading).

The solemn promise and pledge of the covenant consecrates us to 'our side' of the agreement, undertaking to be holy and faithful witnesses of God's love, nourished and strengthened by the body and blood of Christ. The decision, last century, to restore Holy Communion under the form of wine to all at Mass has several reasons for being welcomed; not the least of these benefits is the opportunity it gives for us to make a personal declaration of our fidelity to the covenant by communicating with Christ's blood, the very sign and seal of the covenant.

Mass is the centre of our lives as Christians and Catholics. The Second Vatican Council has told us that and has introduced many reforms in the manner in which we celebrate the liturgy. This has been done to enable us more easily to participate as fully as possible in the celebration of the Eucharist. But the problem remains and becomes more obvious – fewer and fewer people attend. We all know that Mass is not celebrated to entertain people. It is to enable believers to live as Jesus lived by their experiencing, in the Mass and in a concentrated form, what Jesus lived and died for. But if more and more people do not find that the Mass provides them with that, does there need to be a further and even more radical reform of the way that we celebrate Mass? Or would it be complacent to attribute their absence to their own fault?

The first reading today (Exodus 24:3-8) is the account of Moses leading the people to follow God's instructions to sacrifice animals, with their blood reckoned a sign of the covenant between God and his chosen people.

The letter to the Hebrews (9:11-15) teaches us that Christ's sacrifice is the fulfilment of the Old Testament sacrifice. In the earlier sacrifice, it was only animals' blood that was shed; now it is Christ's. The latter is more effective since it not only gives external reconciliation (as the former did) but also the complete removal of sin. Also, the Temple and the Holy of Holies were human constructions; the sanctuary which our high priest enters is heaven itself.

Sundays in Ordinary Time

SECOND SUNDAY IN ORDINARY TIME – Year B

John 1:35-42

Last Sunday we read Mark's account of the baptism of Jesus, since during Ordinary Time we are in the year of Mark. However, Mark's narrative of Jesus at the Jordan among disciples of John the Baptist is brief and does not contain some details found in the gospel of John and which form today's gospel.

The day after Jesus' baptism, John the evangelist tells us, John the Baptist was talking to a couple of his followers when Jesus passed. The Baptist pointed out Jesus to his followers, calling Jesus the Lamb of God. If in fact this was the title which the Baptist used on that occasion, it may have reference to the 'Servant of the Lord' about which Deutero-Isaiah has four 'songs' (cf. also Isaiah 53:7). At any rate, two of John's followers (one of whom is Andrew, the future apostle) are interested enough in the newcomer to follow him. There then occurs a brief exchange between the two and Jesus, which ends with them spending the evening, and maybe also the night, with Jesus. The meeting had taken place about 4 pm. Next day, Andrew told his brother Simon that they had found the messiah (a laudable claim after such a brief acquaintance) and brought him to Jesus. The gospel reports only that Jesus 'looked hard at him' and gave him a new name, a name which means a rock (and which, until then, was not used as a name for men). The two details of Jesus' reaction to Simon, and because both are recorded in the gospel, suggest that already Jesus had a special part for him to play in his divine mission. (The verses immediately after those of today's excerpt tell us that Jesus met and recruited two others – Philip and Nathanael/Bartholomew – and then left to begin his work in Galilee (1:43-51).)

The directness of Jesus' invitation to these disciples of John the Baptist is impressive and the apparent swiftness of their agreement is equally so. It would seem that they were persuaded not by any detailed description by Jesus of the work that he wanted them to do, but rather by the magnetism of his personality. This was a man whom they were glad to follow; they seem to have had little hesitation, and perhaps no choice! Hence, some questions arise.

How did you/I/we respond to the invitation of Jesus to become followers? Or perhaps alternatively, when we invite others to join us as followers of Jesus, is the appeal that we make in the name of Jesus attractive or not? Do people feel drawn to Jesus by what they see in us or hear from us? Do they know about the plan to build God's kingdom? Do we live with the values with which Jesus lived, so different from those so widespread today, and especially in our affluent, selfish and greedy culture?

I sometimes wonder if, as a result of our upbringing and especially if we attended a Catholic school, our relationship to God is founded mainly on a series of do's and don'ts. In that case, it is hard for us to be free of fear. There is a place for fear but, if in a normal family the relationship between parents and children is a healthy one of love, trust, kindness and encouragement, something similar should characterise our relationship with God the Father, mediated through the Son, our brother.

God's plan for building the kingdom involves each one of us and my part in that plan is my vocation. So how do we discover the call God is asking us to follow? When he was on earth, Jesus solved that problem for the apostles. He called them in a way that they apparently could not refuse. The call of Samuel (today's first reading) is much more typical, in the sense that it needed discernment. For us, discernment can involve a catalogue of resources – prayer, thought, discussion, advice, example; also our abilities, preferences, personal circumstances and responsibilities. The process of discernment is important, sometimes difficult and even may result in a wrong choice which can be corrected. To be specific, the Church in many countries is at present experiencing a great dearth of those choosing priesthood; but can that be attributed to God failing to issue the call – or is there another explanation?

The first reading is from the first book of Samuel (3:3-10.19) and tells the touching tale of God's call of the young Samuel, the future leader of Israel. It is a very appropriate choice to partner today's gospel. From it, we learn the gentleness and patience of God's call and the boy's ready response when, with the help of Eli, he discerned it.

Each of the three years of Ordinary Time begins with several Sundays in which the second reading is from the first letter of St Paul to the Corinthians. This year, there will be five extracts, from week two to week six.

In today's extract (6:13-15.17-20), Paul pleads that, since our bodies make up the Body of Christ, fornication is a sin that must be carefully avoided. Our bodies are temples of the Holy Spirit and given to use for the glory of God, not for sin.

THIRD SUNDAY IN ORDINARY TIME – Year B

Mark 1:14-20

Have you noticed how quickly Mark gets into his task? While Matthew and Luke spend some time recounting stories from our Lord's infancy and childhood (and even the time before that) and John provides us with profound thoughts on Jesus as the Word of God, Mark starts 'The beginning of the Good News about Jesus Christ, the Son of God'. Then, after some information about John the Baptist, a brief description of the baptism of Jesus and an even briefer description of his forty days in the desert, Mark immediately gets to the very heart of his story. 'Jesus went into Galilee. There he proclaimed the Good News from God. "The time has come", he said, "and the kingdom of God is close at hand. Repent, and believe the Good News"'.

There it is in a nutshell. Three points: God's kingdom is at hand; it is good news; repent and believe. They sum up the message for which the Son of God has become human. Let's consider the three points.

'God's kingdom is at hand'. Jesus did not come primarily to teach us various doctrines; nor did he directly announce a list of moral do's and don'ts. He came to tell us of God's plan for saving humankind from sin and its result – deprivation of eternal life. The plan is called God's kingdom or reign because it will have God as its centre and, as its members or citizens, those who live according to God's values.

'It is good news'. If the plan is not about doctrines or rules and regulations, what is it about? The answer is that it envisages a different way for us to live, a way that shuns greed, selfishness, rivalry, hostility and violence and that seeks to be generous, thoughtful, caring, just and peaceful. It is a way that will bring justice for those who are poor and deprived because others are rich, that will bring peace and freedom for those who are victims of violence or enslavement, that will bring a changed life for those who are victims of the misuse of power. Jesus will proclaim this Good News not only in words but also in the example of the way he lives. And the Good News is, above all, that Jesus is here to bring us eternal salvation, eternal life with God. (It is useful to remind ourselves that, strictly speaking, the word 'gospel' means the Good News which Jesus brought, not a book in which we read about it.)

'Repent and believe'. We are called to repent of our sinful ways, both actions and habits, alone or with others, with a repentance that is genuine and lasting; a repentance that is truly a conversion of life. We are to believe in the truth of the Good News with trust that God will grant us what is promised; and we are to share that faith and trust with others by word and example. Moreover, we are all called to get engaged in building the kingdom.

Mark then begins his story in detail. The first four disciples (and who are to be four of the twelve apostles) are recruited. The call from Jesus comes suddenly (and, if it were from anyone else, we might consider it impulsive and unplanned), and is accepted with equal speed. It implies a complete and permanent abandonment of the previous way of life and employment and the immediate adoption of a totally new direction of life.

The details of the call of those first disciples do not provide a blueprint for ourselves, but the basic fact of the call is repeated for each one of us. The baptism that we received, most of us in infancy, contains that call to share our faith; and our awareness of the call gradually develops. The manner of life (married or single, clergy or laity, parents or not) will differ but each of us is asked to share his or her faith and to do so as courageously, as correctly and as frequently as is reasonable. It is not only by example that we can fulfil this responsibility. Parents, teachers and priests have also to do so in words; and so should we all!

This matter has already been considered last week and there is no need for repetition. But mention of last week affords the opportunity to note that John, alone among the evangelists, tells us that, while Jesus was with John the Baptist at the Jordan in Judea, he met some of John's disciples, including Andrew and Simon Peter. If they became disciples of Christ at that time, why was it necessary for Jesus to call them again at the lakeside? Various answers can be suggested – different oral traditions of the two evangelists, or the first call was not definitive, or the disciples were waiting for Jesus to arrive back in Galilee. We have to leave the answer uncertain.

The first reading (Jonah 3:1-5.10) tells us of God's order to Jonah to preach repentance to the Ninevites. Jonah obeys, his preaching is successful, God cancels the punishment intended for Nineveh. The episode is a sign of God's call to new disciples. (The story is not historical. Jonah is sure that his preaching will be useless and so, when he is proved wrong, his confusion is a warning to us against overconfidence.)

The first Christians generally expected an early *parousia* (the Greek word which denotes the end of the world and the second coming of Christ). St Paul (1 Corinthians 7:29-31) gives his own opinion that, if the supposition is true, we should not be distracted by other concerns.

FOURTH SUNDAY IN ORDINARY TIME – Year B

Mark 1:21-28

Much of Jesus' ministry in Galilee took place around the shores of Lake Tiberias (also called Lake Gennesaret or, most commonly, the Sea of Galilee). Capernaum, lying on the northern shore became his headquarters and it is likely that, when he was there, he stayed in Simon Peter's family house. It is in the synagogue at Capernaum that today's incident took place.

Mark reports the event as being the first occasion on which Jesus taught publicly and miraculously healed a person. As far as his teaching is concerned, we are not told its content, although it is safe to presume that it was on the kingdom of God which he had come on earth to establish. This would require changes in people's behaviour to end selfishness and injustice, to live in mutual acceptance and without rancour, and to treat the poor with fairness and dignity.

What Mark does report, however, is that Jesus taught with authority 'unlike the scribes' and that his teaching deeply impressed the listeners. There is a significant phrase in the report given by Mark: the people spoke of his teaching not only as authoritative but also as new. The point is made that Jesus, in his way of teaching and in its content, was different from the scribes. The scribes were the scholars and intellectuals of the Jews and had an impressive knowledge of the law (given by God to the Jews). Most were Pharisees and therefore interpreted the law strictly, their teaching being quotations from the law and the traditions of the Jews. The scribes were seen as influential leaders, so that Jesus (whose teaching was 'new' and 'with authority') was seen by them as a threat to the respected position they occupied. In addition, there are many times when Jesus runs foul of them for daring to heal or do other work of mercy on a Sabbath.

The healing on this occasion does not attract the attention of a scribe but it does cause a commotion in the synagogue. We are told that a man 'was possessed by an unclean spirit' and that the spirit loudly objected to being expelled by Jesus. The victim went into convulsions before the spirit left him. This type of healing happens several times in the gospels and causes us to be surprised at the frequency with which possession by spirits occurred. It may be that some at least of the cases were persons with diseases such as epilepsy and which, in those days, were presumed to be possession by spirits; on the other hand, it is possible that, because of the presence of Jesus, the Son of God, Satan was especially active. We really do not know. Undoubtedly, the cure added to the people's astonishment and we are told that they were at a loss for an explanation.

Matthew and Luke tell us more about the content of Jesus' teaching than Mark does. It is clear even from Mark's gospel, however, that both the content and the style of Jesus was not only novel but also to the people's liking. The final sentence of the reading today confirms this, since we are informed that his fame spread quickly throughout the neighbouring towns and countryside.

Christ passed on his ministry of teaching with authority to the Church. It is a duty that has to be fulfilled by many people. Clearly, it is one of the principal responsibilities of the pope and of bishops and priests. Priests should be grateful for having to share their faith with those in their pastoral care, recalling that this duty must be fulfilled with proper knowledge, training and updating and in a manner that attracts the attention of their listeners; the content should be appropriate and with due discipline regarding frequency and duration. For teachers and parents, the latter being the first and most important of the teachers of their children, the duty laid on them is also a serious one. It is not really enough to rely on what was learned many years ago or what one thinks is correct or if the presentation is boring and unattractive. All of us with the responsibility of handing on the faith and sharing the Good News of the kingdom need to pray for God's guidance and a share in divine wisdom.

In one of his great discourses reported in the book of Deuteronomy (18:15-20), Moses assures the people that, in the promised land, God will raise up for them a teacher; he will come from among the people themselves and will speak in God's name. Christians reckon that this divine promise is fulfilled in Christ, the messiah and teacher.

Continuing directly from last week's second reading, and presuming that the *parousia* is near, Paul (1 Corinthians 7:32-35) remarks that, while those who are married cannot give undivided attention to 'the Lord's affairs', the unmarried can and are therefore better placed to prepare for the Lord's coming.

FIFTH SUNDAY IN ORDINARY TIME – Year B

Mark 1:29-39

Today's gospel extract resumes where last week's left off. From it, we get some details of Jesus' private life – he has the brothers James and John as his close friends; he is also familiar with the other brothers, Simon (to whom Jesus gave the name Peter (John 1:42; Matthew 16:18)) and Andrew; in fact, he certainly eats in Simon's house and may indeed live there when not on the road.

On that Sabbath evening a crowd called at the house, bringing many people with different illnesses and many others troubled with evil spirits; the sick he cured, the devils he expelled. Mark notes for the first of several times that Jesus forbade anyone (the evil spirits here, elsewhere the healed) to speak publicly of the wonders he performed. His reason for the prohibition is that, at the time, the popular notion of the messiah was of a nationalistic leader who would free the people from Roman rule – an idea in complete contrast to the truth and one that would be very dangerous. This insistence by Jesus is usually called the 'messianic secret'.

To be healed of our infirmities, whether spiritual, psychological or physical, is a great and hugely welcome grace to receive. Even though Jesus is no longer visible in our world and even though we do not live when or where he was, the grace of healing is still available and received. I do not speak of healing in miraculous ways but of healing in normal circumstances, through the sacraments, prayer, medical people's skills, modern and constantly improving remedies. And, if we are honest, we need healing not only in illness and pain but also because of weakness through exhaustion, stress, worry, sadness and even aging itself. So often God's healing hand can be detected when we are healed, even in normal and non-miraculous ways.

Today's passage ends with two further pieces of information that tell us of important elements of Christ's life. He made a habit of prayer to his Father, often in a quiet place so that he could be on his own; and he insisted that his ministering should be widespread and not restricted merely to Capernaum or the nearby coastal towns.

In having a regular habit of prayer and alone by himself, Jesus has a practice which he regarded as essential so that he could know the will of his Father as he laboured to establish God's kingdom on earth. Incidentally, or perhaps deliberately, he is also giving us an example for ourselves to follow. The need for us, if we would be faithful to our call from God, is to spend time that allows us to be with God through silence and meditation. It has been asserted that most of us Christians do not know how to be alone with the Father. We talk easily about God, but hardly know how to talk with him. We arrange and attend meetings, get involved in projects and commitments, get tired and harassed by nonstop work. We are always busy. Can we not recall and return to the times when we used to withdraw and spend time in the peace of God's presence?

The book of Job is regarded as a sublime expression of a man's acceptance of illness and misfortune, and both totally undeserved. Job meditates on his misery, speaks and even complains to God about his condition, and eventually is able to see it as God's will, not understood but accepted. Today's extract (7:1-4.6-7) illustrates Job's feelings and patience and makes clear the longing for an explanation – which the coming of the messiah will help to provide.

In the second reading (1 Corinthians 9:16-19.22-23), Paul reflects that his call from God to preach the gospel is one that he fulfils freely and gladly. His only reward is the satisfaction of sharing with others the Good News of God's loving plan of salvation.

SIXTH SUNDAY IN ORDINARY TIME – Year B

Mark 1:40-45

The verse of Mark's gospel immediately before today's extract notes that Jesus went 'all through Galilee' but the only detail recorded of that is this cure of the leper. The disease, its variety and diagnosis are the subject of the thirteenth chapter of the book of Leviticus (the third book of the Pentateuch); the fourteenth chapter deals with the purification, both physical and ritual, of the disease. It is sufficient to note that, under the term 'leprosy', many different kinds of skin disease were included, some serious and contagious, others not; and that ritual purification and its supervision were tasks committed to the priests.

The fate of a person with genuine leprosy was indeed miserable. Not only was the disease progressive and eventually fatal, but the sufferer was condemned to exclusion from all normal society and all contact with others, and his life became one of constant degradation, destitution and humiliation. The encounter, then, between Jesus and the leper (today's gospel) has aspects not at first sight evident. The sufferer, being ritually unclean, should not have gone near Jesus, and Jesus also infringed the law by allowing him to do so. In addition, the man was in such a low and desperate state that he approaches Jesus and makes his request kneeling in humble but reckless misery. With genuine concern, Jesus responds to the man's plea and cures him; but we should note that, as he does so, Jesus touches him – a blatant infringement of the law.

The episode shows Jesus as one whose compassion is immediately aroused by the wretchedness of the leper, both because of the disease and also its ritual consequences. Furthermore, in stretching forward to touch the leper, Christ is declaring that the legal prohibition of that action is not compatible with God's love and care for everyone; to conform to the law would be to exclude a person from God and so would be a wrongful act.

The lesson for us is fairly clear. We disagree with the way in which lepers were treated, excluded from human society, by Jewish laws. Yet we ought to examine our consciences. Are we guilty of marginalising people whom we despise, of ostracising those whom we dislike? How do we behave towards people whose manners, conduct or appearance we consider repulsive? Are there illnesses which make us avoid the sufferers? On the other hand, we should see Jesus present in those unfortunate people as well as in those who 'stretch out their hands and touch them'.

There is, at the end of the passage, another example of the 'messianic secret' and of the great difficulty Jesus had in trying to enforce his wish. Even with the best will in the world, the former leper could hardly keep his cure and his totally altered social status a secret, could he? But, although the evangelist informs us that Christ had to change his custom and avoid towns, the people seem to have had little difficulty in finding him.

The first reading is a section of the book of Leviticus (13:1-2.44-46) that affords us a glimpse into the severe penalties visited upon unfortunates contracting leprosy.

In the first letter to the Corinthians (10:31-11:1), Paul invites his readers to copy him, as he copies Christ, in observance of the two great commandments.

SEVENTH SUNDAY IN ORDINARY TIME – Year B

Mark 2:1-12

Two weeks ago, we heard in the gospel that Jesus was going round the villages and towns of Galilee. Mark gives us no details of that journey (unless we include last week's cure of the leper). Now, he is back in Capernaum. Despite Mark's reticence and the 'messianic secret', Jesus has become well known in the town. When we meet him in today's gospel, he is preaching the Good News of God's plan of salvation from sin and from the communal injustices of the time. In the house where he is, the place is packed and there is a crowd outside, also trying to listen to him.

Then there arrive four people carrying some kind of a stretcher on which a paralysed man lies. They are seeking healing for him from Jesus. They cannot get in because of the crowd so, resourcefully but no doubt inconveniently for the householder, they remove tiles from the roof and lower the stretcher right down to the feet of Jesus. Their hopes are fulfilled. Jesus cures the man and forgives his sins and the former paralytic goes home. The reception of Jesus' actions is mixed – the crowd are astonished and they praise God; but some scribes are predictably very critical. Let's reflect on what had happened.

There is a huge contrast between the paralysed man and his friends. Because of his infirmity, he is rendered inert and passive, not only unable to walk but even to speak. The other four take the initiative; they are true friends who, knowing his inability to help himself, will go even to extreme measures in order to help him. Jesus responds to their appeal, made not in words but in their actions, and immediately frees the man from his pain and immobility. 'Get up; pick up your stretcher; go off home'. The man is cured and he does what he is told. The gospel does not report any words of his; perhaps he was too amazed to speak and express his thanks or perhaps Mark presumes that to report what he said was superfluous. We do not know.

However, Jesus had, even before raising him to physical normality, said to him, 'Your sins are forgiven'. These words were noted by some scribes who were present and they were scandalised. Scribes were men who had been trained in the teaching and rules of Judaism, respected experts who were members of the Sanhedrin, the supreme tribunal of the Jews with 71 members who met twice weekly; it had judicial, political and religious functions and powers. The annoyance of the scribes who were present that day is understandable since they rightly knew that only God can forgive sins. What they did not know was that Jesus himself is divine as well as human. For them, a blasphemy had been uttered by Jesus; the fact that he had brought healing and happiness to a sufferer and a sinner as well as immense satisfaction to his anxious friends was not of concern to them.

This story of forgiveness and healing can perhaps make us conscious that God is still anxious to show such mercy. If the four friends represent our parishes or other communities, are there needs and opportunities which exist and of which we can take advantage? Visiting the sick is an obvious chance; visiting the no-longer-active Catholics is another, though more delicate, possibility. Certainly the completion of such initiatives would be sacramental celebrations of reconciliation and anointing. Such experiences would strengthen the faith of us all and bring our communities great satisfaction and joy.

The first reading today (Isaiah 43:18-19.21-22.24-25) is an assurance from God to the Israelites. They are soon to be freed from exile and God will also free them from their sins. God invites them to a new beginning, putting the past behind them.

Following five weeks of second readings from Paul's first letter to the Corinthians, we begin eight weeks with his second letter (1:18-22). He teaches that Jesus is the 'yes' (that is, the fulfilment) to all the promises God makes. In a Trinitarian statement, Paul asserts that the Father assures us of Christ's work for us and the presence in us of the Spirit, the divine pledge of further gifts to come.

EIGHTH SUNDAY IN ORDINARY TIME – Year B

Mark 2:18-22

This gospel passage is not an easy one to understand. However, the basic point seems to be that the presence of the bridegroom/messiah has precedence over the observance of the Old Testament Law. However, Jesus' disciples will fast when he is no longer visibly with them (a qualification that may be a later addition to explain the Christian practice of fasting).

The contrast between fasting and feasting is expressed by the contrast between the conduct of John the Baptist's disciples and those of Jesus. This contrast is founded upon the different teaching of the two leaders. John the Baptist's message is about God's severe judgment to come; it is essential, therefore, to repent and to live a hard life of penance. This message is exemplified in the life and practice of John himself who lives as an ascetic in the desert and gives no indication of gentleness either in the way he treats himself or in his attitude to others.

The lifestyle of Jesus and his message are very different. He speaks of a God who is our Father, who seeks the salvation of us all and offers mercy and forgiveness to sinners. The behaviour of Jesus himself exemplifies this picture of God. He does not live in the wilderness but in towns and villages, he mixes and eats with sinners, he is welcoming, he heals, forgives and is merciful. He preaches not asceticism but loving conduct that seeks people's happiness. The kingdom of God which he proclaims is, as the liturgy confirms, a kingdom of 'justice, love and peace'.

Some of us may have been brought up with the idea that God is above all a severe God, one who takes account of all our sins and that, on the day of judgment, these sins will weigh heavily against our chances of eternal life. This seems to have been a prevalent view of God at certain times, so that our main response was one of fear and dread. Certainly, God gives us the freedom to choose between love of him and rejection of him. But Jesus, the Son of God, has surely done enough, by his words and actions while among us, to assure us that the divine plan is one of forgiveness, healing, mercy and love. Better even than we know ourselves and our constant weaknesses, God is fully aware of them. He understands human frailty and our propensity to sin. He is a loving, caring, merciful parent who has adopted us as his children. If he is prejudiced at all, it will certainly be in our favour. Don't take God for granted and behave as you like as if judgment were a mere formality; but, on the other hand, trust the God who made us and keeps us in being so that we can enjoy one another's company in heaven.

The prophet Hosea lived in the eighth century BC. He was the first to use the metaphor of marital love to describe the love of God for his people (as in the first reading, 2:16-17.21-22).

In the second reading, in his second letter to the Corinthians (3:1-6), Paul suggests that, if he needed a letter to recommend himself, it could well be the Corinth Christians themselves, a testimonial letter written by Christ. Through God's gift, he has been enabled to make them a 'letter' of the Holy Spirit.

NINTH SUNDAY IN ORDINARY TIME – Year B

Mark 2:23-3:6

Today's passage gives us the description of two further clashes between Jesus and some Pharisees (i.e., those who followed a strict and rigorous interpretation of the law). The first occasion occurred when the disciples of Jesus were picking ears of corn as they were walking through a cornfield on the Sabbath; the second was in a synagogue when Jesus healed the withered hand of a man who was there.

In the first clash, Jesus cites the case (reported in the first book of Samuel 21:2-7) of David and his men, almost a thousand years previously, who, because they were hungry, ate loaves reserved for the priests – a more serious transgression than that of which Jesus' friends were being accused. Then Jesus states a legal principle: 'the Sabbath was made for man, not man for the Sabbath'; presumably, therefore, the personal needs of people have to take precedence over an unconditional observance of the Sabbath regulations. But

Jesus expresses this principle in a way that inflames the Pharisees' anger by describing himself as 'Son of Man'. This phrase in itself literally means only 'a man' but it was used in the Old Testament by Ezekiel and taken up by Daniel and given the meaning of 'someone special'. Jesus may well have been using it in the sense of 'messiah' since, when he uses the term of himself, it is usually when he is declaring an important truth.

The second case seems less trivial. Again there are some Pharisees present who, though they were silent, were clearly displeased that Jesus was infringing the law in its rigorous sense by healing a hand that was shrivelled and useless. Although the question with which Jesus is reported to have challenged them seems somewhat irrelevant since not to have healed the man might not have been termed 'to do evil' and certainly not 'to kill', he is clearly exasperated with their interpretation of the law.

Not to have restored the use of his hand to the man just because it was a Sabbath (the only day that Jesus and the man met) would seem to have mocked God's intelligence as well as the divine compassion. (The final sentence today speaks of the Pharisees plotting with the Herodians. These latter are people who were active supporters of the rule, under Roman supervision, of Herod Antipas, tetrarch of Galilee.)

There are still many Jews who treat the Sabbath day of rest as forbidding every possible type of activity that might be construed as work, even to switching on a light. In the Catholic Church there used to be a rule forbidding 'servile work' on Sundays (which was interpreted as manual work undertaken at another's bidding). However, the present Code of Canon Law (canon 1247) states: 'the faithful . . . are also to abstain from such work or business that would inhibit the worship given to God, the joy proper to the Lord's Day, or the due relaxation of mind and body'. The interpretation of this law is left to the individual; clearly, it is not a very restrictive regulation. Nevertheless, many Catholics deplore the Sunday opening of shops because it deprives those who are thereby forced to work on Sundays of the freedom to worship or to spend the day with their families.

When we consider the gospel extract used today, we should keep in mind the words of Jesus that 'the Sabbath was made for man, not man for the Sabbath'. This is an application of a dictum that laws are made for man, not man for laws. Laws are necessary for order and convenience but they must not take precedence over people's wellbeing; they must not destroy, but rather serve, the welfare of people, especially the weakest.

Those who make laws as well as those who operate them usually insist that they are acting exclusively for the benefit of those who are subject to them; but experience shows that this is sometimes a false claim. Today, therefore, is an opportunity for those of us who exercise any authority, whether in the family, in school, in civil society or in the Church to examine our consciences and to listen to those whom we expect to be obedient; and to try to ensure that we are genuinely and honestly doing what is for the good of those in our charge.

The Old Testament Law (Deuteronomy 5:12-15) that no work should be done on the Sabbath is appropriately the first reading today.

In the second reading (2 Corinthians 4:6-11), Paul says that the light of God's glory, a glory that shines on the face of Christ, is visible to us. It came to the Corinthians by Paul's teaching, but he is only the earthenware jar which holds the light whose power comes, not from him, but from God.

TENTH SUNDAY IN ORDINARY TIME – Year B

Mark 3:20-35

The passage chosen for today's gospel reading is somewhat complicated and, in parts, obscure. The passage opens with Jesus being kept very busy by so many people wishing to hear him or to seek his healing help. Some kinsfolk, being told of this, declared he was 'insane' (verse 21). The word used is stronger than the translation ('out of his mind'), that might denote merely that his commitment was extraordinary.

The scribes were men who, after many years of study, were formally recognised as expert interpreters of the meaning of Scripture; they were also consulted on judicial matters and were members of the Sanhedrin, the 71-strong highest court of Judaism. 'Beelzebul' is 'Baal the prince' and, though a pagan god, is here used as a name for Satan, the prince of devils. The accusation of the scribes is easily refuted by Jesus, who infers that he himself is the one who has broken into Satan's house.

The extract reports that Jesus says that all sins will be forgiven and then adds that he makes an exception: blasphemy against the Holy Spirit will never be forgiven (verses 28-29). This last point is difficult. Blasphemy against the Holy Spirit is a sin which, as well as denying that Jesus' power over devils comes from the Holy Spirit, ascribes his power to 'an unclean spirit'. Some scholars, in trying to explain verse 29 suggest that blasphemy against the Holy Spirit is so deeply embedded in those guilty that it is ineradicable and thus unforgivable; they have blocked themselves from the entry of God's saving grace.

The final section (verses 31-35) of today's reading probably is a continuation of the first section (verses 20-21). Jesus does not deny the kinship of extended family but asserts that, in the kingdom of God, there is a higher grade of kinship or brotherhood and one which makes demands on a disciple that transcend family bonds. The Church teaches that, by baptism, we have become adopted children of God.

This point continues to have relevance in our day. It can apply to anyone who is a committed disciple of Christ and is in a situation, either transient or long lasting, in which duty to family is 'trumped' by the exigencies of another situation. The most evident of such instances will probably be those that occur to men and women consecrated in religious life. It is good that, nowadays, such a vocation does not normally involve a permanent separation from one's family. Priority or precedence among our personal bonds should not mean that the primary bond causes the extinction of the others. In the past, the sacrifice of any further contact with one's own family may have been a heroic choice for the person whose vocation was deemed to require it, but it always seemed to me to overlook the natural bonds of family and, above all, of parents for their children.

In the book of Genesis (3:9-15), the devil having tempted Adam and Eve to sin, God confronts both them and Satan. He imposes a curse on the devil and foretells a conflict between Satan and Eve and between the offspring of both. The final verse is called the *proto-evangelium*, the first indication of God's plan of salvation for humankind.

Despite his physical powers lessening and his awareness that death will come, Paul (2 Corinthians 4:13-5:1) declares his faith that, just as God raised Jesus to life, so he will also raise us to dwell with him for ever in heaven.

ELEVENTH SUNDAY IN ORDINARY TIME – Year B

Mark 4:26-34

The scene is idyllic. Jesus is on the shore of the Sea of Galilee and he is clearly ready to teach the crowds who flock to see and hear him. There are so many people there that, in order to be more visible and audible, Jesus gets into a boat and withdraws a little from the shore. Sitting there, he speaks to the crowd in parables. The principal parable is that of the sower whose seed falls on different kinds of ground with varying results of growth. The parable teaches us that the word of God will have a range of effects, depending on how it is received. This parable is found also in Matthew (13:1-23) and in Luke (8:4-15) and is used, in Matthew's version, as the gospel passage for the fifteenth Sunday in Ordinary Time, year A. Mark follows the parable of the sower (4:1-20) with two short parables, the parable of the lamp (4:21-23) and the parable of the measure (4:24-25), before coming to the passage used for today's gospel.

Today's extract gives us another two short parables, both tending to teach the same lesson. First, seed that is sown will germinate and grow until the fruit is ready to be harvested – and it will do so of its own accord or, at least, without constant nonstop attention. Second, the mustard seed is tiny but, when fully grown, it is surprisingly large from such an insignificant start. Both illustrate the kingdom of God which Jesus came to establish or plant in the world and which, from very small beginnings, will imperceptibly grow into something very large, bearing abundant fruit and giving shelter to many.

The meaning of the final two verses is somewhat obscure and therefore disputed among scholars. Perhaps we can say that the final verse is linked with Jesus' policy of not revealing his kingly purpose to the crowds lest they mistake him for the patriot who will free them from Roman occupation. Moreover the full explanation given to the chosen disciples would include not only the meaning of the parables but also the revelation of the plan of God's kingdom, made known to them at times in the course of Christ's public ministry.

Reflection on today's passage helps us to appreciate the value of small and humble beginnings. Seeds should be planted, not disdained because they seem tiny and inert. They have an intrinsic ability to grow that can be unexpected and surprising. It is not always a wise decision, nor is success always guaranteed, when schemes are begun with huge and expensive inaugural ceremonies and publicity.

The teaching of Jesus' parables and the example of his activities show the value of small, almost unnoticed, starts for even great plans and impressive results. Nor need we, as his disciples, always look to others to show us how we can do useful things. Our love, care and concern for others does not need heroic gestures on our part. Something as insignificant as a smile to a lonely person, a consoling word to someone bereaved, a gesture of support to a person in trouble – these are tiny seeds of God's kingdom in a sad and lonely world where the joy of small things is so often forgotten.

The first reading is from Ezekiel (17:22-24), a prophet of the sixth century BC. The text refers to the prospect of an end to the Israelites' exile in Babylon and a return to their own land. Christians see the words as a prophecy about messianic times and therefore closely related to today's gospel.

St Paul (2 Corinthians 5:6-10) looks forward with confidence to being at home with the Lord. He knows that, for all of us, eternal life will be conditional on a judgment of our time on earth.

TWELFTH SUNDAY IN ORDINARY TIME – Year B

Mark 4:35-41

The narrative of Jesus calming the storm (and the apostles' fear) may be a personal recollection of Simon Peter, passed on to Mark and then copied by Matthew (8:23-27) and Luke (8:22-25). It describes a memorable occasion on the Sea of Galilee (Lake Tiberias) in the evening, says Mark, of the day on which Jesus had taught the people in parables as they stood on the shore with Jesus already in the boat (last Sunday's gospel). The Sea of Galilee is normally tranquil but can lull the unwary into a false sense of security. Jesus was exhausted and fell asleep, despite the storm. The apostles became very afraid and, in their panic, wakened Jesus. He rebuked the gale and the rough waters; there was an immediate calm. Jesus reproached the apostles, implying that their fear was due to their lack of faith. They, meanwhile, express astonishment that Jesus can control even the elements created by God.

The event has always been considered as having clear significance with the boat being an image of the Church. It may not be only the elements which are frightening those in the boat; the fact that they were crossing to the eastern shore of the lake, a shore inhabited by pagans who were probably hostile, may well have created a sense of unease in them from the very start.

The significance of the image retains its relevance for us today, of course. Both the storm buffeting the boat and threatening to capsize and sink it, as well as the possible dangers of an unknown future, remain to frighten us. No need to elaborate on those reasons for alarm at the present. And is Jesus still with us? Presumably he is, but has he fallen asleep? We need to show our need for him. Yet justifiably, he can make the same accusation about us as he made that evening on the lake: not just the rhetorical question, 'Have you no faith yet?' but even more directly, 'How is it that you have no faith?'

These are questions that we must ask ourselves. We know the answers and we also know that Jesus can calm any storms that buffet the Church as well as our needless fears, provided, of course, that we believe and place our trust in him.

The Church today brings to mind not only the apostles in the boat making their way across the lake in the teeth of the storm but also another situation with some similarity – the Jews escaping from Egypt and enduring the rigours and fears of the long trek through the wilderness. We may take courage from the successful completion of the journey in both cases. And remember that several times in the Sinai desert there were calls from some, fortunately not prevailing, to go back to Egypt rather than forward to the promised land!

In a short excerpt from the book of Job (38:1.8-11), the first reading reminds us that God created and still controls the elements and, in particular, the stormy seas.

Paul reminds his readers (2 Corinthians 5:14-17) that, with Christ risen, we live in a new creation. At the thought that Jesus died for all, Paul is overcome with gratitude.

THIRTEENTH SUNDAY IN ORDINARY TIME – Year B

Mark 5:21-43

Jesus is back on 'his' side of the Sea of Galilee, probably in Capernaum. The two miracles reported in today's excerpt from Mark's gospel present a strong contrast. Perhaps most notable is the contrast between a person with dignity, reputation and authority (Jairus, the synagogue official) and another person, a woman, poor, timid, ritually unclean because of haemorrhaging, unknown, ignored and, if known, rejected (and the evangelist does not give her name or where she came from). Jesus grants the requests of both. For his concern and help, there are no favourites and no barriers.

Let's consider the healing of that woman's bleeding. She is desperate because so many attempts have been fruitless; she is ashamed and hopes that she will not draw attention to herself and even that he will not notice. However, she has to reveal herself to Jesus who responds with kindness and a complete restoration of her health.

There are many people today who, apart from physical recovery, long to approach Jesus and seek spiritual healing from him. They are burdened with secret worries which they have shared with no one. Afraid to confide in anyone, resigned to their condition, feeling both guilty and condemned to remain thus, they need help but do not know how to get it, not daring to seek advice, let alone healing. There are even some who are convinced of guilt when, in fact, they have been victims. Will they ever have peace? Will they find a willing and sympathetic counsellor? Will they ever dare to ask? That brave woman in the gospel, whose faith, said Jesus, had restored her to health, is the example and guide that they need.

The approach to Jesus by Jairus is very different from that of the woman. She is hesitant, ashamed, tentative and secretive; he is open, public, unashamed and trustful. But faith is an element which Jesus requires in order to proceed in both cases. He recognises the woman's faith and tells Jairus that it is required. (The messengers apparently did not have faith – 'Why put the Master to any further trouble?' is their advice, which Jairus ignored.) When Jesus says that the girl is not dead but asleep, we cannot know with certainty if he means this to be taken literally; or did he mean that, although she had died, her death was not definitive and final? The latter is arguable since the verb in 'got up' (verse 42) is the cognate of the noun frequently used in the New Testament for Christ's resurrection.

Two other points in Mark's account should be noted. First, the three apostles whom Jesus took with him to Jairus' house were Peter, James and John, the same three as he allowed to accompany him to his transfiguration. This suggests that, in both instances, Jesus wanted the events to contribute to their instruction. Second, despite the presence of many witnesses from the family and the mourners, Jesus once more requests that 'messianic secrecy' be observed.

We do not ask Jesus to restore the dead to life as he did during his visible presence on earth. Despite the grief that always comes with bereavement, we know that it is God's will that each of us should die and at a time of his deciding. Further, even those whom Jesus restored to life after death were alive again only for a limited time; their resurrection was not like that of Jesus. So, when we are bereaved, he will help us to be comforted in our sorrow and reassured in our faith; this is particularly true in the sadness that naturally occurs when the death is that of a child.

The first reading is from the book of Wisdom (1:13-15; 2:23-24). The first century BC author writes that 'death was not God's doing' but came through the devil's scheming.

In the second letter to the Corinthians (8:7.9.13-15), Paul asks the people to send aid to those in need. He cites the example of Jesus and his generosity to us. The request is that they should send from their surplus, and not so as to impoverish themselves.

FOURTEENTH SUNDAY IN ORDINARY TIME – Year B

Mark 6:1-6

This passage tells the story of Jesus' visit to Nazareth and to the synagogue there. It was a visit that went badly wrong. Matthew (13:53-58) gives a very similar account of the event. Luke (4:16-30), however, gives the impression that, at first, Jesus received a very enthusiastic reception from those at the synagogue, enthusiasm that then turned sour. He says that Jesus was lucky to escape alive. It may well be that Jesus made more than one visit to Nazareth and to the synagogue there and that Luke has combined the story of two visits, one successful and the other the reverse.

Let us consider today's gospel narrative. The story is a painful one to read or to hear. Right from the start, there seems to have been an absence of the normal welcome which Jesus received on arrival at a village; nor are any sick brought to be healed. The people are sceptical and suspicious, then downright opposed. Jesus feels rejected and despised; his usual practice of healing thwarted by their lack of faith, except for a few people whom he cured.

The questions that were asked may have been merely because of their astonishment and consequent curiosity; on the other hand, the report that 'they would not accept him' suggests a more hostile mood. The term 'son of Mary' (verse 3) is the only instance in the New Testament of Jesus being described thus. His 'brothers' is a reference to the wider family. James (not an apostle) may have been the first bishop of Jerusalem; nothing is known of the other three.

In our country nowadays, Jesus is frequently rejected or, perhaps more accurately, ignored. It seems a tragic apathy, especially since many of the 'missing' are young, have been at Catholic schools and have parents who are 'active'. The blame is probably not entirely the fault of 'the lapsed'. Have they received proper evangelisation and catechesis? Is peer pressure an influence? Do they know about faith? Is the way in which we celebrate that faith, especially at Mass, so uninviting and unattractive?

What about us – how do we treat Jesus? Unconsciously, we may be treating him carelessly – although we are adults, our attitude towards him may still be infantile; we may not be looking for anything from him that moves us or disturbs us or changes us. We may be so familiar with his story that we forget he is alive and present in our midst. And a final thought or, rather, a postscript. Persons whom we have known for years and who have achieved some success – we must fight the temptation to be envious and therefore to treat them with disdain and avoid recognising their achievements. That would be mean-spirited, rather like the Nazarenes.

In the first reading, Ezekiel (2:2-5) tells of being sent by God to prophesy to the Israelites because they are rebellious, defiant and obstinate.

The final extract from Paul's second letter to the Corinthians (12:7-10) recounts how, to keep him humble despite the revelations he had been given, God gave him what Paul calls (without being more specific) 'a thorn in the flesh'. He accepts this willingly because, with the power of Christ in him, it is when he is weak that he is strong.

FIFTEENTH SUNDAY IN ORDINARY TIME – Year B

Mark 6:7-13

Scripture scholars regard this passage as a new stage in Mark's narration of Christ's public ministry. The principal information in it is that 'the Twelve' are no longer merely accompanying Jesus but are working in his name but not directly with him. The excerpt informs us of some of the guidance which Jesus gave them for their mission. The authority he gives them is restricted to commanding unclean spirits; the people are to be healed, not ruled. The Twelve are to live simply and frugally, the staff denoting that he expects them not to settle down anywhere but to remain constantly mobile, dependent on local hospitality.

A few remarks on this reading. First, between last Sunday's gospel and today's, Mark inserts the information that Jesus 'made a tour round the villages, teaching' (6:6b), as if to insinuate that Nazareth had been a disappointing exception. Second, while Mark's account has Jesus telling the Twelve to carry staffs, Matthew and Luke have Jesus forbidding staffs, presumably to stress their minimum baggage. Third, Mark omits Jesus' prohibition of going to gentiles or Samaritans (Matthew 10:5), perhaps because he is anticipating the later unrestricted practice. Fourth, on Mark's mention of the use of oil for healing the sick (6:13): although Jesus did not use oil or command the Twelve to do so, this mention (and, of course, James 5:14-15) prefigures the sacrament of the sick.

The mission of the Twelve is only the first instance of a practice that has continued in the Church, and not only with 'foreign missionaries' but a duty that belongs to us all, and especially to parents, teachers, priests and bishops. To carry out that mission properly and responsibly, we need to have undertaken preparation, both remote and proximate; moreover, it demands prayer, witness of lifestyle as well as the necessary knowledge. It is a sacred trust, a function of our sharing in the priesthood of Christ and possessing the presence and gifts of the Holy Spirit.

The first reading (Amos 7:12-15) has one of the earliest prophets (mid-eighth century BC) bravely justifying his mission, received from God, against accusations that he is an interfering nuisance. The life of a teacher is not a bed of roses!

The second reading is the first of seven extracts from St Paul's letter to the Ephesians (1:3-14). The passage is a sublime paean of praise to God because of his hidden plan of salvation for the world through Christ, a mystery now revealed in all its wisdom.

SIXTEENTH SUNDAY IN ORDINARY TIME – Year B

Mark 6:30-34

This gospel passage is the conclusion of last Sunday's when the Twelve were sent out to preach. You may notice, however, that the lectionary omits verses 14-29 of chapter 6.

Those verses mention that Herod Antipas, the tetrarch of Galilee, had heard rumours about Jesus and that he began to wonder if this were John the Baptist, risen from the dead. Having mentioned this, Mark then gives an account of the beheading of John the Baptist by Herod at the behest of Herodias.

Today's verses paint the picture of an attractive Christ, anxious to give the apostles a break from their duties and a chance to discuss their experiences as missionaries. But the plan is frustrated by the anxiety of the crowds to be with Jesus, to listen to him. They guess rightly where he and his close disciples are going; in fact, when he arrives, they are already waiting for him. Jesus, surely with the approval of the apostles, abandons his plan to be alone with them and begins patiently to speak to the crowd of the Good News he was sent by the Father to proclaim.

Resting from one's labours is perfectly justifiable, indeed necessary. We cannot continue concentrated work of whatever kind without a break, brief or extended as required. Even if uninterrupted work over a long period were physically possible, our minds do need to relax; otherwise, the quality of our work deteriorates. Nonetheless, planned breaks do sometimes have to be cancelled or postponed when unexpected events occur and need attention. Today's gospel illustrates that as well as offering us some consolation when events conspire against us. We are in good company! As Robert Burns wisely writes: 'The best-laid schemes o' mice an' men gang aft agley, an' lea'e us nought but grief an' pain for promis'd joy!'

An extract from the prophecy of Jeremiah (23:1-6) provides the first reading. At that time, around 600 BC, Judah was in dire straits internally and in grave danger from outside. The leaders have been negligent shepherds, but God promises that he will gather and restore the flock himself and that he will send them a wise and honest leader. Christians see these verses as referring to a future messiah.

In the letter to the Ephesians (2:13-18), Paul speaks of the work of Christ. He has brought Jews and gentiles together, established peace between them and reconciliation with God. He has made all of us 'one single new man in himself' and given us 'in the one Spirit our way to come to the Father'.

SEVENTEENTH SUNDAY IN ORDINARY TIME – Year B

John 6:1-15

For five weeks the readings from Mark's gospel are suspended, being replaced with passages from the sixth chapter of St John's gospel. The break is considerably less complete than might be thought since today's reading is John's account of the encounter that Jesus had with the crowd who had followed him when he had intended to spend some quiet time with the Twelve, in other words, last week's gospel passage from Mark.

Today's excerpt is mainly John's account of the miracle of the loaves, an event which all three synoptic gospels also report (Matthew 14:13-21; Mark 6:32-44; Luke 9:10-17). John says that crowds followed Jesus, impressed by his healing of the sick; for John, the wonder-works of Christ are seen as 'signs'. The text mentions the setting – a hillside, evoking Mount Sinai and God's revelation to the Israelites; and the time of year – near Passover, with its connection to the Eucharist. In fact, since the fourth gospel does not mention Jesus giving bread and wine to the apostles at the Last Supper, this 'sign' can be regarded as the Passover meal of Jesus, celebrated with any and all who chose to be present, attracted as they were by an inadequate faith in Jesus.

It is Jesus himself who raises the practical issue about the people's need to eat – evidence of the awareness that Jesus had of others as well as his thoughtfulness. Although our desire to imitate Jesus will mostly be concerned with sharing our faith with others and encouraging others to participate in the Eucharist, it is helpful to note this example of Christ's concern for people who need to satisfy their bodily hunger. In today's world, there are many millions undernourished, some starving, including infants and children. Even in our own country, food banks have become a necessity in our towns. It is a tragedy and also a scandal. Not only is so much food wasted by the affluent, but could we not be more generous with our money so as to feed the hungry?

A further couple of observations on today's text. Among the Twelve, it is Andrew who has been practical enough to find out the possibilities for distributing food although his report is a pessimistic assessment (verses 8-9). The description of the multiplication of the loaves and fish uses verbs which have allusions to the Eucharist (verses 11-12), and this is done intentionally.

Verses 14-15 have no corresponding verses in the synoptic accounts, but they are important. First, the people regard the miracle as a 'sign' that Jesus is a 'prophet' like Moses and one who was expected; and second, the crowd are so impressed that they want to make Jesus their king or earthly messiah, an idea that so horrified him that he immediately made his escape.

Verses 16-23 of chapter 6 are omitted from the Sunday gospel extracts. They tell us that the disciples took a boat for Capernaum and that the weather was stormy. When near their destination, they saw Jesus walking on the water (Matthew and Mark reporting that he got into the boat). Meanwhile, the crowd had spent the night where they had eaten and, next day, rather unsure where Jesus had gone, they guessed (rightly) that he was probably in Capernaum. The narrative then resumes next Sunday.

The first reading (2 Kings 4:42-44) relates how God wonderfully increased the amount of food which Elisha (ninth century BC) possessed, allowing him to feed one hundred men.

In the letter to the Ephesians (4:1-6), Paul insists on the 'unity of the Spirit' which the disciples possess and must preserve – one Body, one Spirit, one Lord, one faith, one baptism, one God who is Father of all.

EIGHTEENTH SUNDAY IN ORDINARY TIME – Year B

John 6:24-35

At least some of those whom Jesus had fed with the loaves and fish (last Sunday) have made their way to Capernaum and found him there. Then John reports a dialogue between them and Jesus which, in fact, is a gradual unfolding of his teaching on 'the bread of life' and the Eucharist.

They ask when he arrived in Capernaum. His reply is not an answer to their question but rather he tells them that their reason for seeking him is mistaken. They are wanting more material bread to eat but Jesus, on whom the Father has set the seal (of the Spirit who gives divine power), is offering them the food that lasts for ever. The crowd asks what they have to do to receive that food and Jesus tells them that they have to believe in him whom God has sent.

The Jews then ask him for a sign to justify his claim because, after all, God had already given their ancestors bread when they were in the desert, escaping from Egypt. Jesus retorts that the true bread from God is not the manna (which only sustained the body and for a period) but that which comes from God and 'gives (lasting) life to the world'. That's the bread they want, they say, to which Jesus declares that he is that bread who will unendingly satisfy the hunger and thirst of anyone who comes to him and believes.

An important point is only implicit in the exchange between Jesus and those who have sought him in Capernaum because he has attracted them. The people are Jews who, in the Old Testament, have been taught of the need to keep the law which God gave to Moses. So they ask Jesus what work they have to do (verse 28) and what work he will do to prove his authenticity (verse 30). But the essence of Christian discipleship is not doing things but belief in Christ. We need to remember that following Christ is not primarily obedience to a list of rules and observances laid down for us but belief in Jesus Christ which gives us a trusting and loving relationship with him and leads us to think, act and live like him so that we continue to build God's kingdom on earth.

The dialogue between Jesus and his hearers will continue in the gospel passages of the next three Sundays. At the moment, we have reached the stage at which Jesus declares that the food and drink of eternal life is belief in him, 'the bread of God come down from heaven and giving life to the world' (verse 33).

The first reading is from the book of Exodus (16:2-4.12-15) and relates the event referred to in the gospel today. To the complaints of the Israelites in the desert that they are starving, God tells Moses that he will send them quails and manna, meat and bread, in abundance.

In the letter to the Ephesians (4:17.20-24), Paul teaches that following Christ demands a complete conversion of life, becoming 'a new self' of goodness and holiness.

NINETEENTH SUNDAY IN ORDINARY TIME – Year B

John 6:41-51

The encounter in Capernaum continues between Jesus and some Jews who had been at the event when Jesus fed thousands with five loaves and two fish. Last Sunday, Jesus had said to the people that he is the bread of life, sent by God; and that those who come to him and believe in him will never hunger nor thirst.

In today's excerpt, those taking part in the meeting begin to grow more sceptical. They know who his parents are, so how can he claim descent from God? Again, Jesus responds but not directly. Instead he states that, to come to belief in him is to be brought there by the Father; and it is he who alone can communicate the teaching of the Father because he alone has come from him. Jesus then reiterates 'most solemnly' his teaching that to believe in him is the way to eternal life. Those who were fed with manna are now dead; but those who eat 'the bread of life' from heaven will not die.

Today's passage ends with a declaration that astounds his listeners – he is that bread, those who eat it will live for ever, and that bread is his very flesh.

Today's verses help us to understand that Jesus is not just any source of life for us, but is unique in offering life for ever; that we listen to the Father because only thus can we reach Jesus as we are meant to; that belief in Jesus implies that God is incarnate in Jesus, whose humanity is, in some ways, so ordinary and, in other ways, so extraordinary; and that, with Eucharistic faith, we are equipped to go and make disciples for him.

The passage today has something very important to say to us on the subject of faith; and faith not only in the real presence of Jesus in the Eucharist but all faith in Christ. It is this – that faith is a gift from God. We cannot confer it on ourselves but we can dispose ourselves to receive it. We can pray for faith, we can give God time and opportunity to confer it, we can have some prior information (from others, from our reading, from others' example); and, faith once received, we pray that the gift may never be lost but rather that it may increase in both extension (by our wider knowledge of the details of God's loving relationship with us) and depth (by seeking a more intense and committed imitation of Christ).

From the first book of Kings (19:4-8), we hear the story of an incident in the life of the prophet Elijah (ninth century BC). Fleeing from King Ahab and his pagan wife Jezebel, he is near death from starvation and thirst. However, God's angel restores him with food and water and he is able to continue walking to Mount Horeb (Sinai).

Paul, writing to the Ephesians (4:30-5:2), urges them (and us) to live lives of gentleness and thoughtfulness towards others, in imitation of Jesus and as children of the Father who are sealed with the gift of the Spirit.

TWENTIETH SUNDAY IN ORDINARY TIME – Year B

John 6:51-58

The gospel passage today begins with a repetition of the final verse of last week's extract, in which Jesus asserts that 'the living bread' to be eaten if we seek eternal life is his own flesh. Subsequent verses repeat the statement that has so astonished his listeners. In fact, he goes further and, to eating his flesh, he adds the need to drink his blood, a way of saying that his entire self is received in Holy Communion. The shock felt by the people is increased when Jesus speaks of drinking his blood, because drinking blood was forbidden by the Jewish law (Genesis 9:4; Deuteronomy 12:16).

There is no question of a figurative eating and drinking since, when the real sense of the words is raised in objection, Jesus simply keeps reiterating his statement and makes no attempt to explain to the objectors that they have misunderstood. At the same time, Jesus, while stating that it is truly his flesh and blood that we receive, is not speaking of physically consuming them as if it were cannibalism. Since eternal life is to possess Christ, the Eucharist is an eschatological sacrament, a pledge and foretaste of eternity. Indeed, even the Eucharist now, Jesus teaches (verses 56-57), gives us a sharing in the divine life. The final verse of today's reading is a summary of the whole passage.

If we long to have a better 'quality of life', our desire will not be fulfilled by greater material wealth. But having the relationship with Jesus that he offers in this meeting reported by John – the bread of his word, his teaching; the food of his flesh and blood – will nourish and gradually transform us. We shall know how Jesus lived and shall want to live in that way, trusting in God, aware of human suffering and seeking the true welfare of all.

We speak of the 'real presence' of Jesus in the Eucharist, meaning true presence but 'sacramental', not 'physical'. At the same time, we should not forget that Jesus is also really and truly present in other ways when we celebrate the Eucharist (Second Vatican Council, Constitution on the Sacred Liturgy, §7). In the gift of the Eucharist which Christ has given to the Church, there is much that is beyond our understanding – not only the full explanation of sacramental presence, but also the relationship between the Eucharist and Calvary, especially that the celebration of the Eucharist is truly sacrificial and yet in no way a repetition of the sacrifice of Calvary (since that would mean that Calvary was not fully effective). We generally try to avoid that error by speaking of the Mass as a re-presentation (with a hyphen) of Calvary.

The insistence of Jesus that we should eat his flesh and drink his blood gives weight to the decision of the Second Vatican Council to restore Holy Communion under both forms of bread and wine. The restoration is to be welcomed, not because we thus receive 'more of Jesus' (since, under each species, we receive the now risen and living Jesus, whole and entire and no longer a bloodless body), but especially because it provides communicants with greater access to the symbolic renewal of the covenant between God and humans which Calvary (and the shedding of Christ's blood) instituted.

The first reading comes from the book of Proverbs (9:1-6). The author of this extract speaks of Wisdom inviting anyone who wishes, and especially the foolish, to go to her house and dine there and thus 'walk in the ways of perception'.

In today's reading from Paul's letter to the Ephesians (5:15-20), he urges us to be wise enough to avoid evildoing and to live in a way that accords with the will of God.

TWENTY-FIRST SUNDAY IN ORDINARY TIME – Year B

John 6:60-69

This is the final insertion of passages from John's gospel into the year of Mark and it also brings to an end the narrative that comprises the sixth chapter of the former. Most Scripture scholars believe that that chapter may be a compilation of various teachings that Jesus gave on himself as the bread of life and also, towards the end of the chapter, some explicit Eucharistic teaching. We are reminded that the two nourishing gifts – Word and Eucharist – are offered and accepted in the Emmaus encounter (Luke 24:13-35).

Verses 60-66 report that, having heard what Jesus said, 'some of his followers' (therefore not only some of the curious in the crowd) could no longer believe in him. If they could not believe now, Jesus declares, they certainly would not believe in the meaning of the events that culminated in his return to the Father. He affirms (verse 65) that, to have faith and be a believer, it is necessary to have divine help; he even foresees that, among the chosen Twelve, not all would have faith. This bleak judgment about the many who would not follow Jesus in Galilee is confirmed later in John's gospel (12:37-41); a similar assessment is found in the gospel of Matthew (11:20-24).

Jesus now challenges the Twelve and, as usual, Simon Peter makes the response on their behalf. They believe that the teaching of Jesus points the way to eternal life; and, using the expression 'Holy One of God', Simon Peter shows that the Twelve are advancing in their awareness of the messianic character of Jesus, even if they have not yet realised the fullness of his identity. They have seen and heard him, and they believe. Especially if the narrative in this chapter describes episodes that occurred at different times and places, it is possible that Simon's profession of faith may be John's rendering of the event described in the synoptic gospels as occurring in Caesarea Philippi (Mark 8:27-30; Matthew 16:13-20; Luke 9:18-21).

The teaching of Jesus in this sixth chapter has amazing claims – that he is from God, that he offers food for life without end, that the food is his own flesh and blood. No wonder that many of those who heard him, including some disciples, had had enough. They ceased to have any time for him. The same challenge and the same outcome happen in our day. The crux is that, for faith, there has to be divine grace and that it has to be accepted.

I am not sure if this is well enough known by many people. Do we not need to make it clearly known to enquirers from outside the Catholic Church and for those Catholics who, without rejecting the teaching, have simply drifted away and need to be helped if they are to return? There certainly is a problem of the multitude of non-active Catholics and the need of a long, patient and well presented process to encourage them to consider becoming active again. And, as a start, the information they need has to be available.

To end on a positive and optimistic note. Have you been aware that when, about to receive Holy Communion, we hear the words 'The Body of Christ' and 'The Blood of Christ', our response of 'Amen' is itself a declaration of faith? It means 'Yes, I believe. You, Lord, have the message of eternal life'.

In the first reading (Joshua 24:1-2.15-18), the Jews have finally reached the promised land. Joshua, successor of Moses, exacts a pledge from the people and their leaders that they will be faithful to their God who has brought them safely through their long trek to freedom.

This is the final excerpt from Paul's letter to the Ephesians (5:21-32). He draws a parallel between the union of husband and wife in marriage and the union of Christ and the Church. Each union contributes to a better appreciation of the other. In some parts of his explanation, Paul relies on the contemporary culture (which can be distracting nowadays). The passage ends with a reference to marriage in the book of Genesis (2:24) which he calls 'a mystery' in the sense that it is a hidden prophecy of the union of Christ and the Church.

TWENTY-SECOND SUNDAY IN ORDINARY TIME - Year B

Mark 7:1-8.14-15.21-23

We return to Mark's gospel and a passage that contains more of Jesus' teaching. Jesus is gradually revealing himself as the messiah whose mission is not limited to Israel and who is opposed to the legalism of the religious leaders of the Jews.

The evangelist gives neither place nor time, but today's extract starts (verses 1-8) with some of these leaders who had come to Galilee from Jerusalem and had objected to the disciples eating with unwashed hands, contrary to one of the practices added by Jewish leaders to the law given to Moses. The criticism is ostensibly about the disciples' behaviour but is really an attack on Jesus. He does not give a direct answer but accuses the complainants of hypocrisy by his quotation of a passage from the prophet Isaiah (29:13).

In today's gospel, there follows a short section (verses 14 and 15) in which Jesus is addressing a crowd again, telling them that a person is unclean by reason of what comes out and not by what goes in. This statement was later to have repercussions regarding the dispute on whether gentile converts had to observe Jewish rules of diet.

Finally, Jesus explains (but only when back inside and to his intimates – another instance of the 'messianic secret') the meaning of the statement by giving examples of evil intentions which arise in the heart and so make a person unclean. Twelve vices are listed, the first ten from various of the ten commandments, with pride (the cause of hypocrisy) and folly (the reason for our doing evil) as the final two.

Jesus accuses the religious leaders of hypocrisy, a vice to which other religious leaders have been prone during the centuries. It is sometimes easy to become infected, even unconsciously so, and we may find ourselves condemning what we see in others yet guilty of the same or worse in ourselves. We can also see, in the intervention of those Pharisees and scribes, a readiness to be busybodies, correcting others' behaviour and with a certain malicious intent. They had become accustomed to observe and obey man-made regulations which obscure the values of the kingdom of God and to teach others to do likewise. It would be useful for today's leaders to reflect on their behaviour and to be on their guard lest they are guilty of similar misconduct.

In the first reading (Deuteronomy 4:1-2.6-8), Moses is addressing the people before they cross the Jordan into the promised land. They are to be obedient to the commandments they have received from God, observing all of them but not adding to them.

With today's second reading, we begin five extracts from the letter of St James (1:17-18.21-22.27). We are told that all that is good has been given by God and that he has adopted us to be his children. To gain eternal life, we are to obey God's word with especial emphasis on helping orphans and widows and on avoiding the evils that exist in the world.

TWENTY-THIRD SUNDAY IN ORDINARY TIME – Year B

Mark 7:31-37

Jesus had been in the north of Palestine and on the coast, where he had healed a Syrophoenician woman's daughter. The event was reported in year A, Twentieth Sunday in Ordinary Time (Matthew 15:21-28) and, although it is also in Mark's gospel (7:24-30), it is not read in year B. But it explains the words introducing today's extract. Christ is back in Galilee. A man who is deaf and either cannot speak or has difficulty in doing so is brought to him. Using more gestures and words than usual, Jesus heals him so that he can hear and speak. Despite Jesus' wish that the cure should be kept a secret, the people do not pay any attention to the request but seem to have been extremely enthusiastic. 'Their admiration was unbounded.'

This miracle of the man being given the ability to hear and speak provides a strong indication that the messianic age has come. The kingdom of God is being established and the Good News needs to be heard and proclaimed. In fact, in the sacrament of baptism, there is a rite in which the priest re-enacts the gestures of Christ in the miracle by touching the person's ears and mouth with his finger and saying the Aramaic word which Jesus used: *ephphatha* (which means 'be opened'). The rite declares that the baptised person is now enabled to share in the work of evangelisation.

There is a rather similar symbolism in today's miracle. In the Old Testament, those who resisted God's call were called 'deaf'. Hence, the miracles of curing the deaf remind us that we all must allow Jesus to dispel the 'deafness' we can experience to his call. Moreover, in today's event, the man needs the help of friends to bring him to Jesus, thus reminding us of our duty to help others to faith. The need is great nowadays and the duty sometimes requires much effort and prayer, aspects that also appear in the gospel story. We must not be deaf to the responsibility given us at baptism when we were made followers of Christ.

The first reading is a passage from Isaiah (35:4-7) in which the prophet looks forward to messianic times when God will show his care for the people in many ways, including opening the eyes of the blind and the ears of the deaf – a very appropriate first reading 'partner' for today's gospel.

The second reading comes from the letter of James (2:1-5). He is not either of the apostles but probably the relative of Jesus who is said to have become the first bishop of Jerusalem. He tells us not to show favours to the rich and exclude the poor. The latter are near and dear to God.

TWENTY-FOURTH SUNDAY IN ORDINARY TIME – Year B

Mark 8:27-35

This reading reports the crucial moment of Jesus' mission, the moment when his closest helpers will be tested regarding their awareness of his mission and hence of their continued commitment to him. The event is both the climax of what has already taken place in Jesus' public ministry and the introduction of an awareness of a messiah who is to suffer.

Caesarea Philippi was a village in the extreme north of Galilee, given the first part of its name in honour of the Roman Emperor and the last part because it was established by Philip the Tetrarch and to distinguish it from Caesarea Maritima (Caesarea-on-Sea). The event is reported by the evangelist long after the death and resurrection of Jesus and so it can be admitted that the account in the gospel had those later events in mind; but it would be wrong to suggest that the whole report is a post-resurrection fictitious story.

The three synoptics report the event, but with some differences. Matthew (16:13-23) adds the words of Jesus to Simon Peter making him the rock on which the Church will be built; Luke (9:18-27) omits Peter's remonstrance and Jesus' rebuke.

The question that Jesus asks, 'Who do you say I am?', must have been in the minds of the Twelve as they had observed Jesus' curing the sick, declaring sins forgiven and preaching about his mission of setting up the kingdom. Besides, all with whom Jesus had been in contact faced a similar question. So now the Twelve have the chance to declare their faith in Jesus, probably not yet his divinity but certainly his messiahship. Their response is of vital importance to Jesus, especially for his mission of establishing permanently God's kingdom. He is now given the opportunity to start directing his words and their thoughts to the future and to a messiahship not of power and conquest but of suffering.

On this subject of what lay ahead for him, Jesus begins for the first time to be very explicit in his teaching to the Twelve. He also refers to himself as 'the Son of Man', a title that Jesus uses of himself when he is describing his messiahship, which is to be both of great suffering as Isaiah's 'Servant of the Lord' and, later, of glory in his resurrection and second coming. It may be noted that, in the earliest reports of the resurrection, the phrase used is that 'God raised Jesus' (for example, Romans 4:25), while in later reports, as here (verse 31), the resurrection is expressed as 'Jesus rose'. After Jesus speaks openly to the Twelve about the suffering and death that await him, Peter protests. He still does not understand, or refuses to understand, the type of messiah Jesus is. Christ's rebuke is immediate and peremptory and directed to the hearing of the Twelve.

The final two verses (34-35) are directed not only to the Twelve but also to 'the people' and could therefore have been spoken on another occasion, though relevant to the present occasion. The assertion that his followers will have to take up their cross may be understood in the obvious sense; alternatively, the meaning may be expressed as: 'If you want to be a disciple of mine, repent of your sins and dedicate yourself wholly to God'. Then Jesus adds that, for the sake of eternal life, no sacrifice is too great.

Today's gospel is clearly an account of a climactic moment in their relationship for Jesus and for the apostles. However, we can see the real challenge that confronted them. Although they could now be sure that Jesus was the Christ, the messiah come at last, they still had much to learn about Jesus and the full reality of his being and of the divine plan that was his, and now also to be their, mission. They would come to that awareness only gradually and by being in his presence and listening to his teaching. This is equally true of us, Christ's disciples today. If we want to know and faithfully follow him, we must try to be in his company daily. Faith is a gift of God to us. But our grasp of that gift and our discipleship grow only gradually all during our lives.

The first reading is from the later part of Isaiah (50:5-9), the part not from the eighth century BC but from the sixth (often referred to as Deutero-Isaiah). The reading is the first part of the third 'Song of the Servant of the Lord'.

In the second reading (James 2:14-18), the author, recognising in a Christian the need for faith, insists that good works are also required; otherwise, faith would be dead.

TWENTY-FIFTH SUNDAY IN ORDINARY TIME – Year B

Mark 9:30-37

The lectionary extracts omit most of the ninth chapter of Mark, including the description of the transfiguration. Returning from the mountain and on their way to Capernaum, Jesus makes a second prophecy about his passion, death and resurrection. He does so with great deliberation as he wants to emphasise that his messianic mission will involve rejection and suffering for him and will not be one of earthly power and glory. But the apostles do not yet understand and were apparently afraid to ask him to explain.

On arrival at Capernaum, the group goes into 'the house' (Simon's?) and Jesus discovers that, while walking, they had been arguing about which of them was the greatest. So Jesus has to correct them once again by saying that they have not to vie with one another over status or rank; if any of them is to be first, it will be in service. The instance of Christ's embrace of the little child and of his words as he did so is to insist that to welcome a little child – and, by extension, any 'little one', the weak and powerless, those on the margins – is to welcome Jesus himself; and to welcome Jesus is to welcome the Father.

This lesson has already been taught by Jesus several times. His whole behaviour showed that he sought neither power nor worldly success himself, nor did he court those who possessed them. He had come to proclaim good news to the poor. The apostles were slow to get this message; it was a teaching that the Holy Spirit needed to impress on them. We need to examine our own conduct in this respect. It can be very attractive to seek the affluence and the honours of this world; it can be very tempting to enjoy the company of the wealthy and famous. Please God we shall be faithful to the example of Jesus whose disciples we claim to be.

The first reading (Wisdom 2:12.17-20) paints a picture of the godless, in their dislike of the virtuous man, plotting to hurt, torture and kill him. Let's see, they say, if the God he serves will come to rescue him. The passage is seen by Christians as looking forward to messianic times; it accords with Jesus' prophetic words in today's gospel.

St James (3:16-4:3) teaches that, while wisdom brings peace and goodness to our world, jealousy and ambition bring enmity and violence. We should pray for what we seek; and, if it is not received, that will be because it is not for our good.

TWENTY-SIXTH SUNDAY IN ORDINARY TIME – Year B

Mark 9:38-43.45.47-48

The gospel passage today is taken from a section of Mark's gospel that brings together a number of sayings attributed to Jesus, but probably from different times during his public ministry. The first (verses 38-40) shows Jesus tolerant of someone who is not one of the Twelve (or not a disciple) but is casting out devils, using Jesus' name to do so. Strangely, when similar situations arise after the ascension and the coming of the Holy Spirit, the apostles are very intolerant (Acts 8:18-24; 13:6-12; 19:13-20). Verse 41 ('If anyone gives you . . .') is placed here because it may have been seen as a similar saying to the preceding one.

The toleration which Jesus shows has a lesson for us. It often happens that there are groups or persons authorised to carry out some work or task for the benefit of others.

When someone else is found nonetheless to be performing that work or task, the group may try to put a stop to the 'unauthorised' person. The outsider, the group decides, has no right to be acting thus – he or she is not a member of the group. It is probably too strict to say that in every case the group's view is wrong. But at least, the criterion has to be not the prestige or reputation of the group but rather that God's loving care, mediated through human acts, should not be denied to anyone.

Verse 42 ('But anyone who is an obstacle . . .') is a warning against the serious sin of causing scandal to people with faith. Verses 43-48 are three parallel warnings against sins which originate in different parts of the body – hand, foot and eye. Persons guilty of these sins are threatened with hell, where the punishments are described, quoting the last verse of Isaiah (66:24), as unending worms and fire. This description is derived from Gehenna, a valley outside the walls of Jerusalem and used as a place where rubbish was burned; it was taken as a symbol of the place of torment for the wicked. (Verses 44 and 46 are omitted because they are identical to verse 48 and were added by a later copier.)

The first reading (Numbers 11:25-29) is an excellent illustration from the Old Testament of the virtue of tolerance. During the Israelites' years in the wilderness, a group of seventy were endowed by God with the gift of prophecy. Two others, but not in the group, were also gifted. Despite pleas that the pair should be stopped, Moses refused, adding that he wished that everyone had received the gift.

The second reading (James 5:1-6) accuses the wealthy of being guilty of selfishness and injustice in their treatment of the poor; they will pay in the next life for their evil ways on earth.

TWENTY-SEVENTH SUNDAY IN ORDINARY TIME – Year B

Mark 10:2-16

The gospel passage today finds Jesus in Judea and on the east bank of the Jordan. He gives his teaching on two important subjects: the indissolubility of marriage and the right of children to be in his company.

The first subject arises from a question from some Pharisees who were among the crowd listening to Jesus; the question was put to test him. 'Is it against the law for a man to divorce his wife?' The Pharisees knew that, in the Deuteronomic Code proclaimed by Moses, the implication is that, in certain circumstances, a Jew was allowed to divorce his wife (Deuteronomy 24:1). Some rabbis held that the Code allowed divorce in any circumstances. Since Mark's text is not written for Jews, it excludes divorce in all cases (verses 9-12). Jesus treats the Old Testament permission as due to 'unteachability' or hardness of heart, and not as a commandment from God. He then goes on to give the reason for indissolubility by citing Genesis (2:22-24). Since the woman was taken and made from man, the two have an urge to form a unity. Thus the indissoluble nature of marriage comes from God's will. This teaching of Jesus, as reported by Mark, on the total indissolubility of marriage is not found in the Old Testament or in any rabbinical documents.

With divorce, remarriage and unmarried cohabitation so frequent today, even among Catholics, the teaching of Jesus seems, to a great extent, ignored – and perhaps unknown. The problem is huge and a solution seems distant. Older Catholics are very concerned and offer all kinds of explanation for the situation. Please God that the synod on the subject (and on the related subject of the welfare of families), begun in 2014 and continued in 2015, will bring some light and help to this apparently intractable problem.

The other subject, that of children being allowed to be near Jesus, is less complicated. He speaks of the kingdom of God as belonging to children because they think of God as *Abba*, they trust God implicitly, aware of his unlimited love and safe in his presence. Some see, in Jesus' attitude, a justification of the decision in favour of the baptism of infants.

Since Jesus had recently embraced a child in the presence of the disciples (Mark 9:36-37), it is strange that they should now have tried to prevent children approaching him. They seemed to want to have the power to decide who should be allowed near Jesus. Yet Jesus indicates that it is children, first of all, who should be able to be with him. The officiousness towards children which was shown by the disciples of Jesus two thousand years ago is still to be seen on some occasions today. Perhaps young people need to be disciplined and controlled to an extent, but never to such a degree that they feel excluded from Jesus.

The first reading (Genesis 2:18-24) is from the second or 'Yahwistic' account of creation and includes the description of God's making of woman and the consequent marriage of man and woman so that 'they become one body'.

Today's second reading is the first of seven extracts from the letter to the Hebrews, a first century book addressed to Jewish converts to Christianity; the author is unknown. In this reading (2:9-11), we hear that God's plan to bring us to glory involved Jesus becoming man and submitting to suffering and death. He is the one who leads us, his brothers and sisters by human nature, to salvation.

TWENTY-EIGHTH SUNDAY IN ORDINARY TIME – Year B

Mark 10:17-30

This is the touching account of the rich young man who, although he kept all the commandments of the Decalogue, was conscious that there was still something missing before he could be assured of eternal life. He seeks Jesus' advice and Jesus is impressed with his sincerity. But the advice that the young man receives comes as a great shock; he cannot accept it and he walks away, crestfallen.

The disciples are surprised at the severe demand that Jesus makes as an assurance of eternal life. Even for us the requirement to 'give away all your wealth to the poor and then follow me' seems unnecessarily rigorous. For the disciples, however, there was the added consideration that, in their culture, wealth was a proof of God's favour. Leaving that point aside, we feel that we would have shared the disciples' consternation. Jesus is reported as exclaiming, first, how hard it is for the rich to enter heaven; and then, when he repeats his words, 'the rich' has been altered to 'anyone' which makes the problem even greater. There is some solution in the next remark which Jesus makes: only God, for whom everything is possible, can get human beings, and even the rich, into eternal life.

The episode is bound to make us think seriously about ourselves. We can attempt to calm our worries by suggesting that Jesus was exaggerating or that people of great wealth, as the young man was, find it all but impossible to give everything away. It is, of course, reasonable to be aware that many of us have obligations to support others; and that literally to give away absolutely everything we have would, in present-day culture, be irresponsible. Nevertheless, we are called not to keep wealth that we do not need, first, because it can distract us from being wholehearted followers of Christ, and second, because we are depriving those who are living in poverty. The 'trickle-down' theory of economic prosperity seems no longer to be sustainable. We must not be like that poor but rich young man who 'went away sad'.

This Sunday's gospel ends with Simon Peter (as usual, the spokesman) asking Jesus about those who, like the Twelve, have left everything to follow him. Jesus reassures him. However, it is arguable that his reassurance ends with the phrase 'a hundred times over'; the remainder of the reply attributed to him (recompense in this life) is never found elsewhere as a promise of Christ.

The book of Wisdom (7:7-11) provides the first reading. It esteems wisdom as the greatest of possessions, including all material wealth.

The letter to the Hebrews (4:12-13) extols the powerful effects of God's word. By its ability to discover all our secrets, even our thoughts, it enables God, our judge, to know us and everything about us with absolute thoroughness.

TWENTY-NINTH SUNDAY IN ORDINARY TIME – Year B

Mark 10:35-45

It is surprising to discover that the Twelve, after having spent so much time in Christ's company and having heard his teaching that he was the messiah but who had come in meekness and not in majesty, should still be labouring under various childish and selfish delusions about him and about themselves. They are making their way south to Jerusalem and Jesus has just made his third prediction that 'the Son of Man' will be arrested and crucified and, three days after his death, he will return to life. The Twelve are bewildered and fearful, but they are still ambitious and their thoughts are on what will happen to them.

First of all, it is the two brothers, the 'sons of thunder', who approach Jesus, and apparently ensuring, as they went to speak to him, that the others were not present. They want to have the best two places, right next to Christ in his glory. Jesus seems taken aback at their audacity and lack of anything but their own advantage. Using metaphors for the passion he will endure, he asks them if they too can drink the cup of woe and be baptised (immersed) in the suffering along with him. Although, with great confidence, they reply that they can, he tells them that he is not the one who can grant the favours for which they ask.

Naturally but also selfishly, the others are angry with the two brothers. The pair had no right to attempt, surreptitiously, to reserve the best places for themselves. At this stage, Jesus decides to intervene and to repeat the lesson that they should have learned by now. He reminds them that he had come as messiah, not to rule with severity but to serve with humility. In the kingdom of God, the leaders must be servants of the rest. They must not think of themselves as autocrats or with special honours and privileges. After all, he, the Son of Man, came to serve, not to be served. The final ten words of today's excerpt are based on the verses used in the first reading (Isaiah 53:10-12) but may be a later addition to the gospel.

The teaching of Jesus is basic for discipleship and we are very familiar with it. It makes sense and presumably we agree with it – at least in theory. But in practice, does selfish ambition not enter our thoughts and desires? It can, and no one can claim to be exempt from the temptation. Pope Francis has deplored the spirit of careerism and opportunism that can afflict members of the Roman Curia, 'attempting to show themselves as being more capable than others' (Address to the Roman Curia, 22nd December 2014). It can be found in those who have been given responsibilities, whether great or small, but are still intent on 'advancing higher'. Seeking prestige and control will always destroy the unity of the Christian community; it will also be a grave hindrance to the person who wants to live and act in imitation of Christ.

The excerpt from Deutero-Isaiah (53:10-11) is part of the fourth 'Song of the Servant of the Lord' and is clearly messianic in character. It acclaims God's servant who has atoned for others' sins by his suffering, and who will be rewarded for doing so.

The second reading (Hebrews 4:14-16) begins a protracted teaching on the priesthood of Christ. He is a high priest with personal experience of our human weaknesses, with the exception of sin. Consequently, we can be certain that he will judge us with mercy.

THIRTIETH SUNDAY IN ORDINARY TIME – Year B

Mark 10:46-52

The healing of blind Bartimaeus is the second such miracle recounted by Mark, but the first (8:22-26) is not included in the Sunday gospels. Although this healing is described in Matthew (20:29-34) and in Luke (18:35-43), only Mark names the blind man. The miracle occurs in Jericho, a town near the Jordan and some thirty kilometres east of Jerusalem, the city to which Jesus and the Twelve are going. Bartimaeus calls out to

Jesus, using a messianic title, 'Son of David', the first person not an evil spirit to address Jesus in that way – and a title to which Jesus does not object (despite the 'messianic secret'). Bartimaeus is told that his faith has saved him and, with the sight given him by Jesus, he follows him. This last phrase may mean either that he joins the group accompanying Jesus on the way to Jerusalem or that he begins the journey of discipleship. The man's faith is noted by Jesus, but there is no mention either of a healing gesture by Jesus or of the usual amazement of the onlookers present at a healing.

To hear or read this story is a recurring source of emotion especially for those of us who have, or have had, problems with our eyesight. In particular, if we have had the experience of a restoration of sight or a notable improvement, due to the recent remarkable advances in eye surgery and the skill of surgeons and nurses, we are so grateful to them and to God. We have not had a miracle worked on us, but we certainly can be thankful to God's providence for the skills and improvements from which we have benefitted.

There is, of course, another way in which this miracle for Bartimaeus affects us. Faith is often referred to in terms of vision or blindness. Our faith may be nonexistent or have badly deteriorated. It may also have become a faith that has strayed from following Jesus on the road that he walked and, instead, has become static and even ossified. In that case, it is no longer a genuine following of Jesus along his path of humility, gentleness and service. Today's gospel passage should help us to recognise if we need the Bartimaeus 'treatment' by which Jesus can grant us or restore to us, if we ask, the gift of twenty/twenty faith.

It is worth noticing that the gift of faith was affecting Bartimaeus before he realised it. Consider the determination of the blind man ('he began to shout ... he only shouted all the louder') and his alacrity ('throwing off his cloak, he jumped up ... '). No wonder Jesus told him, 'Your faith has saved you'. More properly, 'My gift of faith, accepted by you, has saved you'. Therein lies a great lesson for us – to want and to seek the gift of faith, to throw aside all obstacles in the way, and to act now!

I heard Pope Francis, in his address at a general audience during the Holy Year of Mercy in 2016, take another approach to this miracle. He likened Bartimaeus to the marginalised and the excluded ('sitting at the side of the road' as the crowd hurried past), ignored until he began to call out, then told to shut up as he was a nuisance. The pope added that Jesus, by his presence, worked a second miracle that day – those following him were converted from regarding the blind beggar as a distraction and an intrusion to showing themselves as agents of mercy. The story is timeless and relevant.

The prophet Jeremiah wrote in the seventh and late sixth centuries BC. In today's excerpt (31:7-9), God speaks through him, proclaiming that the people will be brought back from exile and that God will guide them all, even the blind, so that they will not stumble on the way.

The letter to the Hebrews (5:1-6) continues to 'compare and contrast' the Levitical priesthood and that of Christ. Both are appointed by God to offer sacrifices on behalf of sinners; and being human, they can sympathise with the people. The reading ends with a citation from a psalm in which God declares of the promised messiah, 'You are a priest of the order of Melchizedek, and for ever' (109/110:4).

THIRTY-FIRST SUNDAY IN ORDINARY TIME – Year B

Mark 12:28-34

The lectionary for Sundays in Ordinary Time omits all of chapter 11 and much of chapter 12 of Mark's gospel. Those chapters describe the arrival at Jerusalem, the Palm Sunday entry to the city, and some confrontations with controversial and hostile questioners. Today's reading is something of an exception since it recounts a friendly discussion between Jesus and a scribe.

The scribes were members of the Sanhedrin who were learned in the Scriptures and had the duty of officially interpreting them. The scribe's question, 'Which is the first of all the commandments?' means the most important of them, the 'parent commandment' that was the source of the others. Jesus' reply pleases the scribe because he cites the first verse of the *shema* (Deuteronomy 6:5), the daily prayer of Jews. Jesus then adds that there is a second commandment, also more important than any others, that we must love our neighbours as ourselves. He quotes a verse in Leviticus (19:18) in which Jews were told to love other Jews; the commandment was later extended as no longer limited to loving Jews. The scribe and Jesus commend one another and the meeting ends in mutual satisfaction. Mark's final remark seems like an expression of relief that Jesus was spared from further hostile badgering.

The gospel extract today reminds us that both love of God and love of neighbour are essential. They can be called the two lungs so necessary for both Jews and Christians. It is not possible to love God and either ignore our neighbours or be antagonistic to them; and, of course, refusal to love God is a pathetic state for anyone to be in. May the example of Jesus, as well as his words today, be our guide always.

The first reading could not be more appropriate. It quotes the *shema* as it occurs in the book of Deuteronomy (6:2-6).

In the second reading, the letter to the Hebrews (7:23-28) continues to compare the priests of the Old Law and Christ, the priest of the New Law and Covenant. Jesus is eternal and so therefore is his priesthood; moreover, he is present in the best possible position to continue offering the one perfect victim, the sacrifice of himself.

THIRTY-SECOND SUNDAY IN ORDINARY TIME – Year B

Mark 12:38-44

This extract follows almost immediately after that of last week. It is Holy Week and Jesus is in the temple precincts, teaching the people who gathered round to hear him. In the first place, he has some very severe criticism to make of the religious authorities and who, in that sacred place, were much in evidence. He makes special mention of the scribes. They enjoy being prominent in their official robes and are always ready to take the seats at the front of the synagogue which face the people, as well as anxious to be honoured guests at banquets. Even in the streets outside the Temple, they are keen to be noticed and to receive effusive greetings from the people. Worse than that, they are hypocrites in their pretence of being devout. They are ready to relieve widows of their property, presumably by a show of hypocrisy and a readiness to deceive them. Jesus concludes by declaring that they will be severely punished for their wrongdoing. This wholesale and thorough condemnation of the scribes is thought, by exegetes, to show evidence of later antipathy towards Jewish religious leaders and to be an 'embellishment' of some of the measured criticism which Jesus did make.

The incident of the widow and her small but generous almsgiving, some scholars believe, may have been only a teaching on almsgiving or a parable, either of which may have been developed as if it had been an actual happening. Whatever its origin, it does help to balance a rather unbalanced and negative impression of the people of Jerusalem. Mark's estimate of the widow's donation to the temple funds amounts to a tiny fraction of the daily wages of an unskilled workman. Nevertheless, Jesus commends her generosity, given that she is so poor herself. When people make donations to charities, Jesus' remarks remind us that the value of the gift is dependent not so much on the amount given, as on the donor's own wealth or poverty and ability to donate.

There could hardly be a greater contrast than that between the two incidents in today's gospel extract. The scribes were professionally religious and officially the people's leaders and exemplars. They were to be esteemed and respected, models for others to imitate or at least admire. Yet their religiosity was a sham; they used it to increase their own reputation and to exploit the gullible.

The widow is so different. She seeks no publicity, her actions are hardly noticed. Far from exploiting anyone, she gives away everything that she has. While wealthy people were giving large amounts of money, it was from what they had over; she gave little, but it was 'everything that she possessed, all that she had to live on'.

Those of us who have positions of leadership or of prominence in parishes or dioceses must ponder today's reading very seriously indeed. There may well be, in our lives or in our habits and activities, whether consciously or not, behaviour that deserves criticism and correction; it may have caused scandal or derision in those who notice and judge. It may be behaviour that undoubtedly should not happen. Please God we may be intelligent enough to discern our guilt in this area, if there is any; and the humility to admit its presence and to rid ourselves of it without delay. It seems appropriate to quote the Bard at this point:-

> O wad some Power the giftie gie us
> To see oursels as ithers see us!
> It wad frae mony a blunder free us,
>   An' foolish notion:
> What airs in dress an' gait wad lea'e us,
>   An' ev'n devotion!
>   *(To a Louse)*

On the other hand, there are people of no particular renown who know how to give with exemplary generosity and loving hearts. They are the ones among us who are most like Jesus.

They are truly religious people and, though they do not know it, they are our teachers. May we be wise enough and humble enough to learn.

In the first reading (1 Kings 17:10-16), Elijah is fleeing from the wrath of King Ahab (ninth century BC) and is starving. A widow and her son share with the prophet the little amount of food that she has. God sees that she is fittingly rewarded.

The letter to the Hebrews (9:24-28) teaches that Jesus our High Priest, having suffered death in self-offering, presents that sacrifice to his Father on our behalf. When he returns at his second coming, it will not be to re-offer himself but to be our judge and to give salvation to the faithful.

THIRTY-THIRD SUNDAY IN ORDINARY TIME – Year B

Mark 13:24-32

Towards the final Sunday in Ordinary Time, each of the three synoptic gospels deals with teaching of Jesus to his close disciples on a couple of subjects both in the future. These are, first, the destruction of the city of Jerusalem by the Roman army of occupation in retaliation for an attempted Jewish revolt and, second, the events at the end of the world and the second coming of Christ in the general judgment. It is difficult, sometimes, to know which of these two violent periods Jesus is describing at any one point in his discourse; on occasions, moreover, he seems to be referring to both. Also, the language used is often apocalyptic, that is, with very graphic and indeed symbolic descriptions not to be taken literally. Perhaps the spoken teaching of Jesus to the apostles made a clearer distinction between the two events than the written gospels do. On the other hand, there is a connection between the two disasters, the first being reckoned as prefiguring the second. The discourse takes place with Jesus and the disciples gathered on the Mount of Olives, looking westward across the Kedron valley to Jerusalem laid out before them, the city walls and the Temple both very prominent.

In today's gospel passage, only a part of the thirteenth chapter of Mark ('the eschatological discourse') is read. The first four verses (24-27) refer to the second coming at the end of the world and the following five verses (28-32) can be applied to either or both future events, with some seeming more apt for the destruction of Jerusalem and others for the end of the world. Despite the anticipation of disasters and persecution, the underlying and basic message of Christ's discourse is one of hope, a hope founded on the assurance of God's final victory over evil and the successful establishment of his kingdom.

The passage begins with some apocalyptic language borrowed from Old Testament prophetic writings to symbolise the judgment of God being passed on the world and its inhabitants. Then the 'Son of Man' (Jesus' preferred name for himself when speaking of a solemn moment in the story of God's plan of salvation) comes to earth to inherit the kingdom and to bring together those destined for salvation. This image, presented not as a calamity but as a triumph of Christ and with God's eternal plan now completed, is probably derived from the prophecy of Daniel (7:13-14). In these verses 24-27, it is not really possible to clarify further the meaning of some of the phrases used.

The remainder of the extract (verses 28-32) comprises a parable about the fig tree, two sayings about the end of the world and a warning to be vigilant because no one but the Father knows when these events will take place, but take place they certainly will. Generally, these verses can refer to both or either of the events. Even the second coming may have been mistakenly expected in their lifetime by those who formed 'this generation'. That the knowledge of the timing of the events was known only to God is also found in the Old Testament; the phrase 'nor the Son' may be either a reference to Jesus' human knowledge or to a misunderstanding by someone, then or later and not yet fully aware of the divinity of Jesus.

It is somewhat anomalous that the eschatological theme at the end of the liturgical year should also be the theme in the following couple of Sundays, at the start of the next liturgical year. Neither the destruction of Jerusalem nor the ending of the world as we know it and the second coming of Christ affect us directly. There was, it is said, an upsurge of millenarianism at the approach of the year 1000 (as well as some anxiety about the effects on computers and electronic data as the change from 1999 to 2000 drew near). Today's gospel, however, does remind us of the advisability for each of us to realise that death and judgment can come at any time and quite unexpectedly.

Our celebration of the Eucharist not only looks back to Christ's death and resurrection but it also has its eschatological aspect with many of the prayers asking God to keep us for eternal life. Two of the acclamations after the consecration of the bread and wine contain the phrase 'until you come again' and the prayer following the Lord's Prayer ends with 'as we await the blessed hope and the coming of our Saviour, Jesus Christ'. Nor should we forget that, when we receive Holy Communion, we do so as a pledge and foretaste of eternal life since we are 'called to the supper of the Lamb'.

Firm belief in life after death and an awareness of the resurrection of the dead developed only gradually among the Jewish people. Related to this slowness was the fact that the Jews made no distinction between body and soul. The first reading today is from the prophecy of Daniel (12:1-3), written around 165 BC and therefore quite late in the story of the Jews in the Old Testament. The passage chosen is apocalyptic in genre and is concerned with the end of the world as we know it.

The author of the letter to the Hebrews in today's reading (10:11-14.18) yet again dwells on the superiority of Jesus' priesthood over that of the Old Law. Christ 'has offered one single sacrifice for sins . . . there can be no more sin offerings'.

LAST SUNDAY IN ORDINARY TIME – Year B
OUR LORD JESUS CHRIST, KING OF THE UNIVERSE

John 18:33-37

As happens now and again in the course of year B, John's gospel replaces that of Mark. The episode chosen is from the account of Jesus on trial before Pontius Pilate. John's gospel gives fewer details than the synoptics give of Jesus' appearances before Annas and Caiaphas, but considerably more details than they do of his trial by Pilate. Thus, since Pilate is the Roman governor and the Roman empire extended over much of the known world, the effect is to show Jesus in confrontation with the world.

The Jewish leaders have brought Jesus to Pilate on the grounds that they were not allowed to execute anyone by crucifixion. Pilate's question about Jesus as the king of the Jews must have been prompted by his having heard that that was his claim. Jesus asks how he had heard, but Pilate does not directly answer the question. Then Jesus takes the opportunity of explaining to Pilate the type of kingship that he claimed. In the synoptics Jesus had already shown himself to be the fulfilment of the Jews' messianic and kingly expectations. Now, he states that his kingship is neither political nor nationalistic, nor does he have any military or armed force upon which to call. Finally, in this extract, Jesus identifies himself clearly as a king; by his very presence as well as by his words, he witnesses to the truth and those who seek the truth listen to him.

It is a pity that the extract did not go on for one further verse (verse 38) or even for its first six words: '"Truth?" said Pilate; "What is that?"'. Pilate does not wait for Jesus to reply; he is a sceptic and a cynic and he thinks there is no reply to give. Jesus tells us that he, Jesus, is a witness to the truth. So, in his presence, can we examine our consciences, especially with regard to our following of him? How much of our discipleship is honest and genuine? Is some of it pretence, in an attempt to impress or to deceive?

The first reading is from the prophecy of Daniel (7.13-14), an excerpt referred to last week. The passage, which is obviously messianic and in apocalyptic language, speaks of 'a son of man' being led in triumph to God the Father who confers eternal kingship on him.

The second reading is from the Apocalypse (1:5-8). It describes Jesus as the faithful witness (see John 18:37, in today's gospel reading) who has freed us from our sins and made us sharers in his kingship and priesthood. 'This is the truth' (verse 7) could well be an answer to Pilate's question!

The Seasons and Ordinary Time of Year C

Advent and Christmas

FIRST SUNDAY OF ADVENT – Year C

Luke 21:25-28.34-36

Advent is a time for us to look forward and to be prepared. It is a time of expectancy since the word 'advent' means 'a coming', 'that which is about to happen'. Although our own thoughts are now directed towards Christmas – and the commercial world that we live in does not let us escape from such thoughts, building us up to a state of near-panic and obsession – the liturgy is content to concentrate, for the first half of Advent, on another coming of Christ, his second coming. In fact, there is a close similarity between the Scripture readings used in the final Sundays of year B and these first Sundays of year C, the year in which most of the Sunday gospels come from St Luke.

Today's gospel passage illustrates the point. The scene is Jerusalem, in fact in the temple area. It is the week before the arrest, trial and passion of Jesus. He is talking to his disciples, instructing them. The discourse has two subjects – the forthcoming destruction of the city of Jerusalem and his own second coming on earth at the end of the world. The gospel for today is chosen from the part of the discourse dealing with the latter subject.

It opens with a description of the preliminaries to Christ's arrival at the end of the world. These preliminaries are described in graphic, not to say frightening, terms in the literary genre known as apocalyptic. It is the style used in parts of the Scriptures, most notably in the prophecy of Daniel in the Old Testament and the book of the Apocalypse in the New Testament. The language is dramatic, meant to be understood figuratively and not literally, and therefore difficult to interpret in its literal meaning. At some point, Jesus will appear 'with power and great glory'. When he was visible on earth two thousand years ago, he was meek, humble and gentle; but, at the second coming, he is the triumphant messiah, conqueror of sin and death, saviour of humanity, Christ the King. Those who have been saved are told to be unafraid and to hold their heads high since the full effect of Christ's saving work is about to be revealed.

The gospel excerpt ends with a warning that we must be prepared for the second coming and the general judgment. We have to remain on the alert and be constant in prayer, carefully avoiding any conduct that might allow the second coming to catch us unaware or unprepared. When referring to himself in today's gospel, Jesus uses the title 'Son of Man'. The title appears in the Old Testament, in the prophecies of Ezekiel and Daniel. Although it is basically only a rather verbose phrase for 'man', the prophets use it as a messianic title. Jesus himself copies this and employs it especially when he is making a momentous announcement or describing an important activity of his.

There was an impression among the early Christians that the second coming of Christ was imminent or at least would not be long delayed and would probably occur during their lifetime. This sense shows itself in various places in St Paul's writings and in the gospels, especially, for example, in the passages used for the early Advent Sundays. The name given to Christ's second coming with all the attendant happenings at the end of the world, especially the general judgment, is the Greek word *parousia*, literally meaning 'presence' or 'coming'. As the years went by and the *parousia* did not take place, there was also an increasing tendency among the Christians to cease being constantly watchful; this laxity probably induced the evangelists and others to be all the keener on insisting on its certainty, although when it would happen was unknown. In our days, there is little expectation of Christ's second coming and the end of the world being imminent; but the certainty of death and our ignorance of its date should be enough to convince us of the value of being constantly as prepared as we can.

The first reading today comes from the prophet Jeremiah (33:14-16), writing early in the sixth century BC, dark days when Israel was corrupt and sinful as well as under the threat of Chaldean invasion. Nonetheless, Jeremiah promises a future time of honesty and virtue which will happen when the messiah comes.

In his first letter to the Thessalonians (3:12-4:2), Paul encourages the Christians of the city to continue living good lives and to progress in holiness in the ways he had taught them.

SECOND SUNDAY OF ADVENT - Year C

Luke 3:1-6

Advent is the time at which we prepare for the coming of Christ, but the liturgy seems reluctant to propose that that should mean preparing for Christmas. Last week's extract from Luke's gospel had Jesus telling his disciples that they should be in a state of readiness for his second coming as our king and judge (the *parousia*). Today's excerpt is about John the Baptist exhorting the people to prepare for the coming of the messiah; in other words, Jesus would already be an adult when he would begin to reveal himself as the messiah. So nothing yet about Christmas in the Advent gospels.

There are aspects of John the Baptist's preaching that have relevance for us in our search for holiness. He hears and transmits God's message in the desert, that is, in a place away from worldly distractions and attractions, a place where life is at its simplest and where one can hear God's call. This call is for repentance so that we can be rightly disposed to receive God's forgiveness. John confers a baptism which is to help bring us to that required state of repentance and which is symbolic of a personal conversion and the start of a new way of living. He is aware that he is a herald of the Lord who wants the obstacles cleared away so that he can come to us, as Isaiah prophesied.

Of course, when Christ does come into our lives, the baptism we receive is not that of John. Rather, it is the sacrament of baptism that gives us not only pardon for sin but also an indwelling of the Holy Spirit, and indeed of the Trinity. Moreover, the sacrament makes us sharers in Christ's priesthood, members of Christ's Church and adopted sons and daughters of the Father. So those who became disciples of John the Baptist would hear about the messiah who was coming and would have the perfect opportunity to become disciples of the messiah also. Although now we do not follow that route to Christ, the testimony of John the Baptist retains its power to direct us towards him and to enrich our faith in the divine mission of Jesus Christ.

John's citation from the prophecy of Isaiah (40:3-5) is also to be found in the other three gospels. It originates in what is known as Second Isaiah or Deutero-Isaiah, that part of the prophecy which dates from the sixth century BC. The original sense of the citation is that, just as, centuries earlier, God had led the Israelites through the desert on their way from slavery in Egypt to the promised land, so again he would lead his people from exile in Babylon to their homeland in Israel. This interpretation was widened subsequently by both Jews and Christians to be a proclamation about the messiah whom God would send to lead his people through the wilderness or desert of their lives to the kingdom of God.

It is interesting to note that the historical details which Luke mentions at the start of today's passage permitted scholars to calculate the date of Christ's birth. The first to do so was Dionysius Exiguus in the sixth century and it is from his calculations that we have our numbering of the years. Unfortunately, his calculations were not accurate. We know that King Herod the Great was alive when Jesus was born and we are certain that he died in the year 4 BC, so we have to place our Lord's birth as occurring at some time between 8 and 4 BC, but precisely when is unknown.

The first reading is from the prophet Baruch (5:1-9), an associate of Jeremiah. It speaks of the time when Jerusalem will be a place of peace, integrity and honour. God will prepare the way for exiles to return and the city will enjoy God's protective care and love. We see this passage as explicitly messianic.

In the second reading, Paul assures the Philippians (1:3-6.8-11) of his esteem for their fidelity to the Good News. He looks forward to their faith and love growing even deeper as they await 'the Day of Christ', a reference to the *parousia*.

THIRD SUNDAY OF ADVENT – Year C

Luke 3:10-18

This is a continuation of the gospel reading of last Sunday. John the Baptist proclaimed then 'a baptism of repentance for the forgiveness of sins' in preparation for the arrival of the messiah. Today, the people ask him to tell them exactly what they had therefore to do. John gives several examples which indicate that people should fulfil their duties honestly and show a willingness to help those in need.

To dispel any suggestion that he was the messiah, John the Baptist then declares clearly that he is not; in fact the messiah is superior to him and his power is much greater. He will have the ability to separate the wheat from the chaff; in other words, the good people from those who are evil and thus bound for rejection. Moreover, says John, while he, John, baptises with water, the messiah's baptism will be 'with the Holy Spirit and fire'. The presence of the Holy Spirit is an indication of the divine involvement which the messiah's baptism will have; the meaning of fire in this context is difficult to explain – perhaps to indicate the purifying effect of the Spirit's presence or, alternatively, a reference to the fate of the evil people, the chaff that will be consigned to burn. The extract ends with the statement that what has been reported is only a sampling of the content of John the Baptist's preaching.

It is noticeable that, in telling the people what they have to do in preparation for the messiah, John does not order them to undertake new duties or to change the way they live; nor is there a call to new religious activities. The advice is that they should continue to do what they are doing already, but to do it with thoughtfulness for others and with honesty. This advice is still completely relevant for us. Especially in today's world, where there are so many people who are victims of injustice or who live lives of destitution or in the midst of violence, we must show our concern for them. And this will mean our readiness to share our excess wealth or possessions as well as trying always to ensure that our actions do not, either directly or indirectly, contribute to the sufferings of others. Today's gospel reading is a Lenten call to conversion of life (*metanoia*) that is an appropriate reminder in the midst of Christmas preparations in our affluent world. It also should remind us that everything that we have comes as a gift from God. We need to be thankful. We cannot express our gratitude better than by acting on our reflections in today's gospel.

The first reading is from the prophet Zephaniah (3:14-18). The chosen passage looks forward to an era of liberation for Israel, when God will be present with the people, and bringing peace and prosperity.

St Paul's message (Philippians 4:4-7) is that we should be happy, enjoying the grace of God's peace and trustingly asking God in prayer for whatever we need.

FOURTH SUNDAY OF ADVENT – Year C

Luke 1:39-45

Finally, the chosen gospel passage takes us to the time shortly before the birth of Jesus. Although Mary is pregnant with Jesus, she sets out on the hazardous journey to be with her cousin, Elizabeth, an older woman and herself unexpectedly pregnant. There is a tradition that Elizabeth, along with her husband, the priest Zechariah, lived in Ein Karim, a village in the hills a few miles to the north west of Jerusalem (but now a suburb of the city).

Today's passage provides only the fact of Mary's visit and the words with which Elizabeth greeted her cousin. The remainder of the report, which comprises Mary's response to the greeting (the canticle of the *Magnificat*) and the information that her visit lasted three months, is omitted (Luke 1:46-56). But we are told that Elizabeth's unborn child, the future John the Baptist, leapt for joy in her womb at the sound of Mary's greeting and that Elizabeth experienced within herself the presence of the Holy Spirit.

Elizabeth's greeting of Mary is very fulsome, as was fitting, and some of the phrases she employs are now in the *Hail Mary* and are prayed daily by millions of Catholics. In addition, Elizabeth speaks of Mary as 'the mother of my Lord' and 'she who believed', beautiful titles which take us to the source of Mary's greatness. The former title states the objective reason for her greatness; the latter confirms that greatness by reminding us of Mary's humble and trustful faith in her acceptance of the honour. Both phrases give us material for reflection if we can find some free time from all the things that need our attention in these hectic days. They also encourage us to remember that, like Mary, each of us has received a vocation from God and that, in our desire to fulfil it, we cannot do better than imitate Mary in the total trust which she placed in God's help.

An extract from the prophecy of Micah (5:1-4) dating from the eighth century BC provides the first reading. It tells of a ruler of Israel whose reign will be marked with God's protection. This ruler will be born in Bethlehem, 'the least of the clans of Judah' (a description which, in Matthew 2:6, is quoted as 'by no means least among the leaders of Judah').

The second reading (Hebrews 10:5-10) attributes some words from psalm 39/40:6-8 to 'Christ, on coming into the world'. The author's point is that Christ's sacrifice will be very different from those of the Old Law.

THE NATIVITY OF OUR LORD – Years ABC

Luke 2:1-14	Mass during the night
Luke 2:15-20	Dawn Mass
John 1:1-18	Mass during the day

All Scripture readings are common to years A, B and C. The notes are at year A.

THE HOLY FAMILY OF JESUS, MARY AND JOSEPH – Year C

Luke 2:41-52

On this feast, three different events of our Lord's childhood are chosen for the gospel passages of the three years of the Sunday cycle – the flight into Egypt, the presentation in the Temple, and the finding of Jesus in the Temple. The last of the three, today's excerpt, is the only information we have of Jesus between his infancy and his baptism by John the Baptist.

Jews were expected to go to the Temple in Jerusalem to celebrate three annual feasts – Passover, Pentecost and Tabernacles. However, those who lived far away from the city (such as people from Nazareth) were excused from the second and third festivals. In the circumstances, the vexation experienced by Mary and Joseph when they realised that Jesus was lost is very understandable. Perhaps there was a good reason for Jesus not informing his parents of his plan to remain behind; or maybe it was simply that boys of that age forget that parents are likely to be upset when their child is missing. The explanation of his behaviour given by Jesus, that he had 'to be busy with my Father's affairs', could mean various things but, in general, it seems to say that he had a unique bond with his Father and consequently a duty which was independent of all created bonds. At any rate, the gospel tells us that Mary clearly remembered all that had happened; she would not have forgotten Simeon's warning (year B) that, because of her child, a sword of pain would pierce her soul.

The family of Mary, Joseph and Jesus is so atypical that to assert, without qualification, that they serve as a model for other families is rather unhelpful. However, from today's incident, we do learn certain things. In particular, Jesus shows us that a family should not be so bound up in its own affairs that it is oblivious of other matters that may require attention, either because of God's wish or because of the needs of other human beings. To be followers of Christ, to be a Christian family, requires that we should have the desire to imitate Jesus, to continue the work of evangelisation that he began, that we should be active in enabling people to hear the gospel of salvation. Nor must we overlook our own faith which needs nourishment, our prayer which needs constancy, and our worship which needs involvement.

Parents have the sacred duty of educating their children, not only by ensuring that they benefit from what schools provide but also by their own efforts. I am not referring here to knowledge of the sciences or training in 'the three Rs' but, by example and teaching, to develop an awareness of the values that we should have, especially as disciples of Christ. He teaches us to seek for peace and justice in all its forms, to look out for those who are suffering or in need or excluded and, in general, to grow in the desire to show love for all people through our willingness to serve.

Today is an occasion for us to pray for families where there is conflict and dissension, that they may find the way to reconciliation; to pray for families which are already fractured, that God will protect the members from further harm. And of course, we pray for children, that, like Jesus, they will 'increase in wisdom, in stature, and in favour with God and men'. Our prayerful thoughts and anxieties must include children who are victims of abuse, or are in danger of becoming so. And let us not forget couples who long to have children but are childless. Unfortunately, family life in our day seems to be under such constant and increasing threat that it needs all the support that we can give it.

Alternative Scripture passages are available for the first and second readings today.

For the first reading, either the excerpt from Ecclesiasticus (3:2-6.12-14), written in the second century BC, which encourages children to honour, respect and, when necessary, support their parents; or in the first book of Samuel (1:20-22.24-28), we read that Elkanah and Hannah, though unexpectedly, were given the gift of a son, whom they named Samuel. His parents dedicated him for the whole of his life to the Lord.

For the second reading, the first option is from Paul's letter to the Colossians (3:12-21). He encourages them to live amicably with one another, being kind, compassionate, forgiving and helpful. The extract ends with brief advice for harmonious family life.

The second option comes from the first letter of St John (3:1-2.21-24). In his love for us, the Father has made us his adopted children. By living good lives, we can anticipate even greater favours.

SOLEMNITY OF MARY, MOTHER OF GOD – Years ABC

Luke 2:16-21

All Scripture readings are common to years A, B and C. The notes are at year A.

SECOND SUNDAY AFTER CHRISTMAS – Years ABC

John 1:1-18

All Scripture readings are common to years A, B and C. The notes are at year A.

THE EPIPHANY OF THE LORD – Years ABC

Matthew 2:1-12

All Scripture readings are common to years A, B and C. The notes are at year A.

THE BAPTISM OF THE LORD – Year C

Luke 3:15-16.21-22

We have already heard the first half of today's gospel passage. It formed part of the reading for the third Sunday of Advent. The remainder of John the Baptist's declaration about Christ's superiority and a passing reference to Herod Antipas, a son of Herod the Great, (verses 17-20) are omitted from today's reading which proceeds to record Jesus' baptism.

Luke's wording is almost identical with that of Mark. After the mere statement that Jesus was baptised, both evangelists record that the heavens opened, the Spirit came down on Jesus in the form of a dove and a voice from heaven was heard to say, 'You are my Son, the beloved; my favour rests on you'. The only variations between the two accounts are that Luke says that Jesus was praying when the Spirit appeared; and Mark reports that Jesus saw the Spirit descending like a dove while Luke omits to mention that Jesus saw this happen. Matthew's account is also very similar to that of the other two synoptics.

The fourth gospel reports the baptism of Jesus (1:29-34) but the wording is different from that of the synoptics. The appearance of the Spirit in the form of a dove is reported and John the Baptist's declaration, 'I am the witness that he is the Chosen One of God', words with a meaning not greatly different from those of 'the voice from heaven', reported in the other accounts.

John the Baptist, while awaiting the arrival of Jesus and throughout the time that they were together at the Jordan, was very insistent that his cousin was superior to him and that he was only the herald and not the messiah himself. Perhaps the most important evidence of this difference, again declared by John, is that those who were baptised with Jesus' baptism would receive the Holy Spirit (who had come on Jesus after John baptised him).

Today, therefore, when we are reminded that we have been baptised and that it was Christ's baptism which we received; we should not forget that, in receiving the sacrament, we received, and still have dwelling in us, the Holy Spirit. This is not only a privilege and an honour but should also be life-changing or life-determining. Our relationship to God becomes no longer that of slaves but of adopted sons and daughters. We enjoy a freedom with God so that our observance of God's commandments is not because of fear but comes from the mutual love between us. Religious duties are carried out not as obligations that we must fulfil to avoid punishment but from a real desire to worship a loving God, to thank a generous God, to ask pardon of a forgiving God. This is true not only of us as individuals but also when we gather in the community that is the church.

Today there are alternatives for both the first and second readings.

From the 'Book of the Consolation of Israel' in the second half of the prophecy of Isaiah (sixth century BC), we have part of the first 'Song of the Servant of the Lord' (Isaiah 42:1-4.6-7). This figure, seen by Christians as foretelling Christ the Messiah, is a faithful servant of God who 'brings true justice to the nations'.

The alternative first reading is from the same source (Isaiah 40:1-5.9-11) and also announces the 'Consolation of Israel'. The assurance of a new presence of God with his people refers primarily to the Jews' return from Babylonian exile, but for Christians it is also an assurance of the coming of the messianic age.

The apostle Peter (Acts 10:34-38), after the coming of the Spirit at Pentecost, declares that 'God does not have favourites' and 'Jesus Christ is Lord of all'. Baptism and salvation are for gentiles as well as for Jews.

The alternative second reading is from Paul's letter to Titus (2:11-14; 3:4-7). He teaches that God has sent Jesus to be the saviour of all humanity. This salvation is given to us 'by means of the cleansing water of rebirth and by renewing us with the Holy Spirit'.

Lent and Easter

ASH WEDNESDAY – Years ABC

Matthew 6:1-6.16-18

All Scripture readings are common to years A, B and C. The notes are at year A.

FIRST SUNDAY OF LENT – Year C

Luke 4:1-13

Each year the gospel reading for the first Sunday of Lent is the account of how Jesus, after being baptised by John the Baptist, went into the Judean desert or wilderness and spent forty days there alone. While there, he was tempted by the devil. The gospel passage which is read today comes from St Luke. One characteristic of Luke's gospel is the stress he lays at various points on the presence of the Holy Spirit with Jesus, guiding and motivating him. An example of this comes at the very start of today's passage. We consider the three temptations of the devil, given by Luke in a different order from that in Matthew's report (4:1-11); Mark does not detail the temptations (1:12-13).

In the first temptation, the devil urges Jesus to turn some stones into bread in order to satisfy his hunger. Then, Jesus is tempted to worship Satan in order to gain glory by having power over many nations. Finally, the devil urges Jesus to jump from the high parapet of the Temple wall in Jerusalem as a sign of the divine care given to the messiah. Jesus, of course, spurns each of the temptations in turn. He is the messiah, but he has come not to satisfy his own needs (first temptation), not to be a worldly and powerful monarch (second temptation) and not to seek fame for his spectacular abilities done with the help of God's angels (third temptation). Having survived the devil's blandishments, Jesus was left in peace. (Most exegetes suggest that the temptations all occurred in the desert rather than Jesus being physically moved from place to place.) Luke's account ends ominously: 'the devil left him, to return at the appointed time'.

The three temptations which Jesus endured were designed to appeal to a person's comfort or vanity. These are qualities totally absent from Christ's human nature, of course, but it would be useful to examine our own consciences on the matter and even consider how they may be present in the activities of the local church to which we belong.

In regard to the first temptation, it is obvious that we ought not to overeat; but what about the millions of our fellow humans who never get enough to eat? Do we as individuals or as our parish community do anything to share our plenty with them? The problem of food shortages as well as a lack of nourishing food is no longer found only in poor countries. There are people in this affluent country of ours who have to resort to food banks.

Someone with a desire to use power for his own advantage would be attracted by the second temptation. People have authority to be exercised for the benefit of others, whether in the family or more widely through appointment or election. The latter category includes not only public civil authority, but power and authority in the parish or diocese. God, the supreme authority, treats us always with love and mercy, as Jesus constantly proclaimed and exemplified. He never imposes himself, he acts consistently with gentleness, he attracts to his company the poor, the marginalised, the rejected. In our family and in our parish community, is there an atmosphere of calm, of peace, of acceptance and of mutual help and support?

The third temptation was meant for someone seeking to be a centre of attraction. Many of us have such a desire and it is frequently to be detected where people gather in groups of one kind or another. 'Showing off' is part of it and, while it is perhaps natural in young children, it is unsuitable in grown ups. Yet it exists, does it not? The quest for fame, prestige, honours, promotion – Pope Francis recently spoke about such matters to the Roman Curia. It is a danger for many people, including members of the clergy. And yet, Jesus famously told us that he had come to serve, not to be served.

Resisting temptation can sometimes be very difficult. We all know that to be tempted is not sinful; in fact, unless we have sought temptation, or what are called the dangerous occasions of sin, the time of temptation is a time of trial. It is reassuring to know that we have the presence of the Holy Spirit to enable us to resist, the same Spirit as was with Jesus during his forty days in the desert and his rejection of the temptations of Satan.

The first reading is a passage in the book of Deuteronomy (26:4-10) in which Moses is instructing the people that, when they reach the promised land, they have to make an annual offering of the first fruits of the land to God in worship and gratitude.

St Paul, in the letter to the Romans (10:8-13), teaches that all, gentiles as well as Jews, will be saved if they confess that Jesus is Lord and believe that God raised him from the dead.

SECOND SUNDAY OF LENT – Year C

Luke 9:28-36

Like the first Sunday of Lent with its gospel of Jesus in the desert (each of the synoptics' accounts being given its year), so the second Sunday of Lent follows the same arrangement, the subject being Christ's transfiguration. The three reports are very similar, although Luke (today's evangelist), is the only one to tell us that the three apostles present had to fight off sleep during the transfiguration and alone does not report that their decision, at least at the time, not to share their experience with anyone else was at the request of Jesus. Perhaps more significantly, Luke alone reports the topic on which Jesus spoke with Moses and Elijah – his 'passing', to be accomplished in Jerusalem.

Peter's proposal of erecting three tents is probably connected with the Jewish custom at the feast of Tabernacles. This was an annual feast of rejoicing at the harvest and vintage when the people set up tents (sometimes called tabernacles or booths) for themselves in the fields, these tents being later seen also as commemorating the Jews' years in the desert on the way to the promised land.

Some commentators suggest that Peter's proposal about tents was not followed because the transfiguration was meant to exhibit not the equality of Jesus, Moses and Elijah but that the two earlier figures were, in their way, precursors of the messiah. Since the Old Testament is sometimes descriptively called 'the Law and the Prophets', Moses is understood as representing the law and Elijah the prophets. On this occasion, they share in the reflected glory and brilliance of Jesus, and it is to him alone that the voice of the Father refers: 'listen to him'.

The words of the preface in today's Mass are instructive. 'After he had told the disciples of his coming death, on the holy mountain he manifested to them his glory, to show, even by the testimony of the law and the prophets, that the passion leads to the glory of the resurrection'. The transfiguration, and especially the Father's words, are a reassurance to Jesus himself and to his closest friends that the road to Jerusalem, leading to his suffering and death, were in accordance with the Father's plan.

The transfiguration, with its assurance that suffering is the prelude to glory, can be a paradigm for us in our lives also. During Lent, we exercise self-denial in order to die to selfishness and sin, so that, with the risen Christ we may experience the new life of the baptised, faithful and converted.

Moreover, a somewhat similar pattern can be discerned in many other areas of our lives. We all, from time to time, have bitter experiences, whether through pain, failure, doubt, worry or sinfulness. But, as adopted brothers and sisters of Christ, through him and with him, we are offered the grace of 'Mount Tabor experiences' to reassure us of God's caring providence. Such experiences can come to us in a whole variety of ways, perhaps during Lent, or at a Sunday Mass, or when receiving the sacrament of reconciliation or at any other special moment, great or small.

The first reading is from the book of Genesis (15:5-12.17-18), the first book of the Scriptures and the first of the Pentateuch, the others being Exodus, Leviticus, Numbers and Deuteronomy and which together comprise the *Torah* (the Law). In this reading, God makes a solemn covenant with Abram that he will have innumerable descendants and that they will have all the land from the border of Egypt to the Euphrates.

Paul pleads with the Philippians (3:17-4:1) that they imitate him and remain faithful to Christ's teaching. If we do, Christ, our saviour, will 'transfigure' our bodies so that they become like his.

THIRD SUNDAY OF LENT – Year C

Even in years B and C, the Scripture readings of year A can be used on the third, fourth and fifth Sundays of Lent, if preferred in place of those appointed to be read. If there are to be baptisms at the Easter Vigil, the year A readings should always be used on the three Sundays.

Luke 13:1-9

Nothing is known from other sources of the two events which were the topic of Jesus' comments to the people listening to him, as narrated in today's gospel passage. Both events involved tragic loss of life. The first also had an element of sacrilege in the fact that some people from Galilee had been killed by the Roman authorities in the temple precincts in Jerusalem and their blood mingled with that of the animals sacrificed. Siloam is a pool in Jerusalem, at that time inside the walls of the city; the tower which collapsed must have been nearby.

Jesus makes the point that disasters such as the two mentioned, whether occurring naturally or as the result of people's deliberate actions, are not to be seen as God's way of inflicting his punishment on sinners. Nevertheless, Jesus adds that, since God will punish unrepentant sinners and by his own methods, those who brought up the subject of the disasters should repent.

The gospel extract then recounts one of the parables of Jesus, that of the unproductive fig tree. The parable has some connection with the foregoing teaching about the need for us, sinners, to repent. In fact, however, the parable demonstrates God's patience with us and his reluctance to bring punishment upon our heads. This parable seems somewhat at odds with the reaction of Jesus to the actual unproductive fig tree which he encountered on one occasion near Bethany (Mark 11:12-14; Matthew 21:18-19).

There are still those who, when they experience, or hear about, a disaster or misfortune are inclined to attribute it to God's displeasure for sin or some other kind of bad behaviour. Such reasoning is very misguided but also deep rooted. It is related to the ancient belief that the sins of the fathers are visited on the sons and daughters. Another reaction to a tragedy or accident, and especially if the victims are totally innocent people, is to ask questions such as 'Where was God when this occurred?' or 'Why did God allow this to happen?' God normally allows natural causes or free will to take their courses without his divine intervention to stop them. And such questioning seems to be in danger of setting out on the road to doubting God's goodness and even existence.

The parable of the fig tree would have had immediate relevance for Christ's listeners, given the climate of the country and the familiarity of most of the people with the various kinds of fruit trees that were cultivated. The plans of the employee to give the tree another chance – digging around it to loosen the ground and feed it with manure – translate to the graces that a sinner could be given to help him to produce the fruit of repentance, graces such as conversion of life, aided by prayer, fasting and almsgiving.

Notice also that the three years the owner has waited in vain plus one more year is a short time in comparison to the patience of God who waits a lifetime for our conversion. Sometimes I wonder, since sin is seldom spoken about nowadays, if people can become unaware of it or complacent ('I'm not going to die yet') so that it never enters their thoughts as an issue to be faced.

In the first reading (Exodus 3:1-8.13-15), Moses meets God for the first time and is sent to be the deliverer of his people from slavery in Egypt. God instructs him that, when the people ask who sent him to lead them, he is to say that it is 'I am who I am'.

In the first letter to the Corinthians (10:1-6.10-12), Paul teaches that, despite all the helps which God gave to the Jews on their trek to the promised land, many of them sinned and perished during the journey. All that should be a lesson and a warning for us.

FOURTH SUNDAY OF LENT – Year C

Luke 15:1-3.11-32

The disdain with which the religious elite of the Jews viewed the low types who seemed to be happy in the company of Jesus is the context of what is probably the favourite of all Christ's parables. Let us consider its three characters.

The younger son is selfish and inconsiderate to his father. He is sinful and foolish with the result that his life degenerates to a condition of desperation. Necessity and fear force him to return home and seek forgiveness. Am I that younger son? If so, where am I on that journey?

The father loves both of his sons and shows his love of the younger by his willingness to give him his freedom, by longing for his return, by his ready forgiveness and by his enthusiastic welcome. The father also loves the older son and this is clear from their years together, living contentedly in each other's company. Further evidence of the father's love for his older son is provided by his earnest attempts to explain to him why he has welcomed his brother so unreservedly and by his appeals to him to share his joy at the other's return. The father obviously represents God our loving Father.

The older son thinks that he loves his father and that he has faithfully carried out his duties to his father. Yet, when his brother returns and is welcomed, he is full of anger. Any love for his brother evaporates in his resentment. He is embittered and unhappy at the other's good fortune which he considers totally undeserved. To increase his displeasure, he considers that, not only has the returning sinner been treated with ridiculous leniency but that he himself has been taken for granted and his father has unjustly deprived him of what he should have received to reward him for his fidelity. Am I that older son? Can I change my attitude before it is too late?

Remember how today's reading began. Jesus was telling the religious leaders of the day that, despite the faithful performance of their prayers and duties, despite their punctilious observance of the commandments, they were lacking in love and compassion for those whom they considered less holy than they were. They made no effort to approach them, to help them, to share with them. Their behaviour repelled the unfortunate people who gathered round Jesus. There is a very powerful lesson for us in the attitude of those religious men. We have a duty to evangelise and to catechise; but that will never be successful unless, first of all, we are people who love all our brothers and sisters as God loves them and us, and as Jesus shows us how.

In the first reading (Joshua 5:9-12), the Jews have finally reached the promised land. They celebrate the feast of Passover and begin to enjoy the produce of their new home.

In the second letter to the Corinthians (5:17-21), Paul tells us that, through Christ's work of salvation, we have been reconciled to God. 'It is all God's work', says Paul, and he appeals to us, in our turn, to be reconciled to God.

FIFTH SUNDAY OF LENT – Year C

John 8:1-11

The scene for today's gospel passage is the Temple in Jerusalem during the seven days of the joyful feast of Tabernacles (*Succoth* or Booths, a harvest festival which also commemorated the Israelites' years in the desert wilderness). There is a consensus among scholars that the report of the event is not by John himself (it is not found in many of the early copies of his gospel, and the style is different from John's) but is an insertion by an unknown author, out of context and perhaps referring to a different time of the year. Nonetheless, it is accepted by the Church as 'canonical' (that is authentically part of Scripture).

We can reflect on the event from several viewpoints; either from the particular details themselves; or from the event being seen as typical of the differences between Jesus and the religious leaders of the time; or as an opportunity to consider in general the treatment of women by those who have power or authority. Let us take the various viewpoints in their order.

The book of Deuteronomy decrees death for women who have committed adultery, but the method of execution is unspecified, except for a betrothed virgin who was to be killed by stoning (22:22-24). The purpose of the Pharisees bringing the woman to Jesus follows a familiar pattern – their intention is to trap Jesus into a dilemma, so that any answer he gives to their question will be to his embarrassment. However, Jesus does not give a direct answer, but his response is enough to put an end to the confrontation. What Jesus wrote on the ground (the only example in the gospels of his having written) is unknown. Left alone with the woman, Jesus recognises that she has sinned but with gentle courtesy forgives her, with the admonition that she should give up her way of life.

The incident is a good example of the contrast between the religious leaders and Jesus. Many of the former group (mainly Pharisees and scribes, although there are several examples in the New Testament of those people showing an interest in Jesus and his teaching) saw themselves as rigidly observant of all the commandments and precepts of the law and with a duty of trying to ensure that others were similarly obedient; and, if not, that they were properly corrected and punished. Jesus had a much more relaxed attitude to people. He was non-judgmental, he forgave sinners, he mixed with those who (in the eyes of the religious officials) were disreputable in their employment or conduct, he considered that man-made laws were not of absolute validity in every circumstance, and he taught and preached a way of life and a regime that promised eternal salvation for all. Inevitably, the Jewish leaders considered Jesus an unholy interloper, a fraudulent and loose-living danger to proper religion, even a blasphemer who claimed to have a relationship with God and to have divine powers. For Jesus, his opponents were hypocrites who used their positions and their power to control and oppress the people.

Widening our consideration to the ill-treatment of women in general would be a huge undertaking, well beyond the scope of this book. Perhaps it is sufficient to make two points. The first is that the ill-treatment of women is not only a matter of past history. It is still very prevalent in today's world and women suffer violence, injustice and unfairness in many countries and in many areas of life, ranging from the trivial to the very serious indeed. The second point is to welcome the recognition by many in the Catholic Church, including Pope Francis himself, that the position and treatment of women in the Church must be examined and, where necessary, corrected. There is the question of ordination to holy orders, of course, and that is a special matter different from others; but it is by no means the only area that requires serious and sympathetic examination.

In Deutero-Isaiah (43:16-21), God, who once drowned the army of Egypt in the Red Sea, proclaims that he will provide his people, now in exile, with the roads and water they will need to return to their land.

St Paul, in the letter to the Philippians (3:8-14), reflects on his gift of faith in Christ that enables him to look forward, after he has shared in the suffering and death of Christ, to reaching the perfection of sharing also in his resurrection.

PALM SUNDAY OF THE PASSION OF THE LORD – Year C

Luke 19:28-40
Luke 22:14-23:56

Fuller notes on Jesus' entry to Jerusalem, the Last Supper, his trial, passion and death are found at the corresponding place of year A. The notes here are some observations on Luke's account of these events.

There are several instances in the Old Testament of a royal person entering a town peacefully, mounted on a colt. The disciples and the crowd welcome Jesus with two lines from psalm 117/118:26; but instead of Mark's further quotation from the psalm, calling God's blessing on 'the kingdom of our father David!' and then adding the acclamation 'Hosanna in the highest heavens!', Luke inserts a quotation from the angels' song at Jesus' birth (Luke 2:14). Luke alone mentions the Pharisees' request to Jesus and his reply (19:39-40); it is uncertain whether the request is friendly or not. Jesus' response is a reference to the noise of the future destruction of the city.

In Luke's account of the Last Supper, Christ's discourses are more prominent than they are in Mark and Matthew, as if foreshadowing the discourses in John. Luke also clearly distinguishes the Passover rites (22:15-18) from the institution of the Eucharist (22:19-20). Only John's account has Jesus taken to Annas (the high priest emeritus and father-in-law of Caiaphas). Both Mark and Matthew have Jesus before Caiaphas late at night after his arrest in the garden, but Luke delays the appearance before Caiaphas and the council of the Sanhedrin until the next morning (22:66-71).

Luke provides more details of Jesus' trial before Pilate than do Mark and Matthew, but fewer than John. Luke alone mentions Jesus being taken to Herod Antipas; the source of this information is unknown. When Jesus is returned to Pilate from Herod, the governor-procurator seems very anxious to set him free, according to Luke's account (and John's). Similarly, these two evangelists regard the scourging of Jesus as an attempt to avert the sentence of death. Jesus' remark about green and dry wood, one not meant for burning and the other meant for burning, is a metaphor: if Jesus is not guilty but condemned, then what is to be happen to those who are guilty?

Luke's description of the Calvary scene is somewhat less harsh than Mark's and Matthew's, since he omits the cry 'Why have you deserted me?', he tells of Jesus' pardon for his executioners and the good thief, the bystanders do not jeer but repent at the end, and Jesus dies with a prayer on his lips, (psalm 30/31:5). In this connection, it is interesting that Luke alone relates these three of Christ's 'Seven Last Words'; Mark and Matthew tell of his anguished cry of the opening words of psalm 21/22; only John's account mentions the other three 'Words' (to Mary and John, 'I thirst', and 'It is accomplished').

Today the same first and second readings are used for years A, B and C. Brief notes are given at the appropriate Sunday of year A.

THURSDAY OF THE LORD'S SUPPER – Years ABC

John 13:1-15

All Scripture readings are common to years A, B and C. The notes are at year A.

FRIDAY OF THE PASSION OF THE LORD – Years ABC

John 18:1 – 19:42

All Scripture readings are common to years A, B and C. The notes are at year A.

THE EASTER VIGIL – Year C

Luke 24:1-12

The notes are at year A.

EASTER SUNDAY – Years ABC

John 20:1-9

All Scripture readings are common to years A, B and C. The notes are at year A.

SECOND SUNDAY OF EASTER – Year C

John 20:19-31

The gospel reading is the same as for the corresponding Sunday of year A. The notes are at year A.

The first reading is from the Acts of the Apostles (5:12-16), as is the case for the next six Sundays. Today, we hear that the early disciples were greatly admired and attracted many more people to faith in Christ. The apostles earned a reputation for their ability to heal the sick.

The second reading, as also for the next six Sundays, is from the Apocalypse (1:9-13.17-19). As the name indicates, the style of the book is apocalyptic, that is, cryptic and symbolic rather than narrative or explanatory. It is also prophetic and much of it is concerned with eschatological details, referring to events of the end times. The consequence is that it is often very obscure and difficult not only to understand but even to decipher. It was written towards the very end of the first century AD, by someone called John, perhaps the evangelist himself but more probably a person or persons who knew him.

In today's excerpt, the author introduces himself. He was on Patmos, an island in the Aegean Sea, apparently banished for being a Christian. He has a vision of one who is described in Christ-like details and who orders him to write down what happens in the present and the future.

THIRD SUNDAY OF EASTER – Year C

John 21:1-19

Chapter 21 of John's gospel, the last, is generally regarded as added at a later time since the final verses of the previous chapter seem to be a conclusion to the work. It may have been an afterthought written by John himself or the author may have been one of his followers. The subject of the chapter is an appearance of the risen Lord to some of the disciples. They had been out on the Sea of Galilee at night, fishing but without having had any success. At dawn they are making for land when they spot a figure on the shore.

The story continues. The person on the shore calls to ask if they have caught anything; he tells them to throw their net to starboard; they do so and net a large catch. They recognise that the person advising them is Jesus. Ashore, they discover that Jesus is cooking fish and preparing breakfast for them. They count the catch netted and discover it to be no less than one hundred and fifty-three fish.

The narration then moves to the dialogue between Jesus and Peter, indicating once again the primacy which Peter held among the apostles. 'Peter, do you love me?' 'Yes, Lord, you know I love you.' 'Feed my sheep.' In these or similar words, the exchange continues three times. Finally, Jesus tells Peter that his discipleship will involve following him even to being put to death, the words 'you will stretch out your hands'(verse 18) being a recognised reference to crucifixion. (The Christians for whom the gospel was written, since they lived some decades after Peter's death, would understand the allusion.)

There are a number of details whose explanation we do not know. For example, why had the apostles (at least five of the seven who were out fishing) gone back to their work as fishermen despite the apparently definitive choice made at the start of Jesus' public ministry? Perhaps, in the post-resurrection doubt and confusion, they felt they needed to start earning their living again. Then, although the large number of fish caught symbolises the huge multitude of people to be evangelised, there may be some significance in the precise number but, if there is, it is not known. Again, it is very probable that the triple exchange between Jesus and Peter has reference to Peter's triple denial at the trial of Jesus. Finally, it seems likely that the words 'lambs' and 'sheep' which Jesus uses are interchangeable and do not signify two distinct groups. But the three questions may indicate that Peter is to be the shepherd of every section of the entire flock which belongs to Christ. The passage ends with the words of Jesus: 'Follow me', a phrase which Jesus used when first calling his disciples (Mark 1:17; Matthew 4:19), but now uttered with a meaning which would demand even more of Peter.

Perhaps, however, the principal message that the event conveys is the necessity for Jesus to be present and acknowledged to be present if the activity of the Church is to be successful. If we are not aware of his presence or forget about it, then, like the disciples who caught nothing in his absence, our efforts will be useless. Further, in the darkness of the night the disciples caught nothing. It was only when the light had come that their efforts had success, 'the light' being understood not only of sunrise but also of the need for Christ, 'the Light of the World'.

The first reading (Acts 5:27-32.40-41) tells of the apostles being brought before the Sanhedrin (the religious court of the Jews) accused of breach of the peace due to the disturbance that their preaching had caused. Their defence is that they are fulfilling a duty laid on them by God and that supersedes human regulations. The court's verdict is to admonish them, forbid them to continue their activities and discharge them.

In the Apocalypse (5:11-14), there is a description of the vision seen by the writer. 'The one sitting on the throne' (God the Father) and 'the Lamb' (God the Son) are surrounded by many thousands comprising angels, animals and elders worshipping God, their acclamations taken up by all living things in creation.

FOURTH SUNDAY OF EASTER – Year C

John 10:27-30

Each year the gospel passage for the fourth Sunday of Easter is from chapter 10 of John's gospel. In year A, Jesus calls himself the gate of the sheepfold; in year B, he uses the metaphor of the shepherd. This year, the image is the same but the time is different from the passages of years A and B. The evangelist opens this narrative by stating that the events he is now reporting occurred during the winter feast of Dedication (*Hanukkah*). This feast commemorates the rededication in 165 BC of the Temple, partially destroyed by invading armies during the Maccabean wars. The context of the short passage is a question to Jesus as he was walking in the temple grounds. A group of Jews demanded a clear answer regarding his identity: was he the messiah? His answer is today's gospel reading, which produces a very hostile reaction from those listening to him. They threaten to stone him for blasphemy, since he was claiming to be God. They wanted to have him arrested and put on trial, but Jesus escaped.

In his reply, Jesus had told his listeners that he will lead those whom he calls his sheep to eternal life. He knows them, he received them from the Father, they are secure in his care because, since he and the Father are one, no one can steal from the Father. In this teaching, Jesus also lays down two conditions for being his sheep – we must listen to his voice and we must follow him, conditions which in fact are also true of the relations between a shepherd and his animal flock.

In our times, it is not always easy to discern the voice of Jesus. We live in a world of noise, made not only by machines but also by constant messages, announcements and would-be entertainment and distractions. But there is also the fact that the voice of Jesus, the Good News that he offers, is rather counter-cultural in our times. It is a voice that calls us to service, to selflessness, to gentleness, to care for the poor and the otherwise unwanted and neglected, to take up our cross daily and follow him.

Nor is the practice of following him easy. It requires courage. It means being guided by the same values as guided Jesus, to trust God the Father as he did, to have the same scale of importance as he had, to be free to act as he did, to serve the poor and the have-nots in imitation of him, and to have the same faith and hope as sustained him even in difficult times and places. The danger is that, although we do not lose sight of Jesus, our standards have become more comfortable, more self-centred, less demanding, more in line with those of the society and culture in which we live.

Those who heard Jesus speaking in the temple grounds that day were outraged at what he was saying. They asserted that he was blaspheming. They may also have known that he was challenging them to a way of life they were not prepared to follow. But God forbid that may also be true of us.

Two other routes for reflecting on today's reading might have been taken. We could have considered those who share Christ's work of shepherding – parents, teachers and priests – and how they should fulfil that sacred trust; or we might have raised the issue of the present serious shortage of priests in our country and what should be done to improve the situation.

The early chapters of the Acts of the Apostles describe the first generation of Christians in Palestine. From the thirteenth chapter, the focus shifts to Paul and his missionary travels. Today's first reading (Acts 13:14.43-52) sees him, with his companion Barnabas, on his first journey and at Antioch in Asia Minor. His presence and preaching in the synagogue produce dissension among the Jewish people of the town and, although some gentiles became Christians, Jewish hostility was strong and Paul and Barnabas were expelled.

The reading from the Apocalypse (7:9.14-17) recounts a vision of 'a huge number from every nation' standing in the presence of the Lamb and ceaselessly worshipping God. They are the martyrs of persecutions, now safe and untroubled because the Lamb 'will be their shepherd and will lead them to springs of living water'.

FIFTH SUNDAY OF EASTER – Year C

John 13:31-35

The scene is the Last Supper, Judas has just left to begin his traitorous work and night has fallen. Jesus begins the long talk to his closest disciples, the apostles, which, as reported in John's gospel, continues with few breaks, to the end of the sixteenth chapter. At once, the notion of Christ's glorification, prominent in the fourth gospel, is introduced. His passion, death, resurrection and ascension are all part of his glorification, a process of exaltation that will redound also to the glorification of the Father. In this way also, the Son is to be glorified directly by the Father when he is taken to sit at the Father's right hand. Note that, when referring to himself (verses 31-32), Jesus uses the title 'Son of Man' which he was accustomed to use when speaking of some solemn moment or stage in his own life.

The atmosphere must have been unusually emotional and Jesus, upset at what lay ahead of him, would also have felt very affectionate and anxious towards the apostles to whom he was bidding farewell, leaving them without the constant guidance of his visible presence which they had had since the start of their acquaintance. He addresses them as his little children as he tells them that he has a new commandment to give them. He could also have spoken of the commandment as a gift. 'Love one another; just as I have loved you, you also must love one another' (verse 34). Today's extract ends with Jesus declaring that this love will be the distinguishing sign so that everybody will recognise that they are his disciples. If the lectionary had continued the narrative, we should have heard the apostles express their alarm. Where was he going? Could they not go too? How can they get there?

It is on 'the new commandment' that we should reflect for our own benefit. First of all, why 'new' when, in the Old Law (Leviticus 19:18), the Jews were told by God that they should love one another? The answer to this question lies in the words which Jesus added, 'as I have loved you'. The love which Jesus asks us to show requires us to learn, throughout our lives, how he loved. His love was selfless, concerned, immediate, unconditional and ultimately sacrificial. It sought not only to comfort the victims but to seek to end the injustices or any causes of people's sufferings. His love was for everyone, but with a special intensity towards those who were otherwise neglected of love for whatever reason.

This is the kind of love to which we are called, both as individuals and as communities. It is a difficult challenge; perhaps we must be content to strive towards perfection rather than achieve it, even during a long lifetime. But we must try, and not omitting to pray for God's grace.

It may be something of a digression, but have you noticed that, when we are invited to consider how we should vote at an election (or, in fact, when we are offered a choice in any public forum), the motives put before us seem to be exclusively those which, we are told, would be to our advantage, never to the advantage of the common good or for the benefit of those in need? In this world, utopia is unachievable but it is depressing that it is presumed that we are not interested in anyone but 'me and us'.

In Acts (14:21-27), Paul and Barnabas continue their mission in various towns of Asia Minor, including a return visit to Antioch in Pisidia (from which they had had to leave hurriedly) to encourage the new Christians there despite the difficulties. They then returned to Antioch in Syria, where they reported on their experiences to the church community there.

At the beginning of the final chapter, the reading from the Apocalypse (21:1-5) presents a vision of the end time. The new Jerusalem comes down from heaven, and God will live there with the saints for ever. From his throne, God announces, 'Now I am making the whole of creation new'.

SIXTH SUNDAY OF EASTER – Year C

John 14:23-29

This is another passage from the farewell discourse of Jesus at the Last Supper, a discourse that begins in the thirteenth chapter of John's gospel and occupies the next three chapters. Listening to what Jesus has to say to them, the apostles begin to feel very bewildered and afraid. It is clear that the time which they have spent with Jesus as he taught and healed in many places and as he trained them to continue his work is coming to an end. At table, he had spoken of being betrayed by one of them and of going away somewhere. It is all very disturbing. Such thoughts and feelings must have made the apostles confused and upset as they heard Jesus speak.

Perhaps with the awareness of Judas Iscariot in his mind, Jesus tells them that, if someone loves him, that person will faithfully obey what Jesus taught and that both the Father and Jesus himself will be present in that person. In fact, it is also the Father's intention to send the Holy Spirit to complete Jesus' teaching and to keep his entire teaching fresh in their minds. Included in these reassuring instructions there are other instances of the intimacy and closeness between the divine Father and Son – the teaching which Jesus gives comes from the Father while it is in Jesus' name that the Father will send them the Spirit.

Today's extract also brings us another occasion for Christ's favourite manner of coping with people's fears. 'Peace I bequeath to you', he tells the apostles. But the phrase is not just empty words. He is making a gift to them, not merely expressing his good wishes. He adds that this gift is unique because it is his peace and his alone. Moreover, their love for him should make his going away good news because he is going back to the Father and will also return to them.

In the middle of the passage (at verse 26), Jesus refers to the Holy Spirit as the Advocate. This is a translation, through the Latin, of the Greek noun *parakletos*. Jesus promises to send the Spirit, the Paraclete, who will enable them (and the Church) to bring to mind and to carry out faithfully all that Christ taught. Another title which Christ gives to the third Person of the Trinity is 'Spirit of Truth', helping us to appreciate something of the mystery of Christ, his actions, his words, his fulfilment of the Scriptures – in fact all that would otherwise remain obscure. This enables the Spirit to be a witness, to bear testimony to Christ. The two titles of the Spirit are closely and unsurprisingly related.

Reflection on these verses from the farewell discourse of our Lord can provide us, the Church today, with real encouragement and reassurance. Our call to evangelise and catechise is daunting; it would be beyond us without divine help. But clearly Jesus intends that his words about the presence and activity of the Holy Spirit should be understood as a gift for the Church as it continues through time, and not concluding when the apostles died.

The words of Jesus (in verse 23) that, 'if anyone loves me, he will keep my word', can be taken to extend not only to one's own personal beliefs and conduct but also to what one teaches others in carrying out the work of evangelisation and catechesis. Consequently, provided we are properly motivated and do what we can to be aware of the truthfulness and accuracy of what we wish to share with others, the work can be carried out confidently and without fear or embarrassment.

It seems to me, then, that today's gospel reading should 'inspire' us (in the literal sense of 'putting the Spirit in us') to remove the reluctance that many feel with regard to sharing our faith with others. In that case, perhaps we shall have the pleasure of attempting something new and fulfilling in order to show our love for our Lord and Saviour.

And let's remember that when we (singly or the whole community) lost the peace that Christ has given us, it is right to seek to regain it by clearing our hearts of resentment, fear and anger and by asking the Holy Spirit to restore Christ's peace to our hearts.

In the first reading (Acts 15:1-2.22-29), the Christians in Antioch are thrown into confusion by some from Jerusalem claiming that, for salvation, Christian men had to be circumcised as had been decreed by Moses. Paul and Barnabas need to go to Jerusalem to discover the alleged demand to have been mistaken.

The author of the Apocalypse (21:10-14.22-23) relates a vision of the new Jerusalem coming down from heaven. Its walls had twelve gates for the twelve tribes of Israel and twelve foundation stones for the twelve apostles. It had no temple because God the Father and the Lamb were themselves the temple.

THE ASCENSION OF THE LORD – Year C

Luke 24:46-53

For this feast, the principal text must be from the first chapter of the Acts of the Apostles (1:1-11). That report forms the first reading in all three years, A, B and C. The synoptic gospels also refer to the event and the three references form the gospels of the three years.

With regard to the date and place of the ascension, the gospels and the Acts of the Apostles offer differing accounts which suggest that the details given are presented for symbolic reasons or to show fulfilment of Old Testament prophecy, and not with the intention of providing factual information. The place named varies between Galilee and the Mount of Olives, near Jerusalem; and the time or date depends on whether Jesus is reckoned to have returned at once to the Father after he rose glorified (though able, when he wished, to be present to the apostles in the glorified state which made him difficult to recognise) or if it is supposed that there was a gap of some (forty?) days between the resurrection and the ascension.

Luke's narrative, without giving any indication of a time lapse between the events, recounts the arrival of the disciples from Emmaus to tell the others what had happened there, the sudden appearance of the risen Jesus himself in their midst and his insistence that salvation was to be 'preached to all the nations, beginning with Jerusalem'. This will be their task, but not until they have been given the Spirit. The narrative then reports that they all went to the Mount of Olives area, where Jesus blessed them 'and was carried up to heaven'. The Eleven worshipped him and returned joyfully to the city.

The report is brief and discloses few details, although it must be remembered that Luke also wrote the Acts of the Apostles. There, the report, given so succinctly in the gospel, is somewhat more detailed (1:1-14). The statement (verse 3) that 'for forty days he had continued to appear to them' may mean, either, that it was only after that time that he returned to the Father, or alternatively, that he retuned to the Father when he rose from the dead and continued to appear on earth for a further forty days.

The point has been made by some writers that one reason why Jesus ceased to be with the apostles in the constant manner as he had been before his death was to ensure that the apostles would assume a mature responsibility for the task they had been given of teaching, healing and sanctifying worldwide. As long as Jesus was visibly with them and leading them, it would be hard for them to feel a mature responsibility and to go out all over the world. Of course, they would not be left unaided – Father, Son and Holy Spirit would be with them – the Spirit in particular being the guarantor that their work would be authentically faithful to the teaching of Jesus.

For today's second reading, there are two options, one from Paul's letter to the Ephesians and the other from the letter to the Hebrews.

In the first option (1:17-23), St Paul prays that God may give us a vivid awareness of the inheritance that awaits us as a result of what God did to save us through raising Jesus from the dead and investing him with all authority as head of the Church, his body.

The second option (9:24-28; 10:19-23) contrasts the priests of the Old Law with Christ, the priest of the new covenant. The former had to enter the sanctuary each year with the sacrifice of the blood of animals; Christ enters once into heaven and into the actual presence of God to present for ever the sacrifice of his own blood. And because of this, we too have the right to enter the sanctuary and by a new opening which is his body.

SEVENTH SUNDAY OF EASTER – Year C

John 17:20-26

The seventeenth chapter of John's gospel is entirely devoted to the prayer which Jesus offers to his Father on the eve of his passion and death. It comes at the end of the long discourse which the fourth gospel locates as an address which Jesus gave to the apostles at the Last Supper. The lectionary divides the prayer into three sections.

In year A, the first part of the prayer has Jesus asking the Father, 'the hour has come: glorify your Son so that your Son may glorify you'. Jesus sees this process of glorification as beginning while he is on earth and particularly in his death on the cross, and being completed in his resurrection, ascension and return in triumph to the Father. The prayer then goes on to pray for his closest collaborators, the apostles. This part of his prayer, interceding for the apostles, begun in the year A gospel reading, is continued throughout the whole of the section read in year B.

In year C, the final part of the prayer shows Jesus widening his petition to include all those who, through his disciples' teaching, will believe in him. His prayer to the Father becomes universal and permanent; it is extended worldwide and down through the ages to us and beyond. The object of his prayer is that 'they may all be one . . . as you are in me and I am in you'. Jesus prays also that he may be present within this unity. He asks for this so that, as he says, 'the world' may believe that he was sent by the Father to be its saviour, that he lives in the glory acquired by his work on earth, and that he has 'loved them as much as you love me'. The prayer ends with Jesus declaring that his work of revealing the Father will go on – it is for this that he has provided for others to continue that mission. And in this way he, and the Father's love for him – a love which is the very basis of their unity – will be present in those who are his followers.

It is natural, and right, that, when we read or hear this prayer of Jesus for his followers to be united, we lament the disunity that exists among Christians. No one knows for certain how much of a scandal (in the strict sense of being a stumbling block or obstacle) this disunity is for those who might be attracted to faith in Christ; unfortunately, it must be a powerful deterrent. But, apart from that, the very fact that unity is Christ's wish and yet it does not exist is wrong. It ought to exist and, at least in theory, we should all want it to exist, but . . . .

The Catholic Church, facing this situation, made this declaration: 'Christ's only Church . . . constituted and organised as a society in the present world, subsists in the Catholic Church, which is governed by the successor of Peter and by the bishops in communion with him' (Second Vatican Council, Constitution on the Church, *Lumen Gentium*, §8). Quoting this declaration, the *Catechism of the Catholic Church* points out that the Council added that 'many elements of sanctification and truth are found outside the visible confines of the Catholic Church . . . and are in themselves calls to Catholic unity' (*Catechism of the Catholic Church*, §819).

A very great deal more could be said on this important subject, but perhaps that is enough at this present place. May we, both individually and as members of our local churches, genuinely do all that we can, by prayer and action, to bring about that sacred unity for which Jesus prayed and which he will always desire for the disciples whom he loves so much.

In the reading from Acts (7:55-60) which provides the first reading, we hear the climax of the story of the deacon Stephen, the first martyr.

The second reading gives us the final verses of the Apocalypse (22:12-14.16-17.20). The author hears the voice of Jesus announcing his second coming on earth, to which the Spirit and Christ's Bride, the Church, in the name of all who long for him, respond 'Come, come Lord Jesus'.

PENTECOST SUNDAY – Year C

John 20:19-23 or
John 14:15-16; 23-26

In the Acts of the Apostles (2:1-11), Luke gives us a description of Pentecost and the coming of the Holy Spirit on the apostles, a description with which we are familiar. It strikes us at first as something of a surprise when we realise that, in one of the options for today's gospel reading, John indicates that the Holy Spirit was given to the apostles on Easter – and he, John, was there! There is apparently a conflict here due principally to the fact that the human authors of the Scriptures were intending to teach the actual mysterious events themselves and not the accurate chronology. When Jesus rose from the dead, it is clear that he lived a different and glorified human existence (the apostles had difficulty in recognising him, he was able to appear and disappear without being seen to make his way in the normal manner, nor was he constantly in the apostles' presence). The conclusion is that, when he rose he also returned to the Father, and that the 'forty days' is not the period before he went to the Father but the period during which he made appearances to the apostles (as well as being with the Father). When he was with the Father, they could together send the Holy Spirit on the nascent Church. Perhaps, then, it may be that, in imitation of the two Jewish feasts of Passover and Pentecost, the early Christians did the same in their (separate) liturgical observances of the resurrection and the coming of the Spirit. Our custom, therefore, of having separate liturgical observance of resurrection, ascension and descent of the Spirit gives us the advantage of being able to reflect more carefully on the meaning of each mystery.

In the first gospel option (John 20:19-23), we hear that Jesus came to the disciples on Easter Sunday evening and, of course, they were overjoyed. His next words are important. He gives them the same mission as the Father had given him – to reach out to those in need, to bring forgiveness and freedom to those who are oppressed by sin or injustice, to give them the new life of the sacraments – and he shows the wounds of his crucified body to show that the task requires total and unconditional commitment. Since he is very aware of their weakness and inexperience and as he will no longer be visibly present with them to lead, he confers on them the Holy Spirit, the Paraclete, the Advocate, literally to be their inspiration in fulfilling their mission even to death.

The gospel links the words of Jesus conferring the Spirit to his giving the Church the power to forgive sin in his name. While this particular privilege is exercised only by those who have a share in Christ's ministerial priesthood, the same Spirit is given to us all in baptism and confirmation in order that we take our share in continuing the mission of Christ and doing so in countless ways.

Prayer addressed to the Holy Spirit is not common in the Church's liturgy, but it does occur, perhaps most notably in the so called sequence (*Veni, Sancte Spiritus*) at Mass on Pentecost Sunday and in various other hymns. Best known of these are *Veni, Creator*

Spiritus and, in English, *Come, Holy Ghost, Creator, come*. And the conclusion of the collect prayers at Mass, although addressed to the Father and through the Son, ends with a profession of faith 'in the unity of the Holy Spirit'.

Given our awareness of the essential work of the Holy Spirit in the Church, it would be no bad thing if our prayers were more frequently said directly to the Spirit. For example, prayer that we be more alive to the presence of Jesus among us, more courageous in following his example, more open to accepting change when it is needed. We might also seek the Spirit's help in being constantly reminded of the teaching and message of Jesus so that our witness does not become routine, uninspired and uninspiring, but rather that the gospel we proclaim is genuine good news for a vibrant community of disciples. And what about the mission of Jesus, now committed to us to continue, the mission of building the kingdom of God, a kingdom of justice and peace, of a more caring world in which, sadly, unfairness and greed and violence are still so evident, of a world of generous love for others and especially for those in need? For many of us, the work of the Spirit in the Church and in ourselves remains in the background, even forgotten. So, 'Come, Holy Spirit' into our thoughts and prayers; make us gratefully aware of your loving presence in our midst.

The alternative gospel reading (John 14:15-16.23-26) is, in part, the same passage as we heard two weeks ago (sixth Sunday of Easter). It comes from the farewell discourse which Jesus spoke to the apostles at the Last Supper. His listeners, at least vaguely aware that Jesus was leaving them and that the authorities wanted to be rid of him, were frightened and confused. So Jesus intended to console and encourage them.

He promises them that, in his absence, the Father will give them another advocate to protect and guide them. Asking them to be obedient to his teaching (which comes from the Father), he promises that he and the Father will come and abide in them. Lastly, the extract repeats the promise of an advocate, the Holy Spirit, to complete his (Christ's) teaching and keep them in mind of that teaching in its entirety.

It is good for us to remember that the Holy Spirit performs the same essential functions in the church today. We, the Church, should be aware of that and make use of the divine wisdom and discernment that are readily available at all times. We may also keep in mind that each of us, having received the Spirit at baptism and confirmation and experienced many times a renewal, a fresh outpouring, of the Spirit in our lives, ought to invoke the guidance of the Spirit much more regularly than we do. Above all, there arise crises, choices, important decisions to be made (and sometimes requiring immediate action) – do we remember the presence of the Spirit on such occasions? Or, when ashamed or embarrassed at our lack of ability to explain our faith or courteously respond to an erroneous accusation about it, should we not have remembered that the Spirit dwelling in us could have inspired us if it had occurred to us to seek the help we needed?

The more we know of God, the better will be our appreciation that we live in the presence of wonderful, indestructible, infinite love – the Father of love who wants us whom he has adopted to call him by that trustful name, Father; the Son who could not have shown us greater love than to die for love of us; and the Holy Spirit of love, always ready within us to help us in every danger, to console us in every sorrow and to guide us through life to the eternal happiness that awaits us in God's presence.

The first reading (Acts 2:1-11) is Luke's familiar account, beginning with 'When Pentecost day came round' and providing a graphic description of the coming of the Holy Spirit and of the galvanic effect it had on the apostles and their preaching.

The lectionary offers two passages as options for the second reading.

An extract from the first letter of St Paul to the Corinthians (12:3-7.12-13) provides the first option. He explains the work of the Spirit, both in the great variety of gifts conferred on different people and in the unity of the multitude of people who receive the gifts, all of whom are united in the (mystical) Body of Christ, all baptised in the one Spirit and recipients of that Spirit.

The other option is from Paul's letter to the Romans (8:8-17). Using both titles, the Spirit of God and the Spirit of Christ, Paul tells us that it is the presence in us of the Spirit that makes us belong to Christ. Indeed, with the Spirit living in us, God, who raised Christ from the dead, will also give life to our mortal bodies. We should live by the Spirit and so, avoiding sin, we become God's adopted children, able to cry out 'Abba, Father!' And, because adopted, we also become 'heirs of God and coheirs with Christ, sharing his sufferings so as to share his glory'.

THE MOST HOLY TRINITY – Year C

John 16:12-15

Since the Blessed Trinity, three distinct and equal Persons but only one God, is the most sublime mystery of all, it is totally beyond our power to understand. Faith, belief, is the only way in which we can know anything about the Trinity; and our belief arises from what God himself has revealed to us. Most of what the Scriptures reveal is concerned not with the interior life of the Trinity and the relationships between and among the Persons, but rather with the activities and relationships between God and creation, including ourselves. These activities and relationships, though perhaps originating in the Trinity, are often attributed, in the Scriptures or by the Church's tradition, to one or other of the Persons. Of course, the human actions of Jesus, who is both God and man, are of him alone and not of the Trinity.

The Scripture passages selected for the gospel readings of the three years A, B and C of the lectionary, show a wide choice. In year A, the choice is an extract from Jesus' words to the Pharisee Nicodemus during their nocturnal meeting (John 3:16-18). Year B gives us the final words of Jesus to the apostles as he bade them farewell (Matthew 28:16-20). This year, the gospel comes from Jesus' long discourse to the apostles at the Last Supper (John 16:12-15).

The extract for this year gives us the arrangement which the Persons of the Trinity reveal (through Christ's words to the apostles) regarding their plan for our salvation. It is a plan that rescues us from our sins and their consequences, restores us to the state of goodness which is acceptable to God and enables us to look forward to eternal life in the intimate presence of God.

Jesus tells us that, while with us as both man and God, he has been implementing the Father's plan which involves, first, establishing a reign on earth of justice, love and peace, a reign that we call the kingdom of God, and which then culminates in his sacrificing his human life and rising from the dead for us before returning to the Father in glory. While on earth, he constitutes his disciples as a community, the Church, to continue this mission of setting up the kingdom of God; when he is no longer visibly directing them in their task, the Holy Spirit will be with them, empowering the Church and its members with the gifts necessary to continue the work that he, Jesus, left to be done.

The first reading, from the book of Proverbs (8:22-31), has the Wisdom of God presenting itself. Particularly stressed is the fact that Wisdom existed before creation began, that, when God was creating, Wisdom was there, 'a master craftsman', always giving pleasure to God as well as now delighted to be in the company of humankind. It is easy to see how Wisdom was sometimes identified with the Holy Spirit and even with Mary, and how John's gospel sees divine Wisdom as God's Word and his Son.

St Paul (Romans 5:1-5) brings all three Persons into his explanation of our relationship to God. He tells us that faith and hope help us to look forward to being with God in glory. Having faith from and in Jesus places us in the state of grace that makes us fit for God's presence and, in our sufferings, having hope is possible because the Holy Spirit is given to us and assures us of the love that God has for us.

THE MOST HOLY BODY AND BLOOD OF CHRIST - Year C

Luke 9:11-17

This solemn feast was inaugurated in the thirteenth century at a time of intense devotion towards the Blessed Sacrament when people wanted to have a special festive celebration of the Eucharist in addition to Holy Thursday, a day on which festivities were overshadowed by the other events of Holy Week. The gospel passage for this feast in year A is the climax of the sixth chapter of John's gospel (verses 51-58) when his listeners are challenged on hearing Jesus say that 'the bread that I shall give is my flesh'. In year B, the account of the Eucharist's institution at the Last Supper is read (Mark 14:12-16.22-26).

Today, we are given the account of the multiplication of the loaves to feed 'the five thousand men'. It is the one miracle narrative reported in all four gospels (Mark 6:30-44; Matthew 14:13-21; John 6:1-13) and in the fourth gospel it is the prelude to the long discourse by Jesus, the climax of which is the corresponding gospel passage for this solemn feast in year A.

The passage brings out the compassionate aspect of Jesus' character for it is he who anxiously discusses what to do about the hunger of the crowd and the lateness of the hour and who then decides how the problem should be solved. More importantly, perhaps, for the present purpose, it is to be noticed that a sequence of verbs in the passage are those very words used in the institution narrative (as well as at the Emmaus story and in our liturgy at the Eucharistic prayer): 'took . . . looked up . . . blessed . . . broke . . . gave'. The fact that twelve baskets were filled with the leftovers may have some symbolic significance (twelve apostles? twelve tribes of Israel? therefore of worldwide importance?). We do not know if the twelve baskets have any particular significance; but the event itself has evident similarity to the Eucharist. It is for this reason that it has been chosen as the gospel reading for today's solemn feast.

The gospels were written to preserve the memory of our Lord, his teaching and his example. The reason is not merely for information's sake or historical purposes but to nourish and deepen our faith and to enable his followers to imitate his ways. These ways have to be the inspiration and model for our lives. We read and listen to the gospels to feel and indeed live like him, to get to know him and love him. These are our motives for celebrating the Eucharist and, in particular, the Liturgy of the Word. And it is in the hope that the readings chosen at Mass will mean more to us that these notes have been prepared and made available.

The first reading (Genesis 14:18-20) tells us of the meeting Abraham had with the king and priest Melchizedek who came with bread and wine and blessed Abraham. He is seen as a forerunner of Jesus, not only because he was a priest and brought bread and wine but also, unlike the Levitical priests of the Old Testament, there is no evidence that his priesthood is hereditary (cf. psalm 109/110:4; Hebrews 5:6.10).

In the first letter to the Corinthians (11:23-26), in the chapter in which he is scolding them for misbehaviour when assembling to celebrate the Eucharist, Paul inserts an account of its institution at the Last Supper ('. . . took . . . thanked . . . broke . . . said'). This is the earliest narrative of the institution of the Eucharist; written around 57 AD, it predates the gospels.

Sundays in Ordinary Time

SECOND SUNDAY IN ORDINARY TIME – Year C

John 2:1-11

Although this is 'the year of Luke', a place in the lectionary is found at its start for the important event at Cana, a miracle in the very early days of Christ's public ministry and recounted only in John's gospel. The first words of the chapter ('Three days later,') are omitted from the reading. The chronology is mentioned mainly for symbolic reasons, to link this first 'sign' of Christ's glorification to come with the full glorification of his resurrection. Jesus is very reluctant to perform the miracle because 'the hour' of his glorification is still in the future. His use of the word 'woman' when speaking to his mother (whom John never names in his gospel) is not a term of insult (it is similar to 'madam') but it is very strange for a son to address his mother with the word. Scholars have offered various possible explanations.

The words which Jesus uses to show his reluctance are a Semitic expression whose exact meaning can be discovered only by the context. So in this case, it is not an outright refusal or an angry rebuke, but merely to inform Mary that, although he will respond to her request and solve the problem, the time of his glorification will be decided by the Father and it lies in the future and not at that moment. Mary seems to understand that, as a result of her request, he will anticipate the time of his full and formal glorification. The large quantity of water at hand is explained by the Jewish ritual of washing before and after a meal. The quality of the new wine symbolises the excellence of the messianic era.

The evangelist describes the miracle as a 'sign', the first of several miracles which, in the fourth gospel, are declared to be signs of the divine mission which Jesus has been given by God. The willingness of Jesus to accede to Mary's request shows the efficacy of Mary's intercession with her son, so much so that it is now recognised as effective whenever she asks him for any favour. And, just as Eve was described as 'mother of all the living' (Genesis 3:20), Mary is seen as 'the new Eve' and a figure of the Church, mother of all those who share the life of Christ (John 14:19-20).

The miracle at Cana can be seen as symbolic of the transformation which Jesus has brought and which he wishes us to experience in our lives. It is the grace or gift of conversion (the Greek word *metanoia* is the technical term) which Jesus offers to allow us to turn away from sinful ways and adopt the values and lifestyle which he exemplified. Moreover, the change of the water into wine is a symbol that our religion should bring happiness to life and that the evangelising or sharing of our faith must not be limited to words but must show that to be a disciple is to have a life that is warm, joyful and fulfilling. It is unthinkable that this sign at Cana could have seen Jesus changing wine into water!

'And his disciples believed in him'. In John's gospel, Christ's miracles are described as signs which show his identity and mission. So today's miracle achieves three results: it enables the celebration to continue; it saves 'the happy couple' from embarrassment and obloquy; and it reveals to his followers Jesus' identity and mission. In this last point, John's gospel differs from the synoptics. For them, the faith of the disciples struggles only gradually to grasp the divine identity of Jesus and the meaning of his mission. In the fourth gospel Cana brings to completion 'a steep learning curve' for the closest disciples. They would continue to see wonderful signs of Jesus' identity and mission, but what they had already experienced in their short time with him had brought them to full faith in him.

In the first reading, Isaiah (62:1-5) is looking forward to the joyful restoration of Israel to its home after being freed from exile in Babylon. The prophet sees God rejoicing with Israel 'as the bridegroom rejoices in his bride' since God delights in his people 'and your land will have its wedding', expressions appropriately chiming with the subject of today's gospel reading.

The early weeks of Ordinary Time each year have extracts from Paul's first letter to the Corinthians as their second readings. In year C, the Sundays from the second to the eighth have passages from the last four chapters of the letter. Today (12:4-11), Paul explains that, since in the Church 'there are all sorts of service to be done', the Holy Spirit ensures that different gifts are given to different people.

THIRD SUNDAY IN ORDINARY TIME – Year C

Luke 1:1-4; 4:14-21

All the gospel passages for the remaining Sundays of year C in Ordinary Time come from St Luke. It is appropriate, therefore, to mention here some of the characteristics of this gospel. Like St Matthew's gospel in year A, St Luke borrows much of his content from St Mark's gospel. But there are parts from other (unknown) sources. Moreover, St Luke's account is often known as the gospel of compassion. This description can be exemplified in a number of ways. It is Luke who reports the two great canticles, the *Magnificat* (1:46-55) and the *Benedictus* (1:68-79), which proclaim God's mercy to those in need; it is in Luke that we find the parables of the Good Samaritan (10:29-37) and the Prodigal Son (15:11-32); he tells us of Christ's consideration for Zacchaeus (19:1-10) and his sorrow for the future fate of Jerusalem (19:41-44); it is in this gospel that we learn of the marked involvement of women in Jesus' ministry.

Luke's gospel begins with a formal preface, introducing the gospel narrative to someone called Theophilus, a name which means 'lover of God'. The identity of this person, if he is a real person, is unknown. We do not even know whether he is a Christian or not. The remainder of the first chapter describes the announcements by angels of the conceptions of John the Baptist and Jesus, followed by the visit Mary paid to Elizabeth when both were pregnant; finally we learn of the birth of John the Baptist and the circumstances surrounding the event. The second chapter is about the childhood of Jesus: his birth, presentation in the Temple, and with the doctors in the Temple. Chapter three tells us of the Baptist's preaching, Jesus' baptism as well as his ancestry back through David, Abraham and the patriarchs to Adam. The first thirteen verses of chapter four outline the incidents while Jesus was in the desert for forty days and nights, after which he went from Judea back north to Galilee to start his public ministry.

Luke mentions that Jesus taught in the synagogues of Galilee and soon acquired a favourable reputation. Typical of Luke is the stress laid on the presence with Jesus of the Holy Spirit. The third Person of the Trinity figures frequently in Luke's writing, in the infancy gospel, in the main part of the book and even in the Acts of the Apostles.

In the synagogue at Nazareth (the unusual alternative word Nazara is used), Jesus very carefully and deliberately chooses a text from Isaiah (61:1-2) in which the prophet proclaims the coming of someone, possessing the Lord's spirit, who will announce good news for those who are poor, captive, blind and downtrodden; it will be a jubilee during which the Lord will rescue all who are burdened with such sufferings. Again, after reading the text, Jesus is aware that the attention of everyone there is on him. He makes the solemn and breathtaking declaration: 'This text is being fulfilled today even as you listen'. That is, I am the person of whom that text is speaking. The next verse (not included in today's reading) reports the approval and astonishment of all present.

In the gospel reading next week, Luke's narrative of Jesus in the synagogue continues for nine more verses, but the atmosphere changes when the people complain that he does not work miracles in Nazareth as he does in Capernaum and that he is no one special but merely from a family well known to them all. Jesus retorts by remarking that, as ever, a prophet is not accepted among his own. The people are infuriated at this insult and would have done physical injury to him, had he not managed to escape. Many exegetes consider that, although Luke's description of the goings-on at the synagogue gives no indication that he is reporting on two or even three separate occasions when Jesus went there, it seems more likely that such was the case.

The other evangelists also report that Jesus went to the Nazareth synagogue, but without the details provided by Luke. Mark (6:1-6) and Matthew (13:53-58) have accounts of a visit to the synagogue in Nazareth some time into the Galilean ministry of Jesus, a visit that resulted in the people being very unimpressed and Jesus surprised at their lack of faith. This clearly refers to the central portion of Luke's report and probably, therefore, to a later visit than the occasion on which the Nazarenes so much admired Jesus and his teaching. The final portion of Luke's narrative may be a sequel to the second visit or perhaps a third and even more unsuccessful visit, or indeed (as has been suggested) it may be intended as a summary of the entire work of Jesus and its outcome among many of the Jews, especially the authorities.

Restricting ourselves to today's extract, we are struck by the passage which Jesus chose to read and with which he identified himself. The Spirit had led him, he said, to preach good news to the poor, and then he uses the specific groups of poor people whom Isaiah lists in order to illustrate the kind of people to whom he would preach the good news of freedom and the recovery of what they lacked. Having stated his programme, Jesus proceeded, in the weeks and months following, to carry it out. His love, both in what he said and in what he did, was for those in need; he constantly scandalised and angered the authorities by consorting with the kind of people they shunned and avoided. Must we not conclude, therefore, that the Church's primary task is not organisation or rules and regulations but what is now called 'a preferential option for the poor'? It would seem that, following that path, we shall be walking in the footsteps of Jesus.

The first reading (Nehemiah 8:2-6.8-10) is an account of the celebration in Jerusalem of the feast of Tabernacles. It is the late fifth century BC, the people have returned from exile in Babylon and, despite Samaritan opposition, have succeed in rebuilding the Temple. (Its predecessor, the first Temple, had been built during Solomon's reign, but was destroyed by Babylonian invaders in 587 BC.) The occasion is a very festive one, Nehemiah being the high commissioner, representing the king of Persia, and Ezra is the priest and scribe who leads the celebration.

In the first letter to the Corinthians (12:12-30), Paul continues to use the example of the human body, a unity but with many parts, all different because with different purposes or functions. This helps to explain the Church, Christ's body, many parts with different ministries, but all aware of the need for having variety as well as maintaining unity.

FOURTH SUNDAY IN ORDINARY TIME – Year C

Luke 4:21-30

This passage in Luke's gospel follows immediately after last week's extract. In fact, it opens by repeating the final sentence of the previous week. But very soon, there is a complete change of reaction in the Nazareth synagogue. First, Jesus was approved by all, 'astonished by the gracious words that came from his lips'. Then there occurs an immediate angry reaction which can be expressed in the phrase, 'Who does he think he is?' It is only this very negative reaction that the other synoptics report and many scholars think that the change is so violently opposed to the previous approval shown by the people that we are dealing with two different occasions.

Jesus responds to the insulting and hurtful response by quoting the saying, 'No prophet is ever accepted in his own country', which only adds fuel to the flames. The saying is verified in the Nazareth synagogue and it is worth noting, in addition to that obvious fact, that Jesus refers to himself as a prophet. And that is what he was; not an earthly king nor a Levitical priest nor a teacher of the law. As a prophet, he is not appointed by any human authority. It is God who inspires the prophet to speak in his name when those with religious or political authority fail to do so. So the prophet will live among the neglected and the victims of injustice, calling attention to their misery and suffering and demanding change.

Since Jesus, in addition to his priestly and teaching mission, was also a prophet, it seems clear that our Church should continue to have a prophetic mission. This task must not be seen as an optional extra to be left to those 'who like doing that kind of thing' or to be something that we can do 'if we have time'. I believe that, in recent decades, we have become much more aware of prophecy as an essential part of our discipleship. Gradually, that theoretical truth is becoming a fact in practice.

Today's extract may also put us in mind of one or two situations that can occur in our lives. For example, the courage needed to stick to our principles and either speak the truth or do what is right, even when we seem to be in a minority of one; or, conversely, the temptation to 'cherry-pick' Christ's teaching and reject what is inconvenient for us; or the temptation to keep quiet and say nothing when we know that we ought to witness to our faith or our moral values.

Jeremiah (1:4-5.17-19) recalls how God called him to be his prophet and, as well as warning him of what he would suffer in speaking in God's name, promised to defend and protect him.

Probably the best known chapter in all the writings of St Paul, the thirteenth chapter of the first letter to the Corinthians is a eulogy on the greatest of God's gifts to us, the gift of selfless love (12:31-13.13).

FIFTH SUNDAY IN ORDINARY TIME – Year C

Luke 5:1-11

Although in today's extract from Luke's gospel, several of the apostles are called by Jesus (three are named: Simon Peter, James and John; and among Peter's companions, presumably Andrew his brother was present), the main focus is on Simon Peter (in Luke, not given the name Peter until later). The scene is the Lake of Gennesaret, another name for the Sea of Galilee. The passage seems to have been collated by Luke in such a way that he uses some elements that are similar to parts of other stories; in particular, the story of the large catch of fish is similar to the scene at the lakeside after Christ's resurrection (John 21:1-11). The fact that Luke places the recruiting of the apostles after Jesus had begun his public ministry is due, some say, to the evangelist's desire to give the apostles' unusually immediate response (as is reported in Mark 1:16-20 and Matthew 4:18-22) the justification of their having some prior knowledge of Jesus' activities.

The relationship between Jesus and Peter is worthy of note. From the start, Peter trusts Jesus. If they, experienced fishermen, had caught nothing all night, it made little sense to continue trying in the daylight; but Jesus told him to do so and Peter complied. He would be a faithful disciple and a trustworthy follower. But Peter is a sinner, which he openly and humbly admits to Jesus; but this does not deter Jesus who does not hesitate to have with him someone who knows that he is a sinner. He tells Peter not to consider himself unwanted or unneeded; he will better understand that the message of Jesus is one of forgiveness.

At the start of every Mass, we all, priests and people, acknowledge in words that we are sinners. It is an easy routine but do we really mean what we say? In particular, those who are priests may, with the help of people's respect for them, run the risk of forgetting the sad truth of what they are saying. Our Church is holy, but it certainly does not follow that the members are not sinners. Hypocrisy is a sad condition for anyone to be in. And it is noticeable that Pope Francis has told us, in a very honest and humble way, that he is a sinner. In this frankness, he is following the example of his predecessor in Galilee.

A few years ago, Pope Benedict XVI called us to a renewed awareness of our duty to be a Church which evangelises. The phrase that he chose as the motto for our efforts comes from today's gospel reading: 'Put out into deep water – *Duc in altum*' (verse 4). I am not sure how successful our efforts were but the more important question would seem to be 'did we try?' and also 'are we still trying?' Evangelising is not an easy thing to do, especially nowadays when matters of faith attract little interest from so many and are frequently the occasion for ridicule. Let us pray that we may not lose heart and that we may see and use any opportunities that arise.

As Jesus called his first apostles in today's gospel passage, so God was calling prophets in preceding centuries. Today, Isaiah (6:1-8) recounts God's call to him, which took place in the eighth century BC.

Writing to the Christians at Corinth, Paul (1 Corinthians 15:1-11) states his mandate for preaching the authentic story of Jesus and his saving work. Speaking of the risen Christ's appearances, he mentions two which are not reported in the gospels: one to 'more than five hundred of the brothers' and another to James. He also adds Christ's appearance to himself (on the road to Damascus) along with three post-resurrection appearances reported in the gospels.

SIXTH SUNDAY IN ORDINARY TIME – Year C

Luke 6:17.20-26

At verse 12 of chapter 6, Luke begins a short introduction to the teaching which Jesus gave to a large crowd and which, in Matthew's gospel, is usually referred to as the Sermon on the Mount. Luke tells us that Jesus went into the hills and spent the night praying to God. The next day, he called his disciples and chose twelve of them (whom Luke names, the first being 'Simon whom he called Peter') to be apostles. He then came down the hill (a variation from Matthew's account) where there was a huge crowd waiting for him. Luke's account of Christ's teaching on this occasion is a great deal shorter than Matthew's (another variation, due to Matthew's system of gathering a number of the teachings and sayings of Jesus into a few extended 'discourses').

Today's gospel passage is on the beatitudes, which Luke, like Matthew, places at the beginning of his report on Jesus' teaching to the expectant crowd. There are obvious differences between this and the more familiar account by Matthew. In the first place, where Matthew gives eight beatitudes, Luke has only four; but Luke then adds four curses, each starting with the phrase 'Alas for you who . . .'. Another major difference is that, whereas the pattern of Matthew's beatitudes is to congratulate the virtuous because they will be rewarded in heaven, Luke's console the rejected with the promise that things will be reversed in heaven. Luke's curses or maledictions each correspond to one of the beatitudes and the self-satisfied are warned that their good fortune will be reversed in the next life.

In spite of, or perhaps because of, their evident challenge to us, the Luke beatitudes are far less commonly quoted than Matthew's, yet they demand serious consideration and especially by us who live comparatively easy lives in the affluent world. As Catholics, we are constantly told of the many millions of people whose conditions of life are truly miserable. We are asked to help materially and to pray for them. But clearly, a great deal more is required before we can be content that enough has been done to share the wealth and the good things of the world. Luke speaks of the poor, the hungry, the sad and those who are hated and rejected; and their opposites whom he cites as the wealthy, the well-fed, the complacent and the esteemed.

In Luke's gospel, the beatitudes and their opposites express the reality of things, how things are in the world. They also represent the behaviour of Jesus who deliberately chose to be with the poor and the marginalised and to show them compassion, while he was very bluntly critical of those who lived complacently, even hypocritically and were contemptuous of the have-nots. When we look at our Church today, it tends to have a middle class appearance that should disturb us. Those poor and unfortunate people whom Jesus befriended and who thronged to Jesus – do their present-day successors imitate them? Is Jesus, present in today's Church, still able to attract them? We may still give them some help and be sorry for them, but they are not present among us. The world is a brutal place for millions. I think that we, today's disciples of Christ, must do more to help and to change an intolerable situation.

Jesus came not only to save us from our sins and lead us to eternal life in heaven, but also to make this world a kingdom fit for God to be with us. He spoke of 'good news for the poor', he made that the aim of his activity, what we now call the 'preferential option for the poor'. He asks us to share his enthusiasm and to continue his work.

In the first reading, the prophet Jeremiah (17:5-8), speaking in God's name, declares that the blessings of a good and happy life will come to the person who puts his trust in God; while the one who relies on human and earthly support will fail to find anything worthwhile.

St Paul (1 Corinthians 15:12.16-20) derides those who deny the resurrection of the dead. If their denial were correct, Christ himself would not be risen and we would still be in our sins. That would mean the unthinkable, that our hope in Christ would only be for this life.

SEVENTH SUNDAY IN ORDINARY TIME – Year C

Luke 6:27-38

Luke reports that, in his teaching, Jesus, immediately after having proclaimed the beatitudes (last Sunday's gospel), goes on to speak of the way that we should treat others. That way should be completely selfless, compassionate and generous. Our love for others should not be restricted to those who love us; even if others have what belongs to us, either because they have stolen or because they have borrowed, we should be intent not on having our property returned but on giving the thief or borrower even more. In general, we should be anxious to treat others with total generosity, never being judgmental about their motives or actions.

This teaching was accepted and practised by many in the early Church, where the distinction, made by St Paul, is between *eros* and *agape*. The former is a love or desire for what will bring advantage to ourselves and the latter is a love or desire for what will be for the benefit of others. In today's gospel passage, Jesus is clearly teaching that his followers should excel in the latter. He gives many examples of how we can behave with selfless love (even though the report sometimes seems to suggest that our motive for acting in that way is for the greater advantages that we shall obtain in the long run).

Is it feasible to preach such generosity and expect the counsel (or precept) to be followed? Undoubtedly it is. Even the meanest of us will, at least sometimes, show kindness to others. So the issue is: how often should we do so? Now and again when we feel like doing so, or oftener, or always as a rule of life which we want to follow? Perhaps the last is a counsel of perfection which requires saintly behaviour. However, we should keep in mind the following lesson which experience teaches.

It is this. When we act with selfless generosity in any of the ways recommended by Jesus, the result is a sense of joyful satisfaction. We do not look to be rewarded in the same 'currency' as we have used or given; it is not a matter of becoming even wealthier than we were. The 'currency' which we acquire is the happiness of knowing that we have made others happy in one way or another, that we have shown love, friendship, forgiveness, thoughtfulness – qualities that we think of as divine! We can call it philanthropy, and so it is. Many of the beneficiaries will never be able to repay us, but that should not enter our calculations. It is enough that Jesus asks us, as his disciples, to act in that way. And experience shows us that he knew what he was talking about. The disciple's love should go beyond the required or the expected.

In the first book of Samuel (26:2.7-9.12-13.22-23), we have an illustration, by David, of the conduct which Jesus was to ask of his followers. Samuel, the last 'judge' to be leader of Israel, was succeeded by Saul, the first 'king'. However, Saul was very unpopular and, before Samuel died, he was told by God to select the man who would be Saul's successor. This was David, whom Saul disliked and tried to kill. David had an opportunity to get revenge on Saul but refused to do so.

Continuing to consider the immortality which Christ acquired for us by his own resurrection, Paul (1 Corinthians 15:45-49) distinguishes between the soul (*psyche*) which all animals and humans have, and the spirit (*pneuma*) which is given to us by the Holy Spirit if we are united to the risen Christ. It is the latter that gives us the destiny of immortality in heaven.

EIGHTH SUNDAY IN ORDINARY TIME – Year C

Luke 6:39-45

Today's extract follows immediately after last Sunday's and, except for four more verses, brings us to the end of Luke's report on our Lord's first discourse, corresponding to, but much shorter than, Matthew's account of the Sermon on the Mount. However, several of the sayings in this passage are to be found dispersed in different parts of Matthew's gospel.

Jesus warns against criticising others' conduct or wishing to correct it when we are not qualified to do so. He calls such foolishness hypocrisy and uses two short parables to illustrate his point. A blind man cannot lead another blind person, nor should a pupil imagine that he can instruct a teacher. (In Matthew's account, Jesus seems to be speaking pointedly about the scribes and Pharisees.)

The second part of the extract sounds somewhat similar to the first, but Jesus is teaching another lesson. He starts by using the example of a tree and its fruit to assert that a person's interior goodness or badness determines that what he says or does will be either good or bad. So, just as we do not look for figs coming from thorns or grapes from brambles, so it is from a good person, not from someone who is bad, that we can expect good things (actions or words).

Perhaps there is another truth that lurks hidden in these reflections of Jesus. Life nowadays is so busy, so hectic, so full of distractions, problems and tensions that it is difficult to find time or place for silence and peace. Yet it is only in the silence and peace of being alone sometimes or being in the presence of God that we can give ourselves the chance to produce something worthwhile. With inner peace, we get the chance to listen to God and, as a result, to be able to release the goodness that lies in our inner selves.

The first reading (Ecclesiasticus 27:4-7) offers a very similar lesson as the gospel, namely, that it is a person's talk which is the best criterion of his worth. Three 'down to earth' parallels are used – the products of a sieve, a kiln and an orchard.

In the final excerpt from his first letter to the Corinthians (15:54-58), Paul encourages his readers to be of good heart since the cause of death is sin which, in fact, has been conquered by the death and resurrection of Christ.

NINTH SUNDAY IN ORDINARY TIME – Year C

Luke 7:1-10

Scripture scholars consider that Mark's gospel is the earliest of the three synoptics and that the principal source of much in Matthew and Luke is Mark. But there are some parts that are found in Matthew and Luke but not in Mark, so the common source of those parts is called 'Q' because its identity is unknown. Today's reading is an example of such passages. It is found in Matthew (8:5-10) and probably also in John (4:46-54), written later than the other gospels. The dialogue in Matthew and Luke is the same, but several of the details are not. For example, in Matthew the centurion goes personally to Jesus, but in Luke he sends two groups in his name. The suggestion is that Luke does not have Jesus making any direct contact with gentiles. Such practice happened, or at least ceased to be exceptional, only after the ascension. The healing also occurs with Jesus not in the presence of the servant, presumably also a gentile, who was ill.

Perhaps the principal feature of the event is the attitude of the centurion, an officer of the Roman army and a gentile. The tone of his messages to Jesus is courteous, but that is to be expected in the circumstances of the situation. But he shows remarkable humility and exemplary faith in Jesus' powers, so much so that Jesus was astonished and told the crowd that was present that he had never met faith like it. It is relevant to keep this point in mind when, at Mass just before Holy Communion, we say the prayer based on the centurion's words. Genuine faith requires that we try to be genuinely humble.

In a passage from the first book of the Kings (8:41-43), it is reported that Solomon (tenth century BC) prayed in the Temple he had newly built that God would answer the prayers even of gentiles who came to worship there. However, the report is probably a sixth century addition, inserted after the Jews returned from exile.

The second reading is the first of six excerpts from Paul's letter to the Galatians (1:1-2.6-10). After reminding the Christians of Galatia (an area of central Asia Minor which Paul had visited and in which he had preached) of his authority, he expresses his dismay that they have tended to revert to some of the Jewish practices which followers of Christ, having received the Good News, should not do.

TENTH SUNDAY IN ORDINARY TIME – Year C

Luke 7:11-17

Only Luke's gospel has this story of Jesus restoring the life of the widow's son. It is neither in Mark nor in Matthew, and Luke' source for it is unknown. However it demonstrates the compassion and tenderness of Jesus, as well as his regard for women, a characteristic that is noticeable in Luke's gospel. This is the first occasion of several in this gospel when the word 'Lord' is used of Jesus. In the Greek version of the New Testament, the word is *Kyrios*, a term reserved for God.

The next episode in Luke's gospel tells of two followers of John the Baptist being sent to find out if Jesus is 'the one who is to come'. The incident is not included in the Sunday lectionary, but it is instructive to note that, in his affirmative reply, Jesus cites the various healing miracles that he has performed, including 'the dead are raised to life'. Clearly, Luke intends those words to refer to the miracle narrated immediately preceding.

The first book of the Kings (17:17-24) provides details of the life of the ninth century BC prophet Elijah. On the occasion reported for today's first reading, he is fleeing from Ahab, king of the northern kingdom of Israel. Ahab had married Jezebel, a heathen who had persuaded him to introduce worship of Baal. Elijah had condemned Ahab for idolatry and, in his flight from the king, had been given refuge by a widow. The widow's son dies but, although she accuses the prophet of being responsible for his illness and death, Elijah implores God to restore the boy's life, which God does.

Paul, in his letter to the Galatians (1:11-19), relates the history of his conversion to show that his teaching has got divine warrant when he denounces the re-introduction of Jewish customs, especially circumcision, among some recent Christian converts.

ELEVENTH SUNDAY IN ORDINARY TIME – Year C

Luke 7:36-8:3

Once again, the event related in today's gospel excerpt is found only in Luke. Jesus has been invited to a meal in the house of a Pharisee named Simon. Presumably the Pharisee is favourably disposed towards Jesus but he is mortified when the woman of bad reputation comes in, unannounced and unexpected, and even more embarrassed at her conduct. He is also astonished that Jesus allows her, a known sinner, to touch him, and begins to doubt if Jesus' reputation as a prophet is correct.

Jesus then explains the situation, first, by a parable. If a creditor forgives the debts of two men, which of them will show him the more love, the one forgiven a large debt or the one forgiven a smaller amount? When Simon correctly opts for the former, Jesus tells him that the woman has shown him (Jesus) much more evidence of her love than had Simon. That proved that she must have had a great many sins pardoned. The other guests are puzzled – who is this person who even forgives sins? But nothing more of the episode is reported; only that Jesus told the woman (whose identity is not revealed to us) to depart in peace because her faith, which had induced him to forgive her, had thereby saved her.

It is not only the kindness of Jesus towards the woman that we admire. The situation was a difficult one for him to deal with, particularly as the woman's sins were complicated by the fact that they were publicly known. It is not only Jesus' compassion that impresses, but also his understanding of the difficult and complex situation which had arisen in the somewhat dramatic circumstances in which they took place. When similar problems suddenly arise and confront us, demanding some action on our part, may God give us the wisdom, discretion and courage to do what is right.

The event is reported only by Luke. The other three gospels narrate (with certain different details among them) a somewhat similar incident. But all three report that it occurred in Bethany and in Holy Week, while Luke's report is of an occurrence in Galilee at the beginning of Jesus' public ministry. There are other variations in the four stories. So did the incident occur on (at least) two occasions? Or has the one happening become embellished with different added details during the years and decades of only oral transmission? We do not know.

Today's excerpt ends with a brief summary of Jesus' ministry 'through towns and villages preaching and proclaiming the Good News of the kingdom of God' (8:1). He was accompanied by the Twelve and by some women who took care of them. Among them was Mary Magdalene, 'from whom seven demons had gone out' – a reference to some illness, physical or mental (and not an implication of an immoral life).

King David's grave sin is the subject of today's first reading from the second book of Samuel (12:7-10.13). David commits adultery with a married woman who becomes pregnant. Her husband is a soldier in the king's army so David contrives to have him killed in battle so that he can marry the widowed Bathsheba. David repents and God forgives him. But the king will have to endure punishment.

In the second reading, Paul maintains his displeasure with the Galatians (2:16.19-21) for their adopting Jewish religious practices again. He tells them that it is not the law of the Old Testament that saves us, but God's gift of faith in Christ our Saviour.

TWELFTH SUNDAY IN ORDINARY TIME – Year C

Luke 9:18-24

As we have seen, Luke's gospel is very faithful to Mark's but, between the previous excerpts and today, he has omitted a large section (6:45-8:26) of Mark. As if in imitation, the lectionary in its turn has omitted a part of Luke's gospel (8:4-9:17). Today's reading, however is of crucial importance, not only for the apostles and disciples but also for the Church down through the centuries. The event is reported both in Matthew (16:13-28) and in Mark (8:27-38).

Jesus and the apostles are by themselves in northern Galilee in or near a town called Caesarea Philippi which lay in the foothills of Mount Hermon. It was built by the local ruler, Philip, son of Herod the Great and married to Salome, daughter of Herodias. The town was named in honour of the Roman emperor, with the ruler's name added to distinguish it from other Caesareas.

After a period spent in prayer, Jesus asks the disciples, first, who do the people think he is and, then, who do they, his close helpers, think he is. Peter is the one who answers for them all. 'The Christ of God', he replies. Jesus responds by asking the group not to divulge this to anyone (an instance of the 'messianic secret' because Jesus expected that, if the knowledge were widely spread, it would be thought that, as the messiah, he would lead a revolt against the Roman occupation and achieve a military and political victory for the people). Instead, Jesus gives them the first of several prophecies about his forthcoming passion, death and resurrection. The information must have bewildered and astonished the disciples, their dismay only made worse when Jesus added that, to be his disciples, each of them would have to follow him every day, and bearing a cross.

Luke's account of the apostles' knowledge of Jesus' identity, 'The Christ of God', is more concise and succinct and less fulsome than Matthew's version. Moreover, Luke omits the incident, embarrassing for Peter, when the apostle protests about a prospect of Jesus' suffering and being put to death; Jesus' rebuke of Peter's well-meaning but misguided objection is very severe indeed.

The Church's faith in the identity and mission of Jesus is absolutely essential. If that faith disappeared, so would the Church. The mission which Jesus entrusted to the Church would be meaningless. We would no longer be open to the gift of the Spirit and the challenges we face would destroy us. For Christians, Jesus is the Christ, the Messiah, and he is the Son of God, indeed God the Son who, incarnate, reveals God to us. He is our Saviour who frees us from the burdens of sin and the punishment of eternal death. And he is Lord, to whom we belong, who is the centre of our lives and of our communities, and who teaches us how to live in order that our world can be the kingdom of God.

If our answer to Jesus' question is the same as Peter's, then it is a declaration that involves renunciation, but also renewal, fulfilment and joy. It means that we want to be a member of a community of faith and therefore also of hope (and prayer) and of love (and service), under the leadership of Jesus Christ.

The first reading is from the minor prophet, Zechariah (12:10-11; 13:1). The second half of his book is from the fourth century BC. Today's first reading is from that part and, though vague and unclear, can be seen as a prophecy about someone whose great sufferings will be a cause of widespread mourning among the people, on whom God will pour 'a spirit of kindness and prayer'.

St Paul tells the Christians of Galatia (3:26-29) that, through their faith in Christ and their baptism, they have been adopted by God without distinction of race, gender or status. They are the promised posterity and heirs of Abraham (who lived before, and therefore outwith, the Old Law which God gave to Moses for the Jews).

THIRTEENTH SUNDAY IN ORDINARY TIME – Year C

Luke 9:51-62

From this point in his gospel, Luke places the remainder of Jesus' public ministry in the context or framework of a journey south, from Galilee and through Samaria, to Judea and the capital, Jerusalem. Almost thirty verses of the ninth chapter have been omitted from the lectionary, some because the events concerned have already been considered in years A or B.

Today's excerpt begins with a problem with some Samaritans, reluctant to show any hospitality to Jesus and his band since they were on the road to the hated city. James and John, impulsive and hot-headed, have to be restrained by Jesus. The gospel then relates accounts (real or fictitious) of three people who wanted to become disciples. The exchanges between Jesus and the three illustrate the demands which being a follower of Jesus entail. In the first case, Jesus tells the volunteer that 'the Son of Man has nowhere to lay his head'; there can be no security or comfort in the worldly sense for disciples. The second person wants, first of all, to go to attend to his father's funeral. However, to stress the urgency and priority that discipleship must have, Jesus uses a play on language that, at first sight, seems idiotic: 'leave the (spiritually) dead to bury their (physically) dead'. The third applicant wants to bid farewell to his relatives, but Jesus tells him that, in the life of a disciple, there is no place for looking back or for retaining ties with the past. Discipleship, therefore, calls for total lifelong commitment with trust in God's caring providence and with courage to accept the same hardships as Jesus did. We cannot plead that Jesus does not tell us what discipleship entails!

Each person who wants to be a disciple of Jesus must judge and decide how these demands are to be accepted and carried out in the circumstances of his or her life. St Francis de Sales wisely pointed out that, for instance, the duties of the mother of a family are very different from those of a priest, that the life of a religious is not the same as that of a bishop, and so on. There is a true heroism in the life of a genuine disciple, no matter who he or she is or how the person is to fulfil the duties and commitment. But we are well aware that the Holy Spirit gives us the appropriate gifts we need for the particular vocation that God wants us to fulfil. Fulfilment of that vocation to the best of our ability is true discipleship.

In the first book of the Kings (19:16.19-21), we hear how Elisha became the successor of the prophet Elijah (ninth century BC). Elijah throws his cloak over Elisha, a sign of his claiming Elisha as his successor. The latter agrees by the definitive gesture of disposing of his plough and oxen. Elijah's reply to Elisha's request to bid his parents farewell is enigmatic. Perhaps it only meant, 'Go; I am not stopping you'.

St Paul (Galatians 5:1.13-18) teaches that Christ has made us free but, lest that liberty degenerate into self-indulgence, we have the Holy Spirit to guide and lead us. In fact, Paul says, the restraints to our freedom can be summed up in one precept: Love your neighbour as yourself.

FOURTEENTH SUNDAY IN ORDINARY TIME – Year C

Luke 10:1-12.17-20

Jesus intends to visit various towns and villages. To prepare for his visits, he asks seventy-two of his disciples to precede him and then to report their experiences to him. Before they set out, he gives them advice and guidance. The instruction is not on the subjects they should discuss with people but on what they should take with them and how they should respond to different receptions, whether welcoming or hostile. Jesus does ask them always to introduce themselves with the words, 'Peace to this house!' The venture must have been successful, at least in general, because the disciples returned very satisfied. Jesus also confirms the outcome of the visits but he counsels that the main reason for rejoicing is not to be the success of their efforts, but rather that God is pleased with the disciples.

The number of disciples commissioned is unclear; some manuscripts say seventy, others seventy-two. Moreover, various suggestions are made to find symbolism in either number, but again without any great conviction. The phrase that Jesus spoke to the returning disciples, 'I have given you power . . .' (verse 19) is seen by exegetes as conferring lasting authority because the previous statement (in the perfect sense) indicates that Jesus has conquered Satan in a definitive fashion.

Reflecting on the passage enables us to draw some lessons that not only help to explain the situation then, but also instruct and encourage us now in the work of evangelising which is the responsibility of us all today.

Jesus 'sent them out' (verse 1), with the words 'start off now' (verse 3), indicating that the Church's primary duty is not to look after itself, preserving the *status quo*, shut in on itself, but rather to think of others and to present God's Good News to the world. The large number sent reminds us that lay people, as well as priests, are called to share their faith. The very severe shortage of priests in our country underlines this point. The fact that the disciples were sent in pairs illustrates Christ's thoughtfulness for them, especially in their inexperience; while the greeting they are to use indicates that evangelising should be done in a gentle and non-threatening fashion. The phrase, 'Cure those . . . who are sick' (verse 9) is surely meant to refer to holistic healing, something that we all need.

'The kingdom of God is very near to you' (verse 9) means that the message should be seen as attractive and the news should be something desirable. If our message is not communicated with humility and respect, it will fail. We must listen as well as speak, our approach must be friendly because we are trying to put people in touch with a God who loves them. We shall succeed in helping to build the kingdom which Jesus established not only by teaching but also by the example of our lives and telling of our own experience.

The extract from Isaiah (66:10-14) comes from the sixth century BC, either at the return of the Jewish exiles or just before the return. The passage, which looks forward to a time of peace and plenty as a result of God's beneficence, can be seen as messianic.

In the final excerpt from the letter to the Galatians (6:14-18), Paul strictly insists that salvation depends only on Jesus and his work of salvation, and not on the precepts of the Old Law. In verse 17, Paul speaks of 'the marks on my body', using the Greek word 'stigmata'. This probably refers not to the modern meaning of the word, but to the marks left through his sufferings for Christ – illness, flogging, stoning – which he compares favourably with the mark of circumcision.

FIFTEENTH SUNDAY IN ORDINARY TIME – Year C

Luke 10:25-37

Jesus' favourite 'tool' when teaching was his use of the parable. That enabled him, when wishing to teach a point that may have been difficult for his listeners to understand or couched in language strange to them, to tell a story or make an allusion whose content was in images familiar to them but which was also sufficiently in parallel with the point he wanted to teach that the people were able to make the connection between the two. Having understood the illustration (the parable), they could then grasp the point or the principle or the doctrine which Jesus wanted to teach.

Scripture experts variously calculate the number of parables in the gospels as being between thirty-five and seventy-two. The difference is because there are a number of very short comparisons or allusions that can be taken as parables, but which some scholars prefer to view as merely similes or metaphors.

Today's gospel parable, the Good Samaritan, even nowadays, vies with the parable of the Prodigal Son as most people's favourite. Yet its popularity is based on the generous care which the Samaritan gave to a stranger in dire need without our adverting to Christ's deliberate choice of the racial identity of the 'hero' of his tale. For us, the phrase, 'a Good Samaritan', is a metaphor for a person who unselfishly helps someone in need; but for the lawyer, a Jew, listening to Jesus, the Samaritans were heartily disliked and regarded with contempt. They were of Jewish stock but had intermarried with pagans, had ceased observing Jewish religious rites and were regarded as heretics. So, for Jesus, the point was not only 'love your neighbour' but also that 'neighbours' are not to be limited to those whom we like or admire. It is a parable that not only urges us to be good neighbours to everyone and especially to those in need; but the parable also has something to tell us about racism and sectarianism.

The introduction to today's excerpt has 'a lawyer' asking Jesus how to gain eternal life. The parallel texts in Mark (12:28-34) and Matthew (22:34-40) describe the questioners being either 'a scribe' or 'a Pharisee' respectively, and they ask about the greatest precept of the law of Moses. Only Luke adds the parable and, since he is writing for gentiles, the lawyer's question is phrased to ask not about the Jewish law (of little interest to non-Jews) but about 'eternal life'. Jesus asks the lawyer to answer his own question. He does so correctly, quoting from Deuteronomy (6:5) and Leviticus (19:18). In the course of narrating the parable, Jesus not only shows the kindness of the Samaritan but also the lack of compassion of two official representatives of the religious authorities who ignored the injured victim. Jesus had reason to know that such people were often so concerned with their own duties and rights that ordinary human courtesy and conduct did not concern them.

The word used in the original Greek text for the phrase rendered in English as 'moved with compassion' (10:33) is a term that literally means 'deeply moved in the guts'. It is used several times about Jesus in the gospels, especially when he was affected by the needs or plight of the crowd. A similar link can occur in some languages today; for example, the Spanish adjective *entrañable* (deeply felt affection or empathy) and the noun *entrañas* (entrails, guts).

In contrast to the priest and the Levite (an assistant in the Temple), Jesus was always ready to exert himself when he encountered those in need; they had to be served, irrespective of whether the law of the Sabbath or the rules of ritual purity were being infringed. The example that Jesus gives should be our rule but, unfortunately, it can still happen that those who are officially charged with religious duties can become remote from the world in which most people live and consequently impervious to their suffering and their need of sympathetic help.

In the first reading (Deuteronomy 30:10-14), Moses is instructing the Jews before they cross the Jordan and enter the land God has promised them. He pleads with them to observe the law, given by voice of the Lord God. Referring to this law of God, Moses says 'the word is very near to you' (verse 14). This use of the phrase, 'the Word of God', is the start of the developing theology which finds its climax and fulfilment in the opening verses of St John's gospel.

The Christians at Colossae had become involved in theories about celestial or cosmic powers. In his letter, Paul does not forbid such speculation but insists that they must never displace Christ from his supremacy, in terms of his human nature, in the order of created things. In today's excerpt (1:15-20), the first of four, he asserts that supremacy 'for in him were created all things' (verse 16) as well as his position as head of the Church because 'he was first to be born from the dead' (verse 18).

SIXTEENTH SUNDAY IN ORDINARY TIME – Year C

Luke 10:38-42

Last Sunday, with the parable of the Good Samaritan, Jesus stressed the need for love of our neighbour. Today, the emphasis is on the need for faith and a relationship with God in the lives of Christians. When he was in Jerusalem (the synoptics mention only one occasion but John indicates that Jesus was there several times during his public ministry), Jesus had made friends, and may well have stayed, with the three siblings, Martha, Mary (not of Magdala) and Lazarus. It is John's gospel that relates the story of Jesus raising Lazarus from the dead (11:1-44); the sisters figure in the account and their characters there seem to confirm the impression given in today's passage.

The words of Jesus to Martha should be seen as explanation rather than rebuke. He is sympathetic to Martha's feelings ('Martha, Martha'), not angry. The exact meaning of his words is somewhat unclear; probably he is telling her that, although she has several things to do, the one thing that Mary is doing has more importance and so she must be allowed to continue. To listen to him and learn what he teaches, being nourished in faith, is the essential characteristic of the genuine disciple.

The episode has something to say to us about the active and contemplative lives of those who feel called to a religious vocation. The two ways are not incompatible and it would certainly be mistaken to laud one by disparaging the other. Both are pleasing to God and both are needed. There are those whose lives incline very markedly to the contemplative state; others follow a reverse tendency and there are those who try to give equal weight to the two ways. The important point is that people should be free to make up their minds on such matters, according to their consciences and their response to the call of God.

Perhaps a more general concern is for people who, either by request or by apparent necessity or by choice, have their lives filled with more and more activity. Excess of work brings stress and anxiety and prevents us having time to know and love Jesus more, to listen to his teaching and be nourished by it. There is not a solution that suits all cases; we must rely on our own wisdom and judgment, but open also to the advice of others. The problem has particular relevance for the situations that arise as a result of the increasing shortage of priests in our country. Personally, when I come to the passages in which Jesus is thought by his relatives to be mad because he seems so busy; or when he goes off on his own in order to pray to his Father but the people discover where he is and want his attention . . . I am always amused and consoled!

I enjoy reading the account of Jesus and the friends with whom he could relax. We do not always think of him enjoying the company of people who loved him and were good to him. Yes, he was divine; but he was also truly human, not just pretending to be. For that reason, he must have been glad to take things easily, not always being on duty, but enjoying the times when he could trust those he was with, have 'small talk' with them, eat a special meal and thank God for the happiness of good company.

The first reading (Genesis 18:1-10) is an account of the hospitality that Abraham and his wife Sarah offered to three unexpected and unknown visitors. Their reward was the promise that they would have a son.

In today's excerpt from the letter to the Colossians (1:24-28), Paul tells us that God chose him to make known the mystery or secret that Christ came to save gentiles as well as Jews. Today's opening verse is variously interpreted by scholars. Perhaps Paul is speaking of the suffering (constant travel, frequent hostility) that he gladly endures in his own task of preaching God's plan of salvation for all.

SEVENTEENTH SUNDAY IN ORDINARY TIME – Year C

Luke 11:1-13

Two of the gospels give us the Lord's Prayer, but with differences. Specifically, Matthew's version (6:9-13) has seven petitions, Luke's has five, omitting 'Your will be done on earth as it is in heaven' and 'Deliver us from evil'. It is likely that the two versions therefore derive from different oral traditions, not from Mark (who does not have the prayer), nor from 'Q' (because of the differences between the two versions). Scholars have theories, for example, that Matthew's source is Jewish and older. The petition in Luke, 'Give us each day our daily bread', refers to an everyday need, whereas Matthew's seems to look forward to one eschatological occasion; but both may have some Eucharistic reference. Luke's 'Do not put us to the test' refers to one great future test from the devil.

The first parable added, verses 5-8 (but not in Matthew), is about two friends, the 'persistence' of one (also can be translated as 'shamelessness' – a stronger word) bringing success because of the bonds of friendship. The point is that the prayer will always be answered. The second parable, verses 9-13 (from 'Q' and in Matthew 7:7-11), is about the relation of a father to his son. It tells us how to pray, not what to pray, and advises faith in God's constant fatherly concern, but that not every prayer will be answered in the way we ask.

The three verbs, ask, search and knock (verse 9) indicate different shades of meaning that can exist in the basic trust that is prayer. 'Ask' is to admit our poverty, an inability to provide for ourselves, true humility. 'Search' is to show a willingness to cooperate in our lives, to help in seeking what we need, not just to sit and expect everything to come without effort. 'Knock' suggests boldness in our prayer, seeing it as important and not to be absorbed in worldly activities.

Some rather basic questions arise. Why pray? God already knows our needs and desires. Does prayer change God's mind? Surely not. So what's the point? Answer: prayer acknowledges God's place in our lives, a relationship of total dependence; and thus prayer builds faith, trust, hope, conformity to God's will.

The specific importance of the Lord's Prayer is brought out by its inclusion and prominence in every celebration of Mass. Although we frequently use it in individual prayer, its plural wording makes it very suitable and effective in communal prayer. And, in view of Christ's prayer for the unity of all his followers, it is good that, at least in this respect, all his followers can unite in the prayer that he taught us.

Abraham prays to God not to punish the cities of Sodom and Gomorrah for their wickedness (Genesis 18:20-32). In those times, the idea of communal responsibility took precedence over individual responsibility. Eventually God agrees that, if there can be found even ten just men in Sodom, he will not destroy it. In other words, although communal responsibility would be the norm, divine mercy could be so prevailed upon that a few good men would win pardon for all.

Paul reminds the Colossians (2:12-14) that in baptism they have died to sin and risen to new life with Christ through their faith in the power of God. All debts due because of the law and any due to sin have gone, destroyed by having been 'nailed to Christ's cross'.

EIGHTEENTH SUNDAY IN ORDINARY TIME – Year C

Luke 12:13-21

Luke has explained the setting in which this gospel passage unfolds: 'Meanwhile the people had gathered in their thousands so that they were treading on one another' (12:1). Someone in that crowd asks Jesus to settle a quarrel between him and his brother about an inheritance. Although there is a section in the Pentateuch to guide rabbis if they are consulted on this kind of subject, Jesus refuses to intervene. But the man's request gives Jesus the opportunity to teach on the folly of greed and to guard against thinking that hoarding ensures one's security. His teaching is by the parable of the rich fool, narrated only in this gospel.

In the parable, the rich landowner is not only foolish but also totally self-centred. His harvest has been so plentiful that he has a great surplus. However, instead of using the surplus to help those who are in need or, in particular, to share some of it with the peasants whom he employs (probably at starvation wages), the farmer's one idea is to keep it all for himself so that his future is, as he presumes, absolutely safe. Then God is introduced into the parable and his verdict is that the man is a fool, but also a sad fool who deprives himself of the joy of sharing, of generosity, of experiencing the fulfilment that comes from helping people in need. As Jesus observes, the man has failed in his selfish aim to make himself rich. He has succeeded only in making himself poor in the sight of God.

The parable and the lesson it teaches are both very topical. Greed and selfishness are still very prevalent in our day. We know how many people still live in abject misery because of their poverty. We also know how many people are intent on getting as rich as possible through exorbitant salaries, profiteering, grossly increased bonuses and sometimes even corruption. Free market economics, unbridled capitalism, the 'trickle-down' theory of wealth creation are unhealthy and even malignant influences. Many of us are hoarders but as long as we hoard such things as letters, photos or even clothes, it is not a serious matter except for those who have to clear up after we die. It is hoarding money that should disturb us. The parable of the rich fool does not demand that we dispose of all our wealth and possessions, but it does indicate that we should not limit our financial planning to sheer selfishness. The economic crisis which has caused such widespread suffering is not just a 'blip' due to greedy bankers. It is a sign of the times which demands the attention of us all. Our lifestyle must change and we must share our wealth.

The book of Ecclesiastes (third century BC) provides the first reading (1:2; 2:21-23). It is a rather gloomy and pessimistic treatise regarding worldly things and, in this excerpt, declares that, though our work may bring us a return and even wealth, 'we cannot take it with us'.

The final excerpt from the letter to the Colossians (3:1-5.9-11) insists that, now we have been given the new life of Christ, we must abandon earthly practices, 'especially greed, which is the same thing as worshipping a false god'.

NINETEENTH SUNDAY IN ORDINARY TIME – Year C

Luke 12:32-48

In the verses prior to today's reading, Jesus has been telling his disciples not to be anxious about their material necessities. The words 'Your Father well knows you need them. No; set your hearts on his kingdom' (verses 30-31) immediately precede today's passage in which the disciples are encouraged to sell and share their worldly goods, and to concentrate on preparing for the next life in heaven. The reading then uses two parables to illustrate the importance and need of being prepared.

The reason for passages like this being included in the gospels can be attributed to the fact that the expectations of the first Christians about an imminent second coming of Christ had been disappointed. Therefore, to thwart the danger of frustration and discouragement, it seemed necessary to keep the people still alert and watchful. A parable that Jesus taught is recalled. It is of servants staying awake for their master who has been at a wedding feast. If he finds them awake and ready, he will show his appreciation in a generous way. Jesus then adds a short parable to the effect that a householder would prevent a burglary if he knew when the burglar intended to come.

Peter's interruption, asking if the parable is only for the apostles or for everyone, can be understood in two ways. First, the apostles are stewards (as it were, head servants) and, as such, the parable stresses that they should carry out their responsibilities dutifully; however, if Peter's question suggested that only the apostles need expect salvation, Jesus ignored it as out of place. Christ then proceeds, changing the parable somewhat, because the servants are no longer only awaiting the return of their master but, if they are stewards, have been given the duty of ensuring the wellbeing of those servants over whom they have authority. The way in which they fulfil their duties will earn either reward or punishment from the master on his return.

The second coming of Christ as our judge at the end of the world as we know it, along with any other phenomena associated with the event, are known collectively by the Greek word *parousia* (literally meaning 'presence' or 'coming'). The New Testament frequently speaks of those times, perhaps because they were thought to be imminent, or maybe just to keep the Christians 'on their toes' because, though not yet happened or imminent, they would surely come and the Christians had better be ready. Nowadays, the warnings about the need to be prepared are still salutary and helpful for us, but with the aim of keeping us prepared for our own death rather than the end times.

The final paragraph of the reading (verses 47 and 48) reverts to the parables and speaks of the punishment of delinquent servants. It seems that, at this stage of the teaching, by 'the servants' Jesus means not so much all those whom he is addressing, but the leaders of the Christian communities. If that is correct, the moral of the teaching need not be restricted to the *parousia* or to our own deaths; it can well be understood as referring to the state of the Church (whether worldwide or local). The Church can become inactive, becalmed, static, somnolent, moribund – there are many adjectives to describe the malady. If this happens, the blame may lie principally with the leaders; but, especially since Vatican II, lay people have been encouraged and, I hope, empowered 'to do something about it'.

The first reading (Wisdom 18:6-9), dating from the first century BC, speaks of God's time of retribution. He will, at the same time, reward the virtuous and punish the evil.

Today we begin four excerpts from the letter to the Hebrews, all four taken from chapters 11 and 12. The book, written in approximately AD 67 by an unknown author, is addressed to a group of Jewish converts to Christianity. This excerpt (11:1-2.8-19) explains that faith is always for a future benefit. As such, God who grants the benefit is pleased by the confident faith of the recipient. The author cites several examples from the lives of Abraham and his wife Sarah.

TWENTIETH SUNDAY IN ORDINARY TIME – Year C

Luke 12:49-53

This gospel passage brings together some sayings of Jesus, not necessarily uttered on a single occasion. The first of the two short paragraphs gives a glimpse into Jesus' deepest human thoughts and feelings as he awaits, with impatience and dread, the events that will be the culmination of his mission on earth. The phrase, 'to bring fire to the earth' is vague; probably the fire that will inflame the hearts of those who will be faithful in their trials and are destined for eternal life. The 'baptism' here refers to Jesus' forthcoming passion with all the sorrow and suffering into which he will be 'plunged'.

The second paragraph is really a cry of disappointment because not all who hear his message will respond. His teaching will produce dissension and division, even in a family, between those who are eager to respond and the complacent, content to remain as they are.

Jesus came on earth to establish God's kingdom but we know that that implies not stability but change, not resignation to the *status quo* but a search for a fair and just society. The kingdom that Jesus builds requires profound and radical change. There is so much misery and suffering caused by wrongdoing and which therefore has to cease. So the change needed is a change in our consciences, a change from complacency and apathy to a vision that promotes activity. This may seem idealistic talk, utopian ambition but, if we take him seriously, it is what Jesus asks of his followers. Discipleship is certainly not escapism but standing up for principles, a posture that can bring problems, ridicule, failure and, in some places, real physical danger. 'Go and announce the gospel of the Lord', the priest bids us at the end of Mass; to which we reply, 'Thanks be to God'. Do we really mean those words? Are we truly pleased to be given that duty?

In the sixth century BC, the prophet Jeremiah (38:4-6.8-10) always spoke the truth when giving God's message. What he said was not always welcome news and at times he became very unpopular. On one occasion, the message was that Jerusalem would fall into the hands of the Chaldean army and so the people, to save their lives, should surrender rather than resist. For this unwelcome advice, Jeremiah was thrown into a deep, dry well. Fortunately, the king ordered that he be pulled out before he died.

Hebrews (12:1-4) tells the Jewish converts to be brave in the face of hostility, to persevere in their new faith and to be inspired by the example of Jesus, faithful despite all the opposition and suffering he endured.

TWENTY-FIRST SUNDAY IN ORDINARY TIME – Year C

Luke 13:22-30

Luke reminds us that, from the gospel of the thirteenth Sunday (9:51), he is describing events while Jesus is making his way from Galilee to Jerusalem. It was not a direct journey but Jesus was teaching as he went and therefore stopping in villages and towns and making detours. We are told that, on one occasion, someone asked Jesus how many people would be saved. Jesus did not answer that question but took the opportunity to say that salvation would not be automatic.

He expresses this by talking about the entrance being narrow. We recall that (in John 10:7-9) Jesus describes himself as 'the gate of the sheepfold'. Therefore, to enter through the narrow door is to learn to live like he did, to take whatever cross we are given and to bear it willingly and patiently, to be sincerely trying to imitate him. We have learned that the way of Jesus is not by scrupulous observance of man-made laws but by fidelity in our love of God and by loving our neighbours through working for a world of justice and peace. Jesus implies that membership of the Jewish race is not a guarantee of salvation, not even membership of the religious leadership and meticulously fulfilling all the many precepts of the Mosaic law.

In our day, therefore, in our efforts to be Christ's disciples, we must remember the example that he gives us. He prayed to the Father, he accepted and carried out the Father's will but, in addition, his life was constantly a reaching out to the poor, the neglected, the despised. He not only helped them and encouraged them, but he served them, he lived with them and, I think that we can say, he was content to be one of them.

The final verse of today's extract is a proverb that can be used in a wide variety of situations. The circumstances in which Luke quotes it are different from the occasions on which it appears in Mark (10:31) and Matthew (20:16, as well as 19:30).

The first reading today is from the final chapter of Isaiah (66:18-21) and therefore dates from the sixth century BC and the end of the exile in Babylon. It foresees a time when God will summon all nations and peoples, and not only Jews in the diaspora, to come together to witness his glory. The text is seen as messianic as well as eschatological (that is, referring to the end time and the *parousia*).

In the letter to the Hebrews (12:5-7.11-13), the Jews are told that, just as a human father will reprimand and even punish his children but still love them, the same is true of God's treatment of us, his adopted sons and daughters. God's correction is, in fact, a proof of his love for us and not a reason for us to be discouraged.

TWENTY-SECOND SUNDAY IN ORDINARY TIME – Year C

Luke 14:1.7-14

The gospels remind us so frequently of the poor relationship that existed between Jesus and Pharisees that it is surprising to find that one of the latter, and a leading one at that, had invited Jesus to eat at his house and in the company of lawyers and other Pharisees. The lectionary omits five verses in which we are told that, in the Pharisee's house, Jesus cured a man with dropsy (an illness in which fluids cause the body to swell), that it was a Sabbath but that the other guests could find no way to object.

The reading today, having omitted that episode, has Jesus correcting first the guests and then the host. It does, at least at first sight, seem surprising to find Jesus doing this. Is his correction of the guests for trying to get the best places not a breach of courtesy? And to tell the host the kind of guests he should invite seems ungrateful and rude. Indeed we might feel that it was no wonder that the Pharisees disliked him.

Exegetes explain Jesus' behaviour by pointing out that, in both cases, he is in fact explaining how things will be in heaven, often anticipated as a banquet. The way things will be at the Father's table should provide a model for us on earth. (Can we take the analogy further, and suggest its application to the manner in which we should celebrate a Eucharistic meal on earth?) Those who are at God's table in heaven are those who are invited because they recognise their unworthiness and their need to be given the grace of salvation. They will then be under no illusion that they ought to be in the places of honour. Meanwhile, when God is the host, his invitations will, of necessity, go only to those who cannot repay or return the favour. God's favours are totally gratuitous and cannot be matched. In fact, we know from Jesus' practice and his words that it is quite literally 'the poor, the crippled, the lame, the blind' (verse 13) who will be invited by God to be at his table.

In the world and in the culture in which we live, it is not easy to show kindness without expecting (if not hoping) for something in return. The person who is the recipient of our generosity will want to reciprocate; it would be discourteous for us to refuse. But there may be some occasions when we can do something that will not bring a return; our time, perhaps, or a piece of work freely and gladly done – and it would be good if we were ready to seize such opportunities whenever they arise.

Ecclesiasticus was a first century BC book written to encourage Jews to remain faithful to their traditions in a prevailing hellenistic, and therefore, pagan culture. In this extract (3:17-20.28-29) the author advises his readers to act humbly and so to please God.

The letter to the Hebrews (12:18-19.22-24) contrasts the fearful drama with which God inaugurated the covenant between himself and the Jews at Mount Sinai with the sublime peace of the heavenly Mount Zion where God, along with the angels and saints, celebrates his new covenant mediated by Jesus his Son.

TWENTY-THIRD SUNDAY IN ORDINARY TIME – Year C

Luke 14:25-33

The gospel passage appointed for today begins with a paragraph on the total dedication Christ wants from those who are his disciples. We are told that great crowds were with Jesus as he made his way (presumably on one of the days during his long journey to Jerusalem). His words are demanding and uncompromising. Discipleship requires that the commitment to following him must have absolute priority. Family commitments must not get in the way (although the use of the word 'hating' is a 'Hebraism' which, in the parallel text in Matthew (10:37), has been toned down to 'prefer'). To parents and siblings (as in Matthew), Luke adds 'wife', presumably because, in the fuller life of the kingdom, there will be different relationships. Luke ends this paragraph on the disciple's life of renunciation by quoting Jesus on the need to carry the cross. For 'carry', Luke alone of the evangelists uses the same verb as is used of Jesus carrying his cross (John 19:17).

This paragraph on the dedication of the disciple is followed by two short parables. However, their subject is somewhat different from dedication, though related. The parables illustrate the need for careful planning and calculation before embarking on any important undertaking. So the conclusion of the parables is that discipleship should not be begun on impulse; we should first count the cost. And the passage ends by declaring the cost – giving up all our possessions.

The teaching of this gospel excerpt has special relevance for those who think that God's call to discipleship is, for them, in the priesthood or in consecrated life. The careful calculation that must take place can start before formal application to the relevant authority and, of course, should continue until a clear decision can be made.

But the same point should be made in the case of groups, communities, parishes or even dioceses which consider entering upon a process of some kind of pastoral or spiritual renewal, an exercise in discipleship that entails both the individual in his or her own personal life and then, presumably, some efforts at evangelisation. The careful planning and calculation would have to include not only the commitment and dedication of the people involved plus adequate preparation for them, but also some thought about those whom it is hoped to encounter in the subsequent work of sharing the faith. Are we in touch with how they think and feel? Do we speak the language they speak? Would our words be so dated as to be irrelevant? And similar issues.

The first reading, from the book of Wisdom (9:13-18), is appreciative of God's gift to us of his wisdom, his 'holy spirit from above'. It is wisdom that gives us insight into the will and intentions of God and thus enables us to please him.

Paul's letter to Philemon (9-10.12-17) is a personal letter to a friend. Philemon owns a slave called Onesimus, whom Paul met after he had escaped. Paul converted him and is now sending him back to his master with the hope that henceforth he will treat him as a brother. (Paul, of course, does not enter the question of the morality of slave ownership.)

TWENTY-FOURTH SUNDAY IN ORDINARY TIME – Year C

Luke 15:1-32

The entire fifteenth chapter of Luke's gospel is used for today's reading. It is devoted to one subject – God's mercy for sinners. The scene is set by the scribes and Pharisees whose criticism of Jesus for being in the company of tax collectors (who had a reputation as fraudsters and swindlers) and sinners in general allows Jesus to respond with three parables in order to explain that God wants to show concern and compassion for such people whom the respectable shun.

The parables of the lost sheep and the lost coin teach the same lesson, namely, that just as a shepherd will search untiringly for one lost sheep until it is found, and just as a poor woman will go to great lengths to find a lost coin, so will God be diligent and untiring in searching for a sinner who has strayed. Moreover, just as the shepherd and the woman will invite their friends and neighbours to celebrate the success of their searches, so also will there be a celebration in heaven over the repentance and return of a sinner. The first parable is also in Matthew's gospel (18:12-14) although there it is used among Christ's instructions to his disciples to be diligent in urging sinners to repent. The other parable is only in Luke, as is the third and very well known parable.

The parable of the Prodigal Son (so called) is also on the theme of the inexhaustible mercy of God. The father's love for his lost son is very clear. He is in his thoughts and hopes before there is any sign of the young man's return. He is on the look-out for the son and, when he spots him far off, he runs to meet him. Pardon is assured and no sins are too great to be forgiven. The reaction of the father when he is reunited with his son is further evidence of the father's yearning. The elder son's contempt and anger is also obvious in his reaction to the father's explanation; he does not even use the word 'father', as the sinner had. The attitude of the elder son towards his younger brother is like that of the scribes and Pharisees towards sinners.

There are some other aspects of the parable that, though less obvious, should be noted. The younger son, in seeking his share of his father's inheritance in order to leave home and in setting off 'for a distant country' is greatly insulting to his father by wanting to rid himself of the father's presence (as sin indicates a similar attitude towards God). His wild life brings no lasting happiness but soon results in regret, disgust and self-loathing at having been so stupid (as a life of sin can so easily do).

The desire for freedom has proved a false attraction and great folly. The sinner's regret is self-pity at first, but the father's love changes it into true contrition. Are there not many of us who would return to be reconciled to God if only we knew how God would receive us? No wonder that the parable of the Prodigal Son is such a favourite!

A few other thoughts come to mind. First, that although we live in a world where only efficiency and success are valued, there is room in God's love for everyone, including the failures, the avoided and rejected, the 'losers'. Second, the lesson that God gives of unconditional acceptance of all is an example that should be followed by us, both as individuals and as members of communities and especially by our parishes. And lastly, God's love for us is freely given, not earned – the same lesson as in the parable of the labourers in the vineyard (Matthew 20:1-16).

In the book of Exodus (32:7-11.13-14), the people begin to worship an idol and offer sacrifices to it while Moses is on Mount Sinai with God. God tells Moses that they must be punished for their idolatry but, after Moses' pleading, God relents.

In the first of three excerpts from the first letter to Timothy (1:12-17), Paul thanks Christ for both the grace of forgiving his past sins and bringing him to faith, and then for calling him into his service.

TWENTY-FIFTH SUNDAY IN ORDINARY TIME – Year C

Luke 16:1-13

Jesus lived a life of poverty and had no interest in material possessions or wish to be wealthy. Those with whom he mixed or with whom he had the greatest sympathy were also poor. Nevertheless, Jesus does have clear views on money and wealth. He often speaks on the subject and points out how it is frequently associated with greed and dishonesty. Today's excerpt illustrates this. It is interesting to note that, in verse 14, the first after this excerpt, we are told: 'The Pharisees, who loved money, heard all this and laughed at him'. Jesus' rejoinder is stern. He brands them as hypocrites, pretending to be virtuous, 'but God knows your hearts'. So let us see what caused the Pharisees' scorn.

Jesus tells the people a parable about a dishonest steward. The man had been wasteful with his master's property and so was to be dismissed. So, since the future was financially bleak for him, he grants favours to several of those in debt to his master by dishonestly reducing the amounts they owed so that they will return the compliment by taking care of him when no longer employed. The parable ends with Jesus saying that, when the master heard of the deceit, he praised the steward not for his dishonesty but for his shrewd foresight.

The observation which follows (verse 8b) may have been made by Jesus on some occasion and is inserted here as apt for the situation; or it may be a later insertion. It is a remark that wishes that, in similar circumstances, good people were equally foresighted. Most of the rest of the excerpt (verses 9-13) recounts various sayings attributed to Christ and collected here as a suitable place for them. The first is vague. It perhaps means that, since having money usually means that it was ill-gotten, the best way of using it is to give it to the poor so that, at the judgment, the poor who have preceded you to the next world will speak in your favour. The final verse of the excerpt (i.e., the last two sentences) insists on the total commitment required of disciples. It is therefore not specifically on the issue of money and its use.

The conclusion that we draw from today's gospel reading is that we must use with care the money and wealth that we possess. To be wealthy, successful in that sense, is not a sign of God's favour or blessing. We have to try to ensure that any use that we make of money is moral and honest; and we have always to remember that the possession of excessive amounts of money when there are people living in penury and destitution is immoral. It is easy to criticise others (the banks, the arms trade, international sports stars as well as so many unscrupulous rich organisations and people) but do not overlook the need for self-examination!

In the first reading (Amos 8:4-7), the prophet (eighth century BC) condemns those who, by oppression, dishonesty and fraud, treat the poor unjustly. God's punishment awaits them.

Paul advises (1 Timothy 2:1-8) that we should pray for everyone since God wants everyone to be saved. It was for this that Jesus gave his life and Paul, 'a teacher of the faith and the truth to the pagans', witnesses to this.

TWENTY-SIXTH SUNDAY IN ORDINARY TIME – Year C

Luke 16:19-31

The parable of the rich man and Lazarus is found only in Luke's gospel, although there are similar stories known in Egypt and in rabbinical literature. The rich man's lifestyle on earth is not only one of luxury, opulence and ostentatious comfort; but also is so self-centred that he is able each day to go past the poor man, starving and ill, without apparently noticing his state and completely indifferent to him. Their respective fortunes change at their deaths. The poor man, we are told, is taken by angels to 'the bosom of Abraham', a Jewish expression for life in paradise; the rich man merely dies and is buried. Next, we find him in hades, *sheol*, and in great torment.

The parable then continues with exchanges between Abraham and the rich man to indicate that there can be no relaxation of the torment, no possibility of escape and no way of warning those still alive on earth of the agony in the next life that awaits the uncaring rich. The dialogue in the parable ends with Abraham closing the discussion by stating that, since the unrepentant rich seem impervious to the warnings of Moses or the prophets, neither will they be convinced 'even if someone should rise from the dead', a clear indication that Jesus knew that he would die in vain for such people.

In our time, there are millions of people like Lazarus. Because of television, we have some awareness of the situation, due to war and other forms of violence, to diseases and the lack of medical and health facilities, to refugees fleeing from persecution or danger, and to the grinding poverty and destitution so widespread in the world. To some extent, we also know that, in our own neighbourhood, people are living in poverty. The unequal and unjust distribution of wealth is a sinful scandal. The temptation is to be so used to these problems that we become inured to them, cease to advert to them, ignore them and live oblivious to them and to the duty we have to show compassion and a desire to do something to help.

Perhaps we should also note that our Church institutions such as Caritas, SCIAF and Aid to the Church in Need deserve as much support as we can give in their attempt not just to help the victims of poverty but also to seek ways to reduce its causes. Popes, and especially Pope Francis, have pleaded with authorities and powers on such areas as economic tariffs, national debts, the arms trade, corrupt regimes and support for dictatorships, without, it seems, much success. It often happens that the only reaction is a rebuke that 'the Church should not meddle in politics'.

The prophet Amos (6:1.4-7) again provides the first reading. The subject is exactly the same as the gospel passage and is a hard-hitting criticism of the hedonistic wealthy. 'The ruin of Joseph' is a reference to conditions in the northern state of Israel.

In the first letter to Timothy (6:11-16), Paul encourages his pupil, now presiding in the church in Ephesus, to continue faithfully in both his conduct and his work.

TWENTY-SEVENTH SUNDAY IN ORDINARY TIME – Year C

Luke 17:5-10

The short extract which provides today's gospel reading has Jesus instructing the apostles on two subjects. To their request for more faith, Jesus replies that it is the quality of their faith that is important, rather than its quantity. Then, he reminds them that, as disciples, they must fulfil all their duties faithfully and well; they should never be satisfied with anything less. To illustrate the point, he uses a parable about what is expected of a servant working on a farm; the servant would expect to have duties both on the farm and also in the farmer's house – he would not think he could relax when only half of his duties were carried out. Luke is the evangelist who most stresses the total commitment asked of disciples. There seems little connection between the two subjects: deeper faith and total commitment, unless perhaps Paul's teaching on justification by faith has influenced the two being placed together.

To return to the apostles' request on faith. We are speaking not of the content of our beliefs, but of the virtue of believing what God has revealed. The latter is a gift from God, not a conclusion thought out by ourselves; it does not need to be justified by human reasoning. It is given at baptism but, for those baptised in infancy, it lies dormant until revived. God gives us (or revives) the virtue of faith (provided we have no objection) usually quite suddenly and to our surprise. It happens during a spiritual experience, either trivial (for example, as we are 'praying' a hymn, or during Mass on a special occasion) or profound (for example, an illness, or the death of a loved person). We suddenly realise that we know and accept some basic truth about Christ – that 'Jesus is Lord' or 'My Lord and my God' or something like that – and that the knowledge and acceptance have come quite spontaneously and yet fully convincingly. On this foundation, we can now build the content of faith.

I think that the previous paragraph can be a help for those who truly long to believe, or who wonder if they have faith or who struggle with the issue. An awareness that faith is a gift from God can comfort those of us who pray: 'Lord, I do have faith. Help the little faith I have' or, in other words, 'Lord, I believe. Help my unbelief' (Mark 9:24) or who cherish Jesus' words to Thomas: 'Happy are those who have not seen and yet believe' (John 20:29).

The first reading has the prophet Habakkuk (1:2-3; 2:2-4), around 600 BC, searching for a solution to the problem of evil. Why does God allow it? Why does he allow evil people to make others suffer? God replies that we must be patient and await an answer.

In the first of four extracts from the second letter to Timothy (1:6-8.13-14), Paul urges him to renew the gift of the Spirit of power and love which God gave him 'when I laid my hands on you' (the essential action of ordaining a priest). Thus he is to be fearless in his witness and faithful to the sound teaching which Paul gave him.

TWENTY-EIGHTH SUNDAY IN ORDINARY TIME – Year C

Luke 17:11-19

The story of the ten lepers is well known and for several reasons. First, we are astonished and moved to pity when we discover the fate that befell anyone who contracted the disease in those days; and to be Jewish involved near banishment and becoming an object of horror. Then, the fact that only one of the ten returned to show gratitude to Jesus and to praise God – 'and he was a Samaritan' – is not forgotten either in the telling or in the remembering.

Some Scripture scholars have wondered whether the story was originally a parable which Jesus told and which gradually developed into an event that really happened. Others, aware that Luke has placed this story in the long section within the context of the journey from Galilee to Jerusalem, are puzzled by the location of a village 'along the border between Samaria and Galilee'. The Greek wording literally means 'through the middle of Samaria and Galilee' but, in the usual derived translation, it means that Jesus was going eastward along the border in order to reach the Jordan valley, from where he would go south to Jericho. However, since it is thought that Luke was vague about the geography of Palestine, perhaps we should not attempt to be too precise.

The gospel makes a point of noting that it was a Samaritan who alone returned (the same emphasis as is laid on the identity of the hero in the parable of the Good Samaritan). He returned, it is said, not only to thank Christ but also to praise God. Jesus then sent him on his way with the words, 'Your faith has saved you' – presumably the faith which all ten had in asking to be healed, but made manifest again only by the man who retuned to praise God.

Many of us have had the experience of recovering from serious illness or injury. Nowadays, with the astonishing advances in medical science in its many branches, as well as the skill and care of the professional workers, the recovery rate is much higher than even a generation ago. Many conditions, also, are curable that, a short time ago, would have been beyond hope. Yet, as well as the human efforts and skills involved, it is good also for us to be grateful to God who has gifted humans with the wisdom and intelligence to bring about such advances. Recovery from illness or injury is not limited merely to the specific cause of the problem being removed; a more holistic healing also occurs and that should lead us to a renewed and closer relationship with the God who shows his love and care in so many wonderful ways.

The first reading is from the second book of the Kings (5:14-17). It is part of the story of Naaman the Syrian (mid-ninth century BC) who was healed from leprosy by bathing in the Jordan, following the advice of the prophet Elisha. The final sentence of the extract is because Naaman, in gratitude, wanted to build an altar in Syria to the God of Israel.

In the second reading (2 Timothy 2:8-13), Paul in prison declares his steadfastness for the sake of the gospel of salvation and in spite of all his sufferings.

TWENTY-NINTH SUNDAY IN ORDINARY TIME – Year C

Luke 18:1-8

The parable of the unscrupulous judge and the importunate widow is found only in Luke, who introduces it with an explanation of its moral – the need to be persevering in prayer. Nevertheless, it can evoke other thoughts and feelings in us, namely, the fact that, especially for people without influence (and a widow is the classic example in Scripture of that), justice is often delayed and even denied by the powerful; while another reaction to the parable is the assurance that God will respond to our pleading, in contrast with human officials.

The meaning of verse 7 is obscure. It may mean that God will allow time for the evil person to repent; or that he will delay some actions until the end time. The meaning of the final sentence, 'At the second coming, will there be any faith on earth?', is also difficult to understand. Certainly, it seems to have little relevance to the rest of the extract.

One of the most common examples of injustice in the world is the difficulty that people without power or influence (and also, in many cases, without money to offer in bribes) experience in getting justice from the powerful. The difficulty may be in long delay or in complicated bureaucratic systems or in the lack of competent help or in sheer unfair or criminal judges or mediators. We are used to seeing long lines of people patiently waiting to receive attention; delays seem endemic throughout officialdom and inseparable from bureaucracy. There is a huge area of suffering, much of it unnecessary, that is inflicted on people without influence.

As well as praying for them and doing what we can to seek an improvement in the treatment offered them, we should take very great care that we are not, perhaps unconsciously, among the guilty. Specifically, I sometimes think that, even in church matters and business, people can suffer through delay or unpunctuality or careless forgetfulness or just sheer lack of consideration. Would it be worth our while to check on our behaviour in this regard or on the bad habits into which we may have fallen? People are often not brave enough to complain to those in authority lest they offend the people from whom they hope for help.

The book of Exodus (17:8-13) relates the story of an attack by the pagan Amalekites on Israel while the latter were on their journey from slavery in Egypt to the new home promised by God. The Israelites prevailed with God's help and due to the resourceful and patient supplication of Moses.

In the second letter to Timothy (3:14-4:2), Paul reminds his former assistant and who now leads the church in Ephesus to be diligent in proclaiming the message of salvation. In particular, he should use the wisdom of the Scriptures (at that time, the Old Testament) in fulfilling the task.

THIRTIETH SUNDAY IN ORDINARY TIME – Year C

Luke 18:9-14

The parable of the Pharisee and the publican, exclusively in Luke, again (as last week's) has an explanatory introduction, stating that Jesus told it to some who thought highly of their own holiness but with a low opinion of everyone else. The parable narrative is straightforward and the two characters, Pharisee and publican, express their attitudes very clearly. The Pharisee is pleased to remind God that he faithfully observes all the precepts of the law of Moses and that, in his own character, he is a paragon of virtue. For good measure, he compares himself with the publican and, of course, greatly to his own advantage since he feels he has to tell the truth about the publican, thereby denigrating the man.

The publican, on the contrary, when speaking about himself, talks humbly about his sinfulness and his need of God's mercy. Hence, we are presented with two contrasting and irreconcilable characters. One has the right attitude, the other's is unacceptable, and it is obvious which is which. Prayer is not self-praise and self-satisfaction. Such piety is merely legalistic. Such thoughts assume that God's mercy is not required; the person has maximum self-esteem and presumes that God has no choice but to reward him. The concluding verse of the excerpt is relevant to the story. It appears several times in the gospels (Matthew 18:4; 23:12; Luke 14:11) because of its wide relevance in many circumstances.

The contrast between the two characters is so extreme that there is a certain element of exaggeration and unreality in them, but the parable should compel us to examine our consciences with humility and perhaps even with shame. Here are some questions that might arise in such an examination. Am I praying to someone real? Do I pray with faith and with real conviction? Am I really aware of my need for God and his mercy? Does my prayer also include praise and thanksgiving?

_{The book of Ecclesiasticus (35:12-14.16-19) declares that God is 'no respecter of personages' and that he has a special concern for people who are poor and without influence but who seek his help humbly.}

_{In the final extract from his second letter to Timothy (4:6-8.16-18), Paul speaks as one conscious of nearing death. He recalls his arrest and interrogation in Rome (soon after he arrived or at the start of his later trial) and thanks God that he was subsequently able to continue his preaching.}

THIRTY-FIRST SUNDAY IN ORDINARY TIME – Year C

Luke 19:1-10

The Zacchaeus episode makes a charming story and a very popular one too. So much so that a high metal fence now surrounds the sycamore which, if not actually the Zacchaeus tree, is fondly thought to occupy the exact spot. Unprotected, the tree had become the object of pilgrims who had ambitions to climb it (for the photograph rather than in the hope of a Zacchaeus experience) or at least to remove part of it to show to their friends at home.

It is, of course, no surprise that Jericho is an attractive town. It is an oasis in the grim Judean desert, it is Palestinian and peaceful, and it has a history counted in millennia. It is therefore a magnet for archaeologists and biblical scholars, for it is where the walls fell down as the Israelites crossed the Jordan to conquer and occupy the land God had promised them. It has other attractions, including its varied and delicious selection of fruit and, in addition to the Zacchaeus episode, the town was also the scene of Bartimaeus being cured of his blindness by Jesus (in Luke 18:35-43, immediately prior to today's passage; at Matthew 20:29-34; and at Mark 10:46-52, where it forms the gospel reading for the thirtieth Sunday in year B).

The basic story of Zacchaeus is of the radical repentance and conversion (*metanoia*) of a man who, being a tax collector, and a senior one at that, and wealthy also, would be presumed by all to be a great sinner. In fact Zacchaeus practically confesses his guilt in his promise to make reparation and in even greater measure than the law of Moses required. The passage ends with Jesus summing up his part in the story with the words, 'The Son of Man has come to seek out and save what was lost'.

The example of Zacchaeus' conversion is impressive. He was a public figure in the town and, with his wealth and his position, had every prospect of a very comfortable life. It was not easy for him to seek the path of change; perhaps even his lack of inches symbolises that he had obstacles to overcome. Despite being established in a profitable way of life and despite the public embarrassment of the change he contemplated, he accepted the opportunity and the grace of God available at that moment. The part which Jesus had in the transformation of Zacchaeus is typical of him. He recognises the man's simplicity and sincerity. He is open, approachable, ready to forgive the sinner and not slow to be seen as a friend enjoying his company and hospitality. Certainly, in the conduct of both Jesus and Zacchaeus in their encounter, there is plenty of good example for all of us as well as the enjoyment of a happy story.

The book of Wisdom (11:22-12:2) thanks God for his love of all that he has created and for the gentle manner in which he corrects wrongdoing.

St Paul wrote twice to the Thessalonians in the years 50-51, soon after his visit to their city. Today's excerpt, the first of three from the second letter (1:11-2:2), assures them of his prayers for continued progress in their faith. He counsels caution in their expectation of an early second coming of Christ.

THIRTY-SECOND SUNDAY IN ORDINARY TIME – Year C

Luke 20:27-38

In Luke's gospel, Jesus has been slowly making his way from Galilee to Judea. He has now completed the journey and is in Jerusalem. He is frequently in the temple grounds, teaching the people as well as being a source of annoyance and threat to the religious authorities. He gets into argument with several groups of these, most of whom seem hostile. Today's gospel reading is the record of a challenge he had from some Sadducees. These were descendants of Zadok the High Priest, a priestly group, generally aristocratic and conservative and known as denying the resurrection of the dead, since that teaching is not found in the Pentateuch.

Today's reading has some Sadducees attempting to use a scarcely possible situation arising because a woman had married seven brothers one after another in an attempt to produce a male heir to keep the family line alive. This is called the obligation of levirate marriage (stated in Deuteronomy 25:5); the precept is vague and it is unknown whether the obligation still prevailed at the time of Jesus.

To the Sadducees' question Jesus replies that, in the next life, people do not marry, they do not have bodies as on earth, they are not going to die and so do not require to be replaced, and they have become God's children. Jesus then clinches his argument by citing Moses who spoke of God as the God of Abraham, Isaac and Jacob, none of them any longer alive on earth – but God is not a God of the dead but of the living. The phrase (at the end of verse 38) 'for to him (God) all men are in fact alive' seems to mean that the life of the resurrected is indeed enjoyed here on earth by the just who are destined for heaven.

The incident in today's reading is also found in Mark (12:18-27) and in Matthew (22:23-33). All three gospels mention that some scribes heard the clash. Most scribes were Pharisees and believed in the resurrection of the dead. Mark and Matthew therefore recount that, at the conclusion of the Sadducees' encounter with Jesus, a scribe (Mark) or a Pharisee (Matthew) asked him, in what Mark indicates was a friendly fashion (though Matthew says the motive was to trap Jesus), which was the greatest commandment of the law. This latter incident is, instead, used by Luke to introduce the parable of the Good Samaritan (10:25-28 and fifteenth Sunday in Ordinary Time, year C).

The gospel reading this Sunday is, for us all, a reassurance that not only is there life after death but also that we can look forward to the resurrection of the body (an article of faith which, of course, is included in the creeds and professions of faith of the Church). A further and useful point is derived from the incident, namely, that although God does not allow his beloved adopted children to cease to exist, neither has he yet disclosed to us what the details of life after death, whether prior to the resurrection of the body or afterwards, will be. All we know is that God has prepared for us a life that is new and will completely satisfy our deepest longing. Our faith is not able to satisfy our curiosity with details, but faith and love should nourish our hope.

The celebration of the Eucharist is both a pledge and a foretaste of our eternal life. In the embolism after the Lord's Prayer in every Mass, we pray to be free from sin and safe from all distress 'as we await the blessed hope and the coming of our Saviour'. And, before receiving the Lord in Holy Communion, we proclaim, in reference to the 'banquet' in heaven, 'Blessed are those called to the supper of the Lamb'.

The two books of Maccabees tell the tale of the persecution which the Jews in Palestine, and especially the family of Maccabees, endured in the second century BC. The first reading (2 Maccabees 7:1-2.9-14) recounts the heroic deaths of seven brothers, executed by the persecutors. The specific importance of the reading is the witness of the brothers to belief in life after death and, since the Jews did not make a distinction between body and soul, to resurrection (of both body and soul).

In his second letter to the Thessalonians (2:16-3:5), Paul urges the Christians of the city to pray for him, for themselves and for the spread of 'the Lord's message'. Particularly noteworthy, in view of the gospel passage today, is Paul's declaration that God has given us 'such inexhaustible comfort and such sure hope'.

THIRTY-THIRD SUNDAY IN ORDINARY TIME – Year C

Luke 21:5-19

In an earlier chapter (17:22-37, but not used in any Sunday gospel reading), Luke speaks of the end time and the coming of Jesus as universal king and judge. In the present chapter, and as with Matthew and Mark, he is reporting Jesus speaking not only of the end time (the *parousia*) but also of the destruction of Jerusalem, including the Temple, by the Roman army putting down a revolt of the Jews in AD 70. He probably gives more prominence to the revolt than to the *parousia*. However, as in the other gospels, it is difficult to disentangle what refers to the one and what to the other. The reason for the difficulty is due, in large measure, to the apocalyptic style of the writing that is used. Images, symbols and metaphors are not meant to be taken literally, leaving the reader to try to decipher the meaning.

In today's gospel reading, there are three paragraphs. The first paragraph (verses 5-7) appears to be fairly clearly about the revolt in AD 70. The second paragraph (verses 8-11) seems to refer to a more distant time, especially since there is a warning that there will be false rumours of Jesus' second coming having occurred. Therefore, perhaps some disasters are foretold that were to take place all over the world as preliminaries to the *parousia*. The third paragraph (verses 12-19) speaks of happenings, probably persecution, to occur prior to the calamities foretold in the second paragraph and which will have to be borne by those listening to Jesus.

He continues his discourse, although not included in the lectionary, and speaks apparently of the siege and destruction of Jerusalem, of cosmic disasters and of the coming of the

Son of Man, at which time 'your liberation is near at hand'. The only indication Jesus gives of when these happenings will take place is in a short parable. 'Think of the fig tree and indeed every tree. As soon as you see them bud, you know that summer is now near'. Jesus ends the discourse by urging that we should stay on the alert, ready 'to stand with confidence before the Son of Man' (21:36).

This gospel reading should remind us to be realistic. The destruction of Jerusalem occurred many centuries ago and, in spite of all the disasters and evils in the world at present, the end times seem to be still far off. Nevertheless, discipleship is never an easy road but always one of struggle and some hardships. We must try to be faithful to the gospel teaching of Jesus and not be distracted by other teachings or revelations. Even though conditions seem difficult and witnessing needs courage, Jesus wants us not to be silent or hidden, but brave enough, especially by the example of our lives, to let it be clear that we are followers of his teaching and his values.

The first reading is from the fifth century BC prophecy of Malachi (3:19-20). The short passage looks forward to a time when evildoers will be removed and 'the sun of righteousness' (perhaps a reference to the messiah) will shine on those who fear God.

In his second letter to the Thessalonians (3:7-12), Paul has heard that there are some of the Christians who are lazy and refuse to work. 'Don't let them have any food' is his advice. He tells them all to be like him and work as hard as they should.

LAST SUNDAY IN ORDINARY TIME – Year C
OUR LORD JESUS CHRIST, KING OF THE UNIVERSE

Luke 23:35-43

In year A, the gospel reading for this feast is our Lord's description of the last judgment with 'the King' separating the good people from the evil on the basis of their care (or lack of care) for those in need; in treating well or negligently those in need, they had, in fact, been treating him (Matthew 25:31-46).

In year B, the gospel reading is the exchange between Jesus and Pilate at the former's trial, when the governor asks him if he is a king (John 18:33-37).

In year C, the scene is Calvary. Above Jesus, on the cross, is the inscription naming him 'King of the Jews'. One of those crucified with him understands the meaning of Jesus' kingship and asks him to remember him 'when you come into your kingdom'.

Luke makes a distinction between the crowd who were merely 'watching' and the leaders who 'jeered'. The taunts and insults were taken up and continued by the Roman soldiers and by one of the men crucified along with Jesus while the other speaks of Jesus' innocence. From the sense of the words the latter uses in asking Jesus to remember him in his kingdom, it seems that he made the request repeatedly. Jesus, in his reply, uses the word 'paradise', a word of Persian derivation meaning a walled garden; it is used occasionally in the Scriptures, both in the Old Testament where it refers to the garden of Eden and in the New, meaning the home of the saints.

The story of the crucifixion of Jesus is the greatest affirmation that Jesus and his kingdom stand for service, love and a total dedication to saving humankind from sin and death. The crucifixion is also an invitation not only to thank Jesus but also to follow him in our dedication to a life and death of service. It was Jesus himself who told us that discipleship means taking up and carrying our cross. We know that bearing the cross can be burdensome and painful. In seeking justice where people are being abused and compassion where there is apathy, we court conflict and rejection. The person genuinely trying to follow Christ must remember that, as he said, he came to serve and not to be served. We must not let the cross or the crucifix give us a sense of release from involvement or responsibility. Rather, it must be a reminder that, even in the prosperous and comfortable society in which we live, we are still called to continue the work for which Jesus gave his life.

In some ways, the situation in which we contemplate our crucified Lord is one of utter degradation and shame. Suffering execution as a blasphemer and troublemaker, in the company of two thieves, with a notice mockingly proclaiming his claim to be a king, deserted by his chosen apostles, jeered by sneering Jewish leaders and Roman soldiers – he is a sorry sight. Yet this is also his exaltation, when we look on him with the eyes of faith, an awareness of the truth and a heart full of gratitude and love. We adore you, O Christ and we praise you, because by your holy cross you have redeemed the world.

The first reading is from the second book of Samuel (5:1-3). After the death of King Saul (late eleventh century BC), the kingdom of Israel split and David for seven years was king only of the southern part. Then the northern leaders went to David and invited him to be their king also. Thus the Israelites were reunited under David, one of the ancestors of Jesus.

An excerpt from Paul's letter to the Colossians (1:12-20) is the second reading. Paul teaches that the Father has made his Son, by his death on the cross, 'the first-born of all creation' in the sense that all creation has become subject to him. Moreover, God has 'created a place for us in the kingdom of his Son' and wanted 'all things to be reconciled through him and for him . . . when he made peace by his death on the cross'.

Solemnities and feasts which can occur on Sundays

THE PRESENTATION OF THE LORD – 2 February

Luke 2:22-40

This feast derives from the visit which the Holy Family paid to the Temple in Jerusalem in accordance with Jewish law and custom. When a child was born, the mother was ritually or ceremonially unclean and had to be purified. If her child was male, her purification took place forty days after the birth (Leviticus 12:2-4). In the case of the first male child in a family, he had to be presented to the Lord (Exodus 13:1-2.13-16) and redeemed by the gift of an animal or animals (for poor people, the offering was two doves or pigeons) for sacrifice (Leviticus 5:7-10 and 12:8). Mary in her maternity and Jesus, both uniquely graced, were not under any divine obligation to comply with the requirements of the law. They did so in order to express humbly their readiness to be in conformity and solidarity with other Jewish mothers and first-born sons (as is also evident in Jesus' circumcision). The whole episode contrives to give an impression of humble acceptance of God's will, a quiet readiness to do what is right, and a sense of the future destiny of the child in which the parents will have their part, although at this moment the awesome nature of what lies ahead is totally uncomprehended.

Simeon is described as 'upright and devout', words indicating that he was conscientious in observing all the moral precepts of the law. The text tells us that the Spirit guided him to the Temple to meet 'the Christ of the Lord', a phrase meaning someone anointed by God for a mission of salvation, in a word, the messiah. The canticle of praise which Simeon utters speaks of God's salvation being for all, not only for Israelites, and is expressed as light, a term that Jesus was to use of himself and is characteristic of the description of divine revelation in the apostle John's writing. The *Nunc dimittis* shows also Simeon's gratitude not just in seeing the child but in becoming aware that God's salvation is at last to take place.

The meaning of the words spoken by Simeon to Mary is not entirely clear. 'For the fall . . .' probably means that the messiah's message will force all people to face up to their sinfulness and, for some, this will be too much while it will lead others to new life. 'And a sword will pierce . . .', for most commentators, is an indication that Mary will share in the suffering experienced as a result of the messiah's mission.

In regard to Anna who served God constantly 'with fasting and prayer', various women in the Old Testament have been seen as 'prophetesses', sometimes by speaking in the Lord's name, but all by lives conformed to God's will. In both religions, Jewish and Christian, widows were respected and were often found in service of the community. Not only did Anna have the satisfaction of meeting the family and seeing the child; she fulfilled her prophetic work by speaking about him to those who were waiting and hoping for the realisation of God's promise of salvation.

The first reading of today's Mass is from the prophet of the fifth century BC, Malachi (3:1-4), who proclaims that, to rouse the nation and restore the virtuous ways that had been lost, 'the Lord you are seeking will suddenly enter his Temple'.

An extract from the letter to the Hebrews (2:14-18) provides the second reading. The Son of God became fully human in order to carry out God's plan of salvation for us by his passion, death and resurrection.

THE NATIVITY OF ST JOHN THE BAPTIST – 24 June

Luke 1:57-66.80

The accounts of the conceptions and births of John the Baptist and of Jesus are very different in their details, but they do have a certain parallel sequence. The announcements that both Elizabeth and Mary are to be mothers are made by the archangel Gabriel, although to the father Zechariah in the first case, to the prospective mother in the other. Both conceptions are unexpected and unusual. The two expectant mothers are cousins and they spend time together during their pregnancies. And as with Jesus, so also with John the Baptist, the story of the latter's conception, birth and first days, narrated in Luke's gospel (1:5-25.57-80), contains several allusions, some explicit, others less so, to persons, events and texts of the Old Testament which are being fulfilled or repeated in the present case. In particular, John is seen as the new Elijah, a man of austerity of life who will preach repentance for sin in preparation for the messiah (cf. Malachi 3:23 and Matthew 17:10-13 as well as Luke 1:17).

Nevertheless, the circumstances of the two babies' births are very different, John being born at home and with the attendance, then or soon after, of relations and neighbours. Jesus, on the other hand, was born far from his parents' home, in great poverty and without any relatives or neighbours in attendance to help or to rejoice with Mary and Joseph. However, shepherds soon heard the rejoicing of angels and, having been informed of the news, they went and visited the parents 'and the baby lying in the manger'.

Let us return to the event being commemorated in today's feast. Luke's account of John's birth and naming follows immediately after the story of Mary's visit to her cousin Elizabeth. Since Luke did not observe any strict chronological order but tended to finish his account of one item or event before starting to describe another, it is quite possible that Mary was present at John's birth even although Luke has already reported that, after a visit of three months, she went home.

The two details at John's birth and circumcision to which Luke devotes most attention are, first, the naming of the baby and, second, Zechariah, filled with the Spirit, proclaiming the canticle *Benedictus* (still sung or recited daily in the Church's official Morning Prayer). Today's gospel passage ends just before the text of the canticle is recorded. Circumcision was seen as the initiation of a male into the covenanted people of God, binding God to fulfil his promises to his chosen people and the people to observe faithfully the law's precepts. In this case, John's circumcision allows his father to decide the infant's name. Contrary to expectations, the name was not to be Zechariah but John and, as he asserted his decision on a writing tablet, the father recovered his speech, silent since the angel's appearance nine months previously.

Today's feast allows us to think ahead and to consider the life and mission of John the Baptist and especially his relationship with Jesus. John insists that he, John, must decrease as Jesus' prominence increases since he is the more important person for whom John was the herald. Even so, Jesus insists on being baptised by John – an event which is celebrated and whose significance is considered each year at the end of the season of Christmas liturgies. Soon after their meeting at the Jordan, Jesus began to proclaim that the Father had sent him to establish God's kingdom and to be the long awaited Saviour.

Today's first reading is from the later part (sixth century BC) of the prophecy of Isaiah (49:1-6). It is the second of the four 'Songs of the Servant of the Lord', usually seen as a prophecy about the awaited messiah, his suffering for others' sins and his final reward from God. At today's feast, however, the excerpt is referred to John the Baptist.

The second reading is an account of Paul's first recorded discourse to an assembly of Jews (Acts 13:22-26). He proclaims that, since God had promised King David that a descendant of his would be the awaited saviour of his people, that promise is fulfilled in Jesus Christ; and to announce the arrival of the messiah, God had sent John the Baptist.

SAINTS PETER AND PAUL, APOSTLES – 29 June

Matthew 16:13-19

Since the two great apostles are honoured jointly today, the liturgy is shared between them. As far as the Scripture readings are concerned, therefore, and since there are no appropriate excerpts in which both saints are prominent, the outcome is that the first reading and the gospel passage are about Peter, while Paul is the central figure of the second reading.

The gospel presents Matthew's description of the climax of Jesus' public ministry. It is an event recorded in all three synoptics, but rather more fully by Matthew. After the disciples had been in Christ's company for some considerable time as he travelled around Galilee, preaching and healing in towns and villages, he takes them north to the foothills of Mount Hermon. There, he asks them what the people who had seen and heard him thought of him; in particular, who did they think he was. Then, he comes to the crux of his questioning – who did they, his closest followers, think he was? It is Peter who answers the challenging question on their behalf. 'You are the Christ, the Son of the living God'. In Matthew alone, and not in the other two synoptic gospels, does the second half of Peter's reply appear; it could well be a later addition in line with a gradually developing faith of the full identity of Christ among the early Christians.

Matthew alone also has Christ's important response (verses 17-20). Although Peter had spoken for all the apostles, Christ's response is directed only to Peter. In it, Jesus declares that Peter was able to confess his master's messiahship only by a revelation from God and not from a deduction by himself or by others. (This offers an indication of how the early Christians thought the messiahship came to be known.) Peter, known until then as Simon bar-Jona, is given his new name, which signifies a rock, and indicates that Jesus wished to build his new community upon Peter, because it is on the solid faith which Peter has expressed that the Church will endure. It is not at all certain, however, that Jesus used the actual word 'church' (which appears in the gospels only here and in Matthew 18:17). Jesus goes on to assure the apostles that the power of *sheol* (not, therefore, 'of hell', but 'of death' since *sheol* was 'the abode of the dead') will not destroy the new community. It is he who established it, he who builds it, he who protects it. It is his.

In conferring on Peter 'the keys of the kingdom of heaven', he is giving leadership and authority since the key was the symbol of office of the chief officer of a court or palace; and here, 'the kingdom of heaven' does not mean a celestial location but rather the community of God's kingdom which Jesus is establishing here on earth. (Matthew, writing primarily for Jews, courteously avoids using the word 'God' and replaces it with 'heaven'.) 'Whatever you bind . . . whatever you loose . . .' specifies Peter's authority, but unfortunately its meaning is obscure. (The same phrase is used of the whole community in Matthew 18:18 and there it refers to the power of excommunication.) Perhaps it is best to clarify the meaning of the phrase when directed to Peter by examining the occasions in the New Testament when the community recognises the powers which Peter uses. It would seem that these powers, though primarily of exclusion from the community, were also used in matters of doctrinal belief and moral conduct. Catholics hold that the leadership and authority which Christ gave to Peter continue also in his successors since it is evident that Christ intended that the community he founded should not end with Peter's death.

The Church today is greatly changed from what it was like in the days of Saints Peter and Paul. Then it was a community of those who had discovered the gospel, who believed in Jesus Christ and who tried to live and behave in accordance with his message, example and teaching. It has to be admitted that, nowadays, most Christians have lost a lot of that joy and enthusiasm as well as the sense of being a community whose members love and care for one another and are anxious to share their faith and their hope with anyone and everyone. For many of us, our being members of the Church is reduced to having been born into a Catholic family, going to church with more or less frequency, not involved in any specific commitment to evangelising or to deepening our own awareness of the teaching of Christ, but ready, as occasion suggests, to criticise what we think are the faults of those who have some authority in the Church. We need to ask the Holy Spirit to renew us and the whole Church, both local and worldwide.

The first reading, from the Acts of the Apostles (12:1-11), gives an account of Peter's escape from prison in Jerusalem. He had been imprisoned by Herod Agrippa I, ruler of Judea (given the title of king by the Emperor Caligula in AD 41, and died 44), but an angel appeared to him the night prior to his trial and supervised his escape. Peter rejoiced at his unexpected release and so did the Christian community. Unfortunately, however, Herod Agrippa gave orders for the guards to be executed (verse 19).

The second reading is about St Paul. In one of his last letters (2 Timothy 4:6-8.17-18), he reflects on his strenuous life of travel and preaching and thanks God for having protected and guided him and for keeping him faithful to the message he proclaimed. He is sure that God will continue to keep him safe until he is received into eternal life.

THE TRANSFIGURATION OF THE LORD – 6 August

Matthew 17:1-9
Mark 9:2-10
Luke 9:28-36

The event which this feast commemorates is also the subject of the gospel reading on the second Sunday of Lent each year. The gospel for the particular year, A, B or C, is the same on this feast and on the second Sunday of Lent: Matthew in year A, Mark in year B, Luke in year C. The texts of the reflections will be found at the earlier dates.

On the feast day, the first reading each year comes from the book of Daniel (7:9-10.13-14). The book was written in the second century BC to encourage the Jews during a persecution by recounting the survival of Jews in similar straits centuries before. The reading is apocalyptic in genre and foresees a time when, in the presence of God enthroned and a huge multitude of saints, a figure 'like a son of man' is brought in and, on him, is conferred eternal 'sovereignty, glory and kingship'.

The second reading for each year is from the second letter of St Peter (1:16-19). That it was written by Peter is very doubtful, despite the claim that he is the author. The reading gives a short account of the transfiguration, followed by a declaration that the event provides a proof of the veracity and reliability of prophecies.

THE ASSUMPTION OF THE BLESSED VIRGIN MARY – 15 August

Luke 1:39-56

Since the assumption of Our Lady into heaven is not recorded in the Scriptures, another subject had to be chosen for the gospel reading of today's solemnity. The choice made is the story of the visit which Mary paid to Elizabeth after word reached her that her cousin, the older woman, was expecting a baby. Elizabeth lived in 'a town in the hill country of Judah'. That vague description fits the place generally supposed to have been where Elizabeth and Zechariah lived, now known as Ein Karim; it is in hilly country but nowadays it is more a suburb of Jerusalem than a town on its own.

The narrative records Elizabeth welcoming Mary with a very fulsome greeting, praising her holiness now greatly enhanced by the child in her womb and telling her that not only was she, Elizabeth, honoured by the visit but the baby she was carrying was also excited and happy. Mary's response to this welcome is the *Magnificat*.

This canticle of thanksgiving contains many phrases from the Old Testament, but it also expresses Mary's own deep faith in God. She extols the mercy and power of God in her human weakness and his loving care for the poor and needy. The second half of the canticle introduces God's ways of bestowing his help on those who are most in need – the humble, the lowly, the hungry, Israel his servant. On the other hand, God dislikes those who are powerful (and, by implication, who oppress the weak), the proud of heart, the high and mighty, the wealthy. This 'preferential option for the poor' is, of course, one of the most prominent values which Jesus taught and practised. It is an illustration of the closeness of Mary's values to those which her Son practised and preached. In our sometimes feeble attempts to imitate the ways of Jesus, we can, with confidence in her sympathetic understanding, ask for her intercession.

To revert to Mary's assumption, the doctrine is solemnly defined as revealed by God and known by us through the tradition of the Church, manifested in the teaching of the doctors of the Church and the constant profession and belief of the members of the Church. The proclamation of this dogma was made by Pope Pius XII on the feast of All Saints, 1st November in the Holy Year of 1950. I was among the many thousands who attended the ceremony, held in St Peter's Square in Rome. The text did not specify that Mary had died or not died, but said that, at the end of her earthly life, she was taken, body and soul, to heaven. Both Jerusalem and 'the House of Mary' near Ephesus in Turkey, claim to have been the place of Mary's assumption; but no one knows for certain which claimant, if either, has right on its side.

In his address on the occasion, the pope expressed the fitness of the doctrine. Just as Mary had been prevented (by an anticipation of the saving work of her son) from contracting original sin and, during her life, was totally innocent of any personal sin, it was also appropriate, indeed perhaps necessary, that the mother of God who, especially, had carried God's Son in her womb for nine months, should not suffer any degree whatsoever of bodily corruption. Mary, therefore, has been privileged to complete her process of total salvation earlier than any other human person. We ask for her intercession especially 'at the hour of our death' and it is right that we should ask her to bless us with a firm faith in 'the resurrection of the body'.

The first reading is from the Apocalypse (11:19; 12:1-6.10) and tells, in symbolic language, of a pregnant woman attacked by a dragon; she flees to the safety of the desert and her child, when born, is taken to God. Michael and the good angels defeat the dragon (Satan) and his angels in battle. The woman is presumed by many Christians to represent Mary.

Today's second reading (1 Corinthians 15:20-26) speaks of the risen Christ who has won resurrection from the dead for all and 'in their proper order' (but without any explicit mention of Mary or her assumption).

THE EXALTATION OF THE HOLY CROSS – 14 September

John 3:13-17

This feast derives from St Helena's discovery, while in Jerusalem on pilgrimage in 330, of the cross on which Jesus had died. A few years later, her son, the Emperor Constantine, ordered the construction of a church at the place where his mother found the cross. That building still forms the earliest part of the basilica of the Holy Sepulchre which encloses the sites both of Christ's crucifixion on the hill of Calvary and the tomb from which he rose on Easter morning. The building's very antiquity plus the many additions and embellishments of later centuries, combined with disagreements among the various Christian Churches which claim a place within the basilica, have resulted in the very unsatisfactory appearance of one of the most sacred churches on earth and its present condition that disappoints and upsets so many pilgrims.

The name of the feast, and especially the use of the word 'exaltation', comes from Jesus' words in today's gospel reading from St John: 'the Son of Man must be lifted up as Moses lifted up the serpent in the desert' (3:13). In John's gospel, the crucifixion of Jesus as well as his ultimate glorification in his resurrection and ascension to the Father are both described as 'being lifted up/exalted'. There are further instances of this double significance of Christ's exaltation at John 8:28 and 12:32-33.

In the present gospel passage, the setting is a meeting between Jesus and Nicodemus, the latter impressed by Jesus' powers and anxious to know more about him. The account which John gives of the meeting begins with a dialogue but develops into a monologue; and it is from this latter part that our excerpt comes. It may be best to go first to verses 16-17 which are the second half of today's reading. These verses make the basic point that God's unconditional love for us urges him to save us and bring us to eternal life; and we can achieve God's purpose if we believe in the Son whom he sent. In the first half of the reading, verses 13-15, Jesus begins by claiming his ability to reveal these truths because he came from heaven and will return there; then comes the important point which is relevant for today's feast.

'As Moses lifted up the serpent in the desert': because the Israelites were dissatisfied with the harsh conditions of life in the desert and became rebellious, God sent a plague of serpents whose bites killed many of the Jews. The people repented and begged for an end to the plague. So God told Moses to make a serpent of bronze and raise it to be seen; thereafter anyone who had been bitten had only to look at the bronze serpent and was thereby saved from death. This is the comparison which Jesus is making: when he is lifted up (on the cross), those who believe in him will be saved for eternal life. Because of its purpose and its effects, the crucifixion is truly an exaltation for Christ in the glory of his victory over sin and death, the triumph of his infinite love for us, as well as in the purely literal sense.

If we wish to imitate Christ in his love for our brothers and sisters and seek to free them from the unjust burdens they carry, we do so not by seeking suffering as if that were a virtue or a remedy in itself. But if our efforts, carried out whatever the consequences, do bring us suffering, then that can be regarded as courageous and creditable, work of an exalted character.

The first reading for today's feast gives us the Old Testament passage (Numbers 21:4-9) to which reference is made in the gospel extract.

The second reading, from Paul's letter to the Philippians (2:6-11), is the early hymn celebrating the double *kenosis* (emptying, humbling) that Christ accepted for love of us and which led to his consequent exaltation in triumph and glory.

THE SOLEMNITY OF ALL SAINTS – 1 November

Matthew 5:1-12

The solemn feast of All Saints originates in the change of purpose of the Pantheon, which had been a Roman temple in honour of pagan gods, but in 610 became instead a church in God's honour and to celebrate the Christian martyrs and other saints not given a specific feast day or mention in the *Martyrologium Romanum*. Since those who practise a life of the beatitudes are promised eternal life, it is totally appropriate that the gospel reading should be Christ's proclamation of the beatitudes as reported by St Matthew. The reflections will be found at the fourth Sunday in Ordinary Time, year A.

The first reading is from the Apocalypse (7:2-4.9-14) and records two visions. First, an assembly of one hundred and forty-four thousand people from all twelve tribes of Israel, gathered to be sealed as servants of God. Second, an innumerable crowd from every nation on earth, identified as martyrs, dressed in robes washed white in the blood of the Lamb and holding palms. They acclaim God and the Lamb and their praise is taken up and continued by all the angels.

The second reading, from the first letter of St John (3:1-3), speaks of God's love allowing us to be his children. Greater gifts, still unknown, await us. We shall see God as he really is and thus become like him.

THE DEDICATION OF THE LATERAN BASILICA – 9 November

John 2:13-22

Each diocese holds a feast annually to commemorate the dedication of its cathedral church. It is fitting, therefore, that the worldwide Church should celebrate a feast to mark the dedication of the cathedral church of Rome (which boldly describes itself as 'Mother and Head of all the churches of the city of Rome and of the world').

All four evangelists describe the scene in which Jesus drives the money changers and those selling animals out of the Temple in Jerusalem. But, whereas the synoptics suggest that the incident occurred only a few days before Jesus was arrested, John's gospel (today) places it at the start of his public ministry. Chronology was not uppermost in the evangelists' intentions but the variation allows us to mention a detail that can confuse us. The synoptics give the impression that Jesus made only one visit to Jerusalem during his public ministry and that was at the end of his Galilean labours and immediately preceding his arrest. John, on the other hand, has Jesus in Jerusalem several times during those two to three years. Most scholars consider it likely that John's information is more accurate chronologically since the synoptics tended to use other criteria when assembling their material for presentation.

John's account is the only one that is followed by a confrontation with those who had witnessed Jesus' angry reaction to the use of the temple precincts for buying and selling. The opportunity of changing money and buying animals for sacrifice was a great convenience for pilgrims, but it should have been available outside the sacred area. Jesus rejects the protests which demanded to know by what right he had acted as he did, but his words about being able to 'raise up this sanctuary in three days' if it were destroyed seemed incredible and nonsensical to his accusers. The evangelist explains that 'he was speaking of the sanctuary that was his body' and that, after his resurrection, his disciples recalled his words.

John wrote his gospel towards the end of the first century, long after Christ rose from the dead and some years after the destruction of the Temple during the failed revolt against the Romans in AD 70. Although for Jews who had not become Christians, the loss of the Temple meant that they no longer had the presence of God in their midst or at least located on earth, for Christians God is to be found in Jesus and, though no longer visible, he remains truly with us. Reflecting, therefore, on the event in today's gospel passage reminds us of this truth and the need for us to be aware of that divine presence, with us always but in a special way when we celebrate the Eucharist.

The first reading (Ezekiel 47:1-2.8-9.12) looks forward to the Jews' return from exile in Babylon in the sixth century BC. The prophet paints a picture of the Temple to be rebuilt, with abundant water flowing from it to make the barren land fertile.

In the first letter to the Corinthians (3:9-11.16-17), Paul explains that Christians are God's sacred temple, built on a foundation that is Christ and with the Holy Spirit dwelling within.

THE IMMACULATE CONCEPTION OF THE BLESSED VIRGIN – 8 December

Luke 1:26-38

There is no mention in the Scriptures of the conception in her mother's womb of the future Mother of God, and even less of the absence (because of God's anticipated redemption) of any trace of original sin affecting Mary. The lectionary, therefore, chooses Luke's account of Jesus' human conception in Mary's womb from which will come his birth in human nature, the incarnation leading to the nativity.

In those days, the calendar dates of events did not seem to matter; or at least, they do not seem to have been recorded for yearly observance thereafter. We celebrate Christ's conception on 25th March because we celebrate his birth on 25th December. We do not know the date of the Lord's birth but there is a credible theory that 25th December was chosen because, 21st December being the winter solstice, 25th was at the start of the annual daily increase in the length of time between sunrise and sunset and therefore was an appropriate day to celebrate (when annual celebration was inaugurated) the birth of 'the Light of the World'. Since, at the time when the date was chosen, there were no Christians in the southern hemisphere, the idea of a midsummer Christmas never occurred to anyone.

Luke is the only evangelist to give us an account of the incarnation. It is noticeable that he also narrates the story of the incarnation of John the Baptist (1:5-25), as if he were urging us to compare the two. In both, the archangel Gabriel was God's messenger to give the very unexpected news to the parents-to-be. But there is a clear contrast between the two events. First, in the locations of the announcements, one in the city of Jerusalem and in the sacred precincts of the Temple, the other in an obscure and even disreputable village far away from the holy city, in the north of Palestine. Then again, in John's case, the parents are elderly and infertile but of good reputation and considerable status since the husband was a priest and both 'scrupulously observed all the commandments' (Luke 1:6); in Jesus' case, the mother-to-be is a young and unknown peasant and, although betrothed and therefore considered married, she conceives not in the normal manner but through the miraculous intervention of the Holy Spirit. The contrast also is seen in the circumstances of the babies' births, John's taking place at home (although no details are given, the neighbours and relations rejoiced with the parents), and Jesus' in the strange and impoverished circumstances which are described and which we know so well, conditions which remind us of the tent in which God's presence dwelt in the time of King David.

Given the choice of the gospel passage, this is an occasion for us to grow in admiration and love for Mary. Particularly, I like to think about her courage in accepting the angel's message, her trust in God since she was faced with the completely unknown as well as the danger of ridicule, and her holiness as the one person in history selected by God to bear his Son to human birth. This can be a day on which we say the *Hail Mary* with great admiration and gratitude. Even more explicitly, we pray: 'O Mary, conceived without sin, pray for us who have recourse to thee'.

The first reading is from the book of Genesis (3:9-15.20). Our first parents have sinned and God curses the devil who, in the form of a serpent, had tempted them. Verse 15 of the extract ('I will make you enemies of each other, you and the woman . . .') is the earliest hint of the divine plan of salvation and is therefore called the *proto-evangelium*. In the phrase 'it will crush your head', the word 'it' is in the masculine form in the Greek text and therefore applied to the messiah; in Latin, the feminine form is used and so Mary is understood, because of her intimate union with her messiah-son. Verse 20 tells us that the name 'Eve' means 'mother of all the living', which alludes to the continuance of the human race despite the offence to God and also, perhaps, may be a vague hint of the sin being passed on through inheritance.

In the letter to the Ephesians (1:3-6.11-12), St Paul teaches that, from eternity, God chose us, through Jesus, to be his children by adoption. God made this determination freely and it was to his glory that the people had put their hopes in a saviour even before Christ came.

Epilogue

We are well aware, nowadays at least, of the importance of the Scripture readings at Mass. The Old Testament passages help us to see the centuries before Christ as a time during which God was preparing his chosen people for the coming of his Son. The second readings allow us to learn the teaching of St Paul (and others) on the meaning for us of the life, death and resurrection of Jesus. Of course, the gospel readings have prime importance. They provide us with detailed information of the very doings and sayings of Jesus himself and, especially in the fourth gospel, we are given some insights into the significance of what he did and said in the furtherance of God's plan of salvation for his creatures.

The fact that there are four gospels is a boon. They are all in agreement over the basic facts about Jesus and, although there are variations in some of the details, that lack of complete uniformity enables us to see that they have a certain independence of origin and are not the result of wholesale collusion. Each gospel has its own 'angle' so that they are portraits of Jesus and his story that, when they are studied together, provide us with a more complete understanding of their subject – Jesus Christ, Son of God made man and our Saviour.

The gospels reveal that Jesus was imbued with Jewish religious traditions but that he was not content to leave things as they were. He had a mission to carry out, setting up the kingdom of God. This would involve change, development that was truly the completion and fulfilment of the Jewish law and its prophets. Nor would the kingdom be like the kingdoms of this world. Its nature was to be one of healing and forgiveness, of care for those in need, of peace and not violence, of mercy and concern for everyone. Those who accept the leadership of Jesus would form a community of disciples. They would be asked to copy him in serving rather than in being served and would be sustained by Christ himself in the Eucharist, by the Holy Spirit and by the divinely inspired teaching of the sacred Scriptures.

For all of this, we can say, 'Thanks be to God'. And for the gospels in particular, 'Praise to you, Lord Jesus Christ'.